C0-DVG-196

New
Parish
Ministries

ST. PATRICK'S SEMINARY LIBRARY
MENLO PARK, CALIFORNIA
94025
DISCARD

Winston Press

BX
1920
.N39
1983

The series of booklets
(published here in book form)

NEW PARISH MINISTRIES

has been made possible
through the interest and collaboration
of many persons involved in parish ministries,
who have given so generously of their time and reflection.
We mention very particularly: Fr. Regis Halloran and
Fr. Pat Byrne, National Office of Liturgy; Claude Poirier, O.P.,
Toronto Pastoral Centre for Liturgy; Sheila Finnerty, G.S.I.C.,
Ottawa Diocesan Centre and Ontario Liturgy Conference; Fr. Paul
André Durocher, St-Antoine-de-Padoue Cathedral, Timmins, Ontario.

New Parish Ministries was originally published by Novalis, Saint Paul University, Ottawa, Canada. This edition is published by Winston Press, Inc., by arrangement with Novalis, Saint Paul University. Copyright © 1982, Novalis. Copyright © 1983, Winston Press. All rights reserved. No part of this book may be reproduced in any form without written permission from the publisher.

Library of Congress Catalog Card Number: 82-63064
ISBN: 0-86683-742-6 (previously ISBN: 2-89088-089-3)

Printed in Canada

5 4 3 2 1

Winston Press, Inc., 430 Oak Grove, Minneapolis, MN 55403

Table of Contents

Introduction

Booklets

Baptism Preparation
First Eucharist, Reconciliation, Confirmation
Marriage Preparation
Liturgy Planning
Readers at Liturgy
Musicians at Liturgy
Lay Presiders at Liturgy
Health Care Ministers
Parish Prayer Groups
Parish Council

Introduction

This book presents a series of ten booklets intended for lay persons and religious involved in a variety of ways in parish ministries. These booklets are available separately but are bound together into one volume for library purposes as well as for the convenience of pastors and pastoral teams.

The reader may desire some brief explanation of the title "New Parish Ministries."

We use the term "ministries" in the wide sense of those services which lay persons or religious are called upon to fulfill by their baptism as Christians. In this series we present ten such ministries which can be undertaken in a parish, in collaboration with the pastor and pastoral team.

We acknowledge that these ministries are not really "new." From the Church's earliest days, lay persons and religious have visited the sick, assisted in the preparation and celebration of sacraments, and aided in the administration of the parish, etc. What is perhaps new is the increasingly new perception we have of the Christian's role — not simply collaborating occasionally in pastoral work but actually being given the responsibility of certain aspects of the Christian life in the local community.

Finally, we present those ministries which take place within the "parish," because the parish continues to play an irreplaceable role within our society — especially that of mediating the faith-life of its people, sacramental symbol and reality.

We wish you every success and blessing in your important work and ministry.

Jerome Herauf
Editor

Baptism Preparation

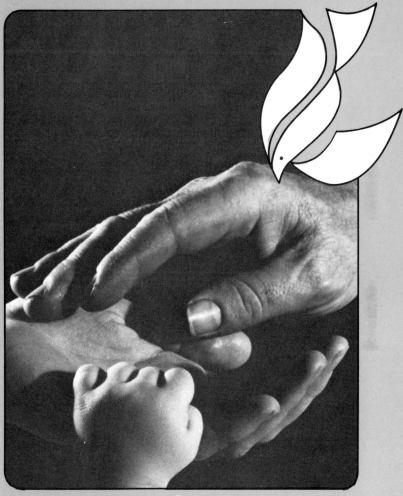

New Parish Ministries

WINSTON PRESS

Contents

New Parish Ministries was originally published by Novalis, Saint Paul University, Ottawa, Canada. This edition is published by Winston Press, Inc., by arrangement with Novalis, Saint Paul University. Copyright © 1982, Novalis. Copyright © 1983, Winston Press. All rights reserved. No part of this book may be reproduced in any form without written permission from the publisher.

ISBN: 0-86683-732-9 (previously ISBN: 2-89088-079-6)

Printed in Canada

5   4   3   2   1

Winston Press, Inc., 430 Oak Grove, Minneapolis, MN 55403

Forming a Baptism Preparation Team

"We appreciate being asked but..."

   "Now where do we begin? Because Jack and I have been parishioners actively involved in the parish and have three children of our own, Fr. Mike has asked us to work with him to form a Baptism Team. Sure, baptism is important to us and we see the need for more people than just the priest to be involved, but where do we go from here? How can we prepare? What can we expect? What is expected of us?"

   This little booklet is written to provide the information that Jack and Sharon are looking for. The aim is to give the practical and necessary help to persons in a growing number of parishes who are launching out into the "brave new world" to which they have been invited.

   Yes, invited. For if parishioners are to become involved in the community project of preparing for baptism, someone in the parish will have to invite them. This someone may be a representative of Parish Council, or a member of the "mission" committee, but most likely the initial invitation will need to come from the parish priest himself. But even with all the best intentions and a good deal of personal experience, the parish priest himself may not have a clear idea on how to proceed. This booklet deals with all aspects of setting up and operating a Baptism Team in a parish.

Please note: The symbols drawn by the artist for pages 14, 15, and 40 may be reproduced for your own usage (e.g. for making banners, etc.).

Ministries of Baptism

Christian instruction and the preparation for baptism are a vital concern of God's people, the Church, which hands on and nourishes the faith it has received from the apostles. Through the ministry of the Church, adults are called by the Holy Spirit to the gospel, and infants are baptized and brought up in this faith. Therefore it is most important that catechists and other lay people should work with priests and deacons in making preparations for baptisms. In the actual celebration, the people of God (represented not only by the parents, godparents and relatives, but also, as far as possible, by friends, neighbors, and some members of the local church) should take an active part. Thus they will show their common faith and express their joy as the newly-baptized are received into the community of the Church.

The Rites, General Introduction, Rite of Christian Initiation, paragraph 7.

As the awareness grows that all in the Christian community are called to serve, more and more persons are participating in the ministries of the community.

It is when the whole community takes on the responsibility for welcoming new members that the phrase "We are the Church" takes on its full meaning.

The formation of a Parish Baptism Preparation Team is a logical place to begin to flesh out the post-Vatican II understanding of the Church as the People of God.

Baptism is, of its very nature, a community project, a project devoid of meaning outside the context of the community. When members of the community take on their roles, each according to their relationship and gifts, then the false image of Church as a private place or as a group where only a few have and take responsibility is dispelled.

A Community Responds

It is when parents, godparents, bishop, priests, deacons, Director of Initiation, Director of Infant Baptism, members of the parish, all take up their distinctive roles in a living, loving community response, that the Church comes fully alive and grows as the Body of the Christ from whom it takes its name. Consistency and clarity of roles is needed if the process of initiation is to take place with understanding and collaboration at all levels.

It is the bishop, first of all, who is responsible for the initiation of all persons: He represents the unity of the Church into which every person is baptized. Diocesan guidelines set the parameters for baptism preparation. At the parish level, the pastor is the bishop's representative.

As the first step in each parish, a Director is appointed from the Pastoral Team. The Director of Initiation is the one responsible for all initiation in the parish. This person is responsible for the Adult Catechumenate Program, the confirmation and first communion preparation, as well as the baptism of infants. It is the new Rite of Christian Initiation of adults that serves as the model for all initiation (see RCIA, CCC, 1974). Whether the director is a member of the Pastoral Team or not, whether lay or ordained, it is important that this person be truly given responsibility. When members of the Pastoral Team and the parishioners themselves understand and respect this position, then direction of the process can be effective.

In larger parishes, it may be helpful to separate the roles of the Director of Initiation into a Director of Adult Initiation and a Director of Infant Baptism. Further, a competent person may be appointed Coordinator of Infant Baptism to help facilitate the entire process.

The following suggestions concerning the role of the Director and Coordinator are not meant to be exhaustive. Here, as well as throughout this booklet, the ideas presented do not indicate that there are no other, or further, possibilities. In fact, as each parish develops its own response, other creative approaches and alternatives will emerge.

Responsibilities of the Director of Initiation
(or of Infant Baptism)

- invites persons to serve on the team (see p. 6)
- ensures team members are prepared for this ministry by personal and team formation (see p. 6)
- oversees the public installation of team members (see Team Resources, p. 16)
- with the team members, plans and implements group sessions (see p. 17)
- with team members, decides on readiness for baptism according to parish, diocesan and universal guidelines
- ensures that a celebrant is chosen for the baptism, and facilitates the contact of the celebrant with the family
- decides on the time of baptism, and plans the baptism with the family (see p. 23,) and team members
- directs the celebration of the baptism
- with the team members, develops follow-up contact with the families of children baptized (see p. 29)
- continuously reviews the baptism preparation process

Responsibilities of the Coordinator of Infant Baptism

(This role may be included in the responsibilities of Director)
- serves as contact person for all infant baptism inquiries
- contacts all families by phone and gets basic information (see p. 7)
- coordinates the assigning of Baptism Team members with families, according to availability and appropriateness
- participates in all team meetings
- coordinates the use of facilities for baptisms, group sessions and team meetings.

The Making of a Team

In contacting persons to form a team, consider the following:

• invite couples that are not over-involved so that this ministry will not be just one more activity

• ensure that persons will not be asked to actually prepare families until they feel and actually are ready to do so

• invite couples who show signs of eagerness and enthusiasm for the baptism of their own child

• invite persons who are ready for a challenge, and show signs of readiness to minister

• invite persons who can work with others and like to work in a team

• invite single persons and grandparents, as well as couples who may be uniquely suited to this ministry

Some dioceses offer a program for the development of parish Baptism Teams. It is, however, the struggle of a group to make a best possible response, that will lead it on a road of self-discovery and improvement.

Regular team meetings, perhaps every other month, can serve to further the growth of individual team members and of the process as well. Prayer, informal discussion, review and evaluation, theological and practical input, brainstorming, refreshments and fun: all can be part of these sessions during the year.

Role-playing the variety of family situations that may be encountered (see p. 7) and sharing personal responses to the discussion questions (see p. 14), can help to enliven and deepen team life. Also, the material listed under Team Resources (see p. 16) offers numerous possibilities. Listening to and viewing audio/visuals (see p. 21) and reading some of the excellent recent publications on Initiation (see Bibliography) will give team members a sound and thorough background, and insure creative expansion in the team approach.

Preparation in the Home

The Initial Contact

The first contact, usually by phone through the Coordinator or parish secretary, may set the tone for the entire process. If the person receiving the call is friendly, doors will be opened. If, when the information is obtained, the tone is one of welcoming and hospitality and not one of skepticism and suspicion, the stage is set for an open response. Families may be unaware of the need to prepare for baptism, but most will react positively, if the process is presented as an opportunity and not as an investigation.

During the initial contact:

● Obtain some basic required information (see p. 38).

● Avoid discussing a date at this time, but note preferences and ascertain why this date is desired.

● Inform the family that members of the Baptism Team will soon be in contact with them.

Each family is unique, and so a great deal of sensitivity is needed to accept every family and respect them as they are. In all situations, we try not to lose sight of the fact that all of us come with weakness and strength.

A Variety of Family Situations

● The young couple who has not been part of a community but is open to the possibility, as the responsibility of new life is awaited.

● The couple who has been directed to call, spurred on by an anxious grandparent worried about the delay in baptism.

● The couple that assumes it has a right to baptism because they themselves were baptized, although they belong to no parish.

● The single parent, hesitant because she is not married, who longs for support and acceptance.

● The couple with three previous baptisms who have nevertheless never deepened their understanding of baptism.

7

- The divorced Catholic father who has joint custody of two unbaptized small children.
- The parishioner who, after a lifetime of parish involvement, fails to see any need for preparation.
- The couple eager to learn and enter creatively into the process.
- The couple who are "shopping around" to find a parish that won't make a fuss about the baptism.

Visiting the Home

You, as Baptism Team members, are reaching out as representatives of your parish, extending the hospitality of the Christian family at a special time of grace. Your attitude must never be one of judgment or condemnation but of welcoming and a sense of privilege at being allowed to be part of this family's life.

If at all possible, the visits should take place in the home of the expectant parents. Arrangements can be made by phone so as to avoid surprise visits. By your visiting their home, the family will be more comfortable and you will be able to talk more freely. It will also help you get a better idea of the family life-style and of the couple's background.

If the couple has already given birth to the child, then stress there is no inordinate haste to have the child baptized — that it is important the occasion be one for which all are well prepared. Inquire about the birth experience. It is beautiful that God has provided for a nine months' preparation time for birth. Certainly, the rebirth also deserves ample time for reflection, prayer and preparation.

The first visit

Before going in, take a moment to ask the Lord to bless you in your service, and to bless the family whose home you are about to enter.

Don't be surprised at a few awkward moments when you first go in. Neither you nor they are sure what to expect.

Break the ice by relating something that occurred to you recently, perhaps a humorous anecdote from your own family life.

Ask the mother about the pregnancy, and be encouraging about this experience.

Don't pepper the parent(s) with questions, but let the conversation move in such a way that you get some indication of their

8

background. They, in turn, will become more comfortable with your presence.

There may be moments of awkward silence, but don't be too quick to fill the void. It takes time for a stranger to become a friend.

Avoid talking about the celebration particulars. Instead, speak about the hopes and expectations the parents may have, and how their faith plays a role in this.

Create a climate that invites openness by avoiding do's and don'ts, meanwhile sharing your own enthusiasm for the opportunities of preparation time.

Presume the parents want to do what's best for their baby and are trying to be good parents.

Let them see you are there as a help and support, and watch to see if there are needs (economic, social, spiritual) that you may be able to help with. Or offer to put them in touch with the proper resources, or qualified person.

Accept refreshments at the end of the session, if they are offered, and use this time to share informally about family life.

Do not stay longer than about an hour, the first time. Thank them for meeting with you.

Leave a copy of questions for further reflection, if you feel they are ready for it. Ask them to write down some thoughts for future discussion (see p. 14). Or, leave a booklet for further thought and discussion by the couple, and let them know that you will follow up on the questions raised at the next visit (see p. 16 and 21).

Leave a copy of the Prayer for a New Parent.

Take a moment, before leaving, to pray for the child and parents, and be sensitive to their own freedom to participate.

Indicate that godparents, grandparents, friends will be welcome at future visits.

As the visits continue, why not:

Bring along some light refreshment as a genuine symbol of neighborliness.

Make an effort to call other children by name and spend some time with the children, if there are any.

Facilitate contact with other groups as the need or desire becomes evident (e.g., St. Vincent de Paul; Separated and Divorced; Religious Education Group).

Enter the process of discovery with the couple rather than be too quick with easy answers.

If you are not sure about a certain question they may have, tell them so — indicate that you will find out more about this or refer them to sources themselves.

Be careful to distinguish your personal point of view from the Church position, where these may differ. Neither pretend to agree, nor push your own understanding as the more enlightened one.

Go through the Baptism Ceremony, using it as an occasion to invite discussion on the meaning of signs and symbols.

Invite the family to participate in a brief prayer time, again being sensitive to their own freedom; avoid creating awkward moments by imposing a style of prayer with which they are not comfortable.

If the family is not involved in the parish, watch for ways to encourage involvement by your willingness to facilitate connections.

The actual preparation will hopefully be the beginning of an on-going friendship. You may be able to participate in the home renewal celebration (see p. 32) and/or simply follow up with the occasional phone call or visit.

Where it is possible, carry through your role to the celebration of the other Sacraments of Initiation, namely Confirmation and First Communion, in this way linking the process of initiation together.

For further content for home visits, see Parent Resources (p. 21) and Group Session Content suggestions (p. 19).

Brochure

In order to encourage families to make contact with the parish at an earlier date, during pregnancy, copies of a brochure may be made and left in the church. They may also be sent to those families that are known to be expecting a baby. The whole parish can take part by advising the Director or Coordinator about families known to be expecting. Copies of the brochure can also be left in local doctors' offices or community centers. The birth of a child is a graced moment that may open a family to renewed participation in the life of the parish.

An attractive cover, perhaps with a picture of a pregnant woman and bold lettering which might read: "Expecting a Baby? We at *(Name of Parish)* care about you and the child to be born." The inside may contain a letter to the parents (like the one below) on one panel. A list of various aspects of baptism preparation and celebration may be included. Along with the Spiritual Rights of the Child, these should stimulate reflection and discussion.

The outside of the brochure should contain a form for the name, address and phone number of the family and the parish's address, along with the suggestion that the information be mailed to or dropped by the rectory.

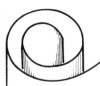
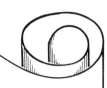

Dear Parents,

You have given life to your child. And as your child grows within, you are becoming eager with expectation. Your child will be welcomed into your family and in your family will grow in "wisdom, age and grace".

This time of waiting is a time for reflection on your role as parents, and the values you share — to which you will introduce this child. It is also an opportunity to reflect on your child's welcome into the Christian community. Now, before the new life takes so much deserved attention in the first few weeks after birth, is a good time to consider preparation for the Baptism of your child. We invite you to contact the parish so that representatives from the Parish Baptism Preparation Team will be able to meet with you, and join with you in the joyful discovery that new life brings.

Spiritual Rights of the Child...

1. The right to know and love God.
2. The right to participate in a living community of faith.
3. The right to those needed resources for spiritual growth.
4. The right to religious and moral education from informed parents.
5. The right to hear the Word of God and have it interpreted.
6. The right to times of silence and solitude to develop a contemplative spirit.
7. The right to active participation in community worship.
8. The right to live in a home with faith in God as the heart of daily life.
9. The right to pray freely.
10. The right to be of service to others.

(Written for the International Year of the Child, by Ann and Gerry Van Regan.)

Discussion Questions

The following questions may be used directly or indirectly in home visits to stimulate deeper reflection on the meaning of baptism. It is sometimes helpful if the husband and wife respond to these separately, in writing, for later discussion together. They may be left with the single parent and discussed at a follow-up visit. Just one section of the questions may be enough for one visit. It would not usually be helpful to hand over the entire list as this may lead to over-simplified responses. This, and all other resources should be adapted according to needs of parish and family background.

Belonging:

In what ways do I express my belonging in my family? (own and extended family)

What groups do I belong to? Why?

In what ways do I express my belonging to the Christian family?

Do I belong to the Christian community of my parents' choice or because of a personal choice?

Am I responsive in expressing my faith in Christ with others?

How is my faith rooted in personal experiences, family experiences, and Church experiences?

What does Church mean to me?

What do I like and dislike about my Church?

Relationship With God:

How does my faith in God affect my daily life?

How does my faith affect my relationship with my children, my neighbors, people around the world?

What is God really like to me?

What do I believe about God?

What do I need to do to please God in this life?

How would I like my children to relate to God?

Prayer life:

In what ways do I pray: individually? with my family?

Why do I need to come together with others to pray in a community?

What do I expect from prayer?

What do I bring of my own life to prayer?

What is my hope for my children's prayer life?

14

Symbols:

What are some symbols that are important to my family? Why?

What do the symbols of baptism mean (e.g., water, garment, oil, candle)?

Why did I choose this name for my child?

How do I express my relationship with God in sign and symbol?

Baptism:

Why is baptism a once-only experience?

Why do I want baptism for my child?

What difference will baptism make to my child?

Evil:

What do I believe about the origins of evil?

How would I explain the meaning of "Satan, Father of sin and Prince of Darkness"?

What do I believe about hell, limbo, and purgatory?

How would I define sin? Do I believe in personal sin? Sin in the world? Conversion?

What do I want my children to grow to believe about evil and sin?

What do I believe about original sin?

Do I ever think of sin? Myself as sinner? My need for forgiveness?

How do I experience reconciliation? Change of heart? Conversion?

Child:

What kind of world do I desire for my child?

What aspects of the world do I hope will never touch my child?

What do I consider the rights of my child?

Are the spiritual rights important to me? (See p. 13).

Which spiritual rights do I consider most important?

What attitudes do I desire for my children — towards life? towards others? towards religion?

15

Selected Resources for the Baptism Team

Baptizing Children (Liturgy No. 73, March-April, 1980. CCCB, 90 Parent Ave., Ottawa, Ontario. K1N 7B1)

Excellent booklet for baptism team members. Looks at the place of baptism in the Church today and the importance of involvement by all — parents, godparents, ministers and parishioners — in the preparation, celebration and continuing care of the baptized.

What Will this Child Turn Out to Be? (F. Lobinger, Published by the Lumko Institute, 1979. No. 13 of the series training for Community Ministries).

Prepared for the African Church, this kit has detailed descriptions for persons involved in preparing parents for the baptism of their infants.

God's Own Child (William & Patricia Coleman, 1977. Twenty-Third Publications, P.O. Box 180, WEST MYSTIC, CT 06388)

This pastoral kit includes a leader's guide and parents' books (ten). Brief articles and questions and discussion pages seek to stimulate parents in active discussion to rediscover the joy of full, shared belief.

We Share New Life (Paulist Press, 1980. 400 Settie Drive, Paramus, N.J., 07652).

A complete baptismal program that includes program director's manual, reflection and activity book, celebrations book and book of activities for children attuned to family togetherness. The program aims at active and joyful preparation.

Baptism (Catherine Fenn, SCJ, Catholic Office of Religious Education, 67 Bond St., Toronto, Ontario)

A program of preparation for the parents and godparents.

The Group Meeting

The group meeting for families presents an opportunity for interaction with other families in the community and for a more formal instruction. This is also an occasion to meet the priest who will be celebrant at the baptism. It is, of course, of utmost importance that the family come to know the priest before the baptism, through the group meeting or by a separate visit. Godparents and other interested persons (such as grandparents) may also be encouraged to attend.

The following is a suggested format for the single group meeting. This meeting generally takes place in the week prior to the baptism, or in close proximity to it. A warm atmosphere should be created for this meeting. To facilitate this, everything should be done to make people comfortable. For example, it should be mentioned in the introductory remarks that mothers should feel free to nurse their children, change their diaper, or rock them in the rocking chair provided.

Pre-arrangements:	Circular arrangement of chairs, background music
	Nametags, childcare if needed, refreshments prepared, audio-visual equipment checked; Baptism Team Members present to greet families; materials to be used ready
7:30 p.m.	Welcome and introduce priest and team
	Open with a prayer (see inside back cover)
	Invite children to their own preparation time
	Facilitator speaks briefly on contemporary understanding of baptism
7:45	Filmstrip/slides/talk (see p. 21)
8:00	Open sharing on challenges and expectations raised by above presentation; if group is large, divide into smaller groups with prepared questions (p. 14)
8:30	Discuss the ceremony, creative participation (see p. 26) Families make decisions on participation
8:45	Children return for closing prayer time
9:00	Close session with refreshments (include juice and nutritious snack for children and all present)

If Children are present (ages 3-12)

7:45	Move into another room
	Learn a song (see p. 39)
8:00	Project and discuss baptism symbols
8:30	Prepare prayer for newly-baptized
8:45	Join group and participate in closing prayer, using song learned, symbols made and prayers prepared
9:00	Share refreshments with adults

Group Sessions

An optional approach is a series of group sessions enabling a deeper and more extensive reflection on the implications of baptism and a building of friendship and community among the families. The following are suggestions for the Aim and Content at these meetings. This Content may also serve as preparation material for persons considering joining the Baptism Team, or for home visits. Format may be similar to that suggested for a single meeting.

SESSION I

Aim:

To create an atmosphere of openness and belonging in order to support reflection on the meanings of pregnancy and birth

Content:

Feelings surrounding pregnancy and birth
Adjustments and expectations
Mystery and challenge of new life to be cared for
Meanings of being named

SESSION II

Aim:

To open up and deepen the understanding of baptism, by a look at the history of its development and the *Rite of the Christian Initiation of Adults*

Content:

History of the Sacrament
Sacraments of Initiation: Baptism/Confirmation/Eucharist, Rite of the Christian Initiation of Adults

SESSION III

Aim:

To reflect on the meaning of the signs and symbols of baptism to enable families to enter the experience of baptism more deeply and creatively

Content:

Biblical meaning of symbols
Signs and symbols of baptism in the Rite
Meaning of these in our life today

SESSION IV

Aim:

To encourage creative participation of families in the celebration of baptism

Content:

The liturgical cycle — Easter Vigil as cornerstone, and Easter Season as season of baptism
Rites of baptism
Possibilities of creative participation of families
Actual decisions on family participation (this may be scheduled with individual families if baptisms are to occur at different times) (see resources on following pages and on page 16)

NORMS FOR CELEBRATING BAPTISM

- *after thorough preparation on the meaning and for the celebration of baptism (see General Introduction, Rite of Baptism for Children #5)*
- *regular participation in a faith community (General Introduction #4)*
- *celebration with the faith community, within the Sunday eucharistic gathering (#9)*
- *celebration in the church building of the faith community (#10)*
- *celebration within the context of the liturgical cycle (#9)*

Exceptions to these norms should be considered for sufficient pastoral reasons.

Audio-Visual Resources

Godparent Gussie (Teleketics, 1229 So. Santee St., Los Angeles, CA 90015.)

Filmstrip on history and development of Baptism/Confirmation using a cartoon format that is very effective; suitable for parent meetings. Utilizing the storyscape approach, this program is based on five 16 mm films: 1. Baptism, Sacrament of Belonging. 2. The Widow's Mite. 3. Godparent Gussie. 4. Water and Spirit. 5. Commitment to Caring.
The kit comes with worksheets containing reproducible activities, reflections and prayers for group use.

Baptism: The Sacrament of Welcome (Winston Press). Filmstrip that builds the bridge between formal ritual and everyday reality.

Welcome to the Christian Community (23rd Publications, 1974, West Mystic, Ct. 06388.) Filmstrip for use with parents, that emphasizes the community aspect and the relationship of baptismal symbols and life.

Signs of Life: Celebrating Sacraments No. 3: Infant Baptism (Our Sunday Visitor, 200 Noll Plaza, Huntington, IN. 46750.)
Filmstrip from a series that follows a family through their experiences in seeking to become part of the Church community. The baptism filmstrip emphasizes the continuing care that baptism promises.

Promise (Winston Pastoral Kit.)

A multi-media baptism program for parishes. Includes two filmstrips, director's manual and activity-centered family book. Contains all the necessary information for a complete baptism preparation program.

The Sacraments of Initiation (NCR, P.O. Box 281, Kansas City, MO. 64141.)
Cassette by Gerard Broccolo, contrasting the traditional meaning of baptism with current trends in pastoral practice.

Resource Books and Booklets For Parents

Religion For Little Children (Christianne Brusselman, Our Sunday Visitor, (1977, 200 Noll Plaza, Huntington, IN. 46750.)
Excellent introduction for parents to the con-tinuing expression of religious meaning in daily life.

In the Beginning, There Were the Parents (Dolores Curran, Winston, 1978.)

A timely series on family issues that concern Christian parents, with a challenge to parents to reclaim their place as primary educators of their children.

Family Nights Throughout the Year (Terry & Mimi Reilly, Abbey Press, 1978, St. Meinrad, IN. 47577.)
"Oodles" of ideas to enjoy as a family, for every week of the year

Family Prayer (Dolores Curran, 23rd Publications, 1978, P.O. Box 180, West Mystic, Ct. 06388.)
A complete guide for praying families, with sample prayers and liturgical suggestions.

A Saint for Your Name (Albert Nevins, Our Sunday Visitor, 1980. 200 Noll Plaza, Huntington, IN. 46750.)
Two books, one for girls, another for boys, with several hundred names of saints, and an account of their heroic lives.

Together at Baptism (Joseph Payne, CSC, Ave Maria Press, 1969, Notre Dame, IN. 46556.)
A book of preparation for baptism including: the rite, alternate prayers and readings, with commentaries for parents.

Infant Baptism and the Christian Community (Charles J. Keating, 23rd Publications, 1972, P.O. Box 180, West Mystic, CT. 06388.)
A book that presents baptism as a challenge to live out and celebrate the sacrament with indications on how to do so.

Touched by God's Promise (Carolyn Puccio and Ann Redpath, Winston Press, 1979.)
A family remembrance gift book to record the event, involve the family, and encourage them to continue the event's meaning.

Prayers for the Domestic Church
A handbook for worship in the home that can be used throughout the year for a great variety of family life experiences. (Forest of Peace Books, Shantivanam House of Prayer, Easton, Kansas. 66020.)

The Liturgy of Baptism

The Adult Catechumenate, as it begins to take its rightful place in parish life, will help sensitize the parish community to the liturgical rhythm of the liturgical year. The Easter Vigil (with its initiation of adults through baptism, confirmation and eucharist), will again take its place as the powerful peak of a community's annual celebration cycle.

Infant baptisms, too, will no longer be scheduled arbitrarily but with reference to the liturgical cycle. (Baptisms during Lent are entirely contrary to this spirit.) It is certainly true that many parishes will not find it feasible to limit infant baptism to the Easter Season. Each Sunday is, of course, a celebration of an Easter People and it is still possible to respect and to be in harmony with the flow of the Church's liturgical expression.

Communities may work toward implementation of the schema on the following page. **Asterisks** refer to readings already in use for the celebration of infant baptism. The readings without asterisks present baptismal themes. The numbering is on a priority cycle, accenting the Easter Season as the season of Baptism.

NOTE: If the celebration of Baptism is taking place outside of the Sunday Eucharistic Gathering, this schema encourages the theme of the Sunday to be recalled and links the celebration to the community worship.

SCHEDULE ACCORDING TO THE LITURGICAL CYCLE

FEAST	Year A	Year B	Year C	PRIORITY SCALE	TIME IN YEAR (approximately)
27th Sunday in Ordinary Time		Mk. 10:2-16*			
30th Sunday in Ordinary Time	Mt. 22:34-40*			10	October
31st Sunday in Ordinary Time			Mk. 9:1-10		
2nd Sunday of Advent	Mt. 3:1-12	Mk. 1:1-8	Lk. 3:1-6	7	December
Baptism of Our Lord	Mt. 3:13-17	Mk. 1:6-11	Lk. 3:15-16, 21-22	8	January
3rd Sunday in Ordinary Time	1 Cor 1:10-13, 17	Mk. 1:14-20	Eph. 4:1-6*	9	January
EASTER SUNDAY	Jn. 20:1-9	Jn. 20:1-9	Jn. 20:1-9		
4th Sunday of Easter (Good Shepherd)	Jn. 10:1-10	Jn. 10:11-18	Jn. 10:27-30	2	April
5th Sunday of Easter	Jn. 14:1-12	Jn. 15:1-11*	Jn. 13:31-33, 34-35	3	
Ascension Sunday	Mk. 28:16-20*	Mk. 16:15-20	Lk. 24:46-53	4	May
Pentecost Vigil	Jn. 7:37b-39a*	Jn. 7:37b-39a*	Jn. 7:37b-39a*	5	
Trinity Sunday	Jn. 3:16-18	Mt. 28:16-20*	Jn. 16:12-15	6	June
12th Sunday in Ordinary Time			Gal. 3:26-29*		
13th Sunday in Ordinary Time	Rom. 6:3-4, 8 -11*			11	July
17th Sunday in Ordinary Time		Eph. 4:1-6*			
18th Sunday in Ordinary Time	Is. 55:1-3		Jn. 6:24-35	12	August
19th Sunday in Ordinary Time		Jn. 6:41-51*			

The baptism experience is enriched by the quality of Christian living expressed by the parish community. Through baptism, the community reveals itself to itself as a sacrament (a living and efficacious sign) of salvation in a given place and time; it is summoned to perform its mission. Because of the close ties between baptism and community, baptism-preparation cannot be conducted in isolation from the rest of parish activity. It must be part of the overall pastoral ministry of the parish community.

p. 48, Item 1, *A Child is Baptized.* Archdiocese of Montreal, 2000 Sherbrooke St. West, Montreal, Quebec. H3H 1G4

Creative Participation in the Ceremony

The celebration of the baptism itself offers an opportunity for creative participation by all concerned. The role of the Director and of members of the Baptism Team should be continued by involvement in the actual celebration of the sacrament. The Director may be responsible for the Opening, the Questioning, the Renunciation of Sin and the Profession of Faith. The Baptism Team members may call the family forward and lead them to the place of baptism. Because the development of Baptism Teams was not sufficiently in place at the time the New Rite was promulgated (1969), the liturgical role of team members is not referred to in the Rite, and diocesan guidelines should be respected here — as in all matters relating to infant baptism.

Participation in Baptism Ceremony by Family

- choice of Readings from Old and New Testament, and of someone to proclaim them

- composition of Prayers of the Faithful, and choice of persons to read individual prayers

- choice of songs (see p. 39) and, when possible, sung by family, friends

- expression by parents, in their own words, of their reasons for presenting their child for baptism

- addition to Litany of the Saints of the names of child's saint, other children's saints, parents', godparents', and grandparents'

- a special banner made with name, baptism symbol, and chosen theme

- baptismal gown sewn with cape, to be used for baptismal garment after baptism

- presentation, blessing, and use of "Children's Bible"

- decision on baptism by immersion or infusion

- baptism stole with symbols, made to be used as a baptism garment and may be retained for Confirmation and First Communion, when further symbols may be added

If there are older children in the family

- children may lay hands on infant at moment of baptism

- the infant's baptismal candle may be lit from the baptismal candle of children

- children may do a reading from their own "Children's Bible"

- children may write and read their own Prayers of the Faithful

- special blessing may be added for the other children

Other rites of special meaning may be included in the celebration

- blessing of stone in family ring

- blessing of cross received as baptism gift

- all present bring a symbol, song,

26

prayer, or other sign of their hope for this child, who belongs to the community

If within celebration of the eucharist

• baking of eucharistic bread (check with celebrant regarding guidelines)

• godparents or parents hold cup for communion

• persons serve as altar servers, eucharistic ministers, etc., according to their regular ministry

• family joins in procession at closing of liturgy

• baptismal candle is placed on altar during Eucharistic Prayer, to indicate connection with Eucharist as Sacrament of Initiation

Further opportunities for creative participation

• a hand-made booklet can be prepared and copied, without great difficulty, personalizing the celebration and serving as a keepsake

• someone may be invited to make a drawing for the cover of the program outline

• parents may compose own credal statement

• baptism candle can be made, and name and symbol for child printed or painted on it

• special blessing may be written in which hopes for child are expressed by mother/father

• family picture (with child to be baptized) placed on "Welcome Board" in church, for all to see

Resources: Rite of Baptism and Rite of the Christian Initiation of Adults

Rite of Christian Initiation of Adults (Study Edition) CCCB, 1974. 90 Parent Ave., Ottawa, Ont. K1N 7B1.

Rites of the Catholic Church, Pueblo Publishing Co., 1976. 1860 Broadway, New York, N.Y. 10023.

The Rite of Baptism, The Liturgical Press, 1970. 74 Engle Blvd., Collegeville, Minnesota. 56321.

Rite of Baptism for Children, CCCB. 90 Parent Ave., Ottawa, Ont. K1N 7B1.

Follow-up on Faith Begun

The process, as it has been outlined here, encourages the incorporation of not only the child, but also the deepening incorporation of the entire family in the community. It is not a single event but an expression of a way of life in faith that continues on. In fact, the baptism is itself a beginning. It is much like birth itself. There is a completion, a coming into a new way of life, but also a start that has a lifetime potential.

As the community watches the child grow, what was celebrated in baptism is brought home to the child and later finds its deepest challenge in his/her life as an adult. The Initiation itself comes to completion with Confirmation and participation at the table of the Lord in Eucharist, but the hope is renewed with each new day.

The parish Baptism Team should be prepared to lead the community in continuing renewal and deepening of the challenge of baptism.

The liturgical season of Lent is a testimony that faith brings us to conversion again and again. As we come to feel more and more at home with the faith we carry within us, it becomes part of all that we are and challenges us to become all that we are called to be in the Risen Lord.

To fulfill the true meaning of the sacrament, children must later be formed in the faith in which they have been baptized. The foundation of this formation will be the sacrament itself, which they have already received. Christian formation, which is their due, seeks to lead them gradually to learn God's plan in Christ, so that they may ultimately accept for themselves the faith in which they have been baptized.

(Introduction, Rite of Baptism for Children, 1969. ICEL, paragraph 3.)

Remembering

As the choice of the day of baptism is made with sensitivity to the liturgical life of the Church, the possibility of remembering the baptism begins to take on more possibilities. Each year, the feast day on which the baptism took place may become a family day of baptismal commemoration. It is possible, then, to use the Readings of the day, or join in the celebration of the Eucharist as a family.

But no matter what the anniversary day, the family can celebrate this "birthday" annually, and highlight it even more on multiple anniversaries — fifth, tenth, fifteenth! Here is a suggested format for a home renewal celebration. Friends and neighbors can also be invited to renew God's baptismal promise in their lives.

It is also possible for the whole parish to choose a Sunday during the Easter Season to gather, together with their families, all those who have been baptized, as a celebration of the community to which all belong. This also serves as a continuing contact with the baptized. Families can be personally invited by the team members who helped prepare them for baptism.

The following suggested outline for the Home Renewal Celebration may be helpful in preparing such a liturgical rite. The renewal of baptismal promises, however, should be reserved to the Easter Vigil and baptism celebrations.

Home Renewal Celebration

The lit baptismal candle(s) of each person present and a large bowl of water are placed on a table. The family bible is also prominently placed there. A short Reading is chosen ahead of time (p. 24).

Songs for the opening and closing are chosen (see p. 39 for suggestions). The family gathers around the table.

Opening Song
Father/Mother:
We gather as a family in the name of the Father, and of the Son, and of the Holy Spirit. May the love of God, who is parent of us all and has given us life, be with us all.
We gather together to recall the great sign of our belonging to Christ and each other — the sign of water which we know as baptism. Baptism is the sacrament that reminds us we are all brothers and sisters, children of one God. We are one family, belonging to the great family of God. Our baptism calls us to forgive each other and is a sign of our own forgiveness. Let us now give to each other a sign of the peace that Christ gives each of us. (All exchange a kiss or a hug and wish each other Christ's peace.)

Reading
Read by one of the children or adults present.

Father/Mother:
Today we remember that (name all whose baptisms are being recalled) were gifted with the sign of baptism by which they became children of the great Christian family to which all are called. Let us thank God for all he is doing for us. (Spontaneous prayer or song).

Anniversary Child:
Let us pray: Lord of life, Jesus our brother, you have called us to live your life. Through our baptism, we have a sign of belonging to you that will never be withdrawn. Help us all to be a sign of life and love to each other and to all those we meet.

Father/Mother:
By water and the Holy Spirit you have given us a share in your life. As I sign my family with this water (dipping hand in water, sign a cross on forehead of each person present), let this be a reminder to us all that you have made us into a holy people, your children, forever and ever.

32

All:

Amen.

While each person holds up a candle, another person prays:

Help us to share our light with others and to receive the light from others. Together, may we be a sign of the kingdom to which we have been called — a kingdom of peace, love and joy.

As we pass our lights in a circle, help us to remember that the life you have given us is to be shared with others.

When candles have been passed around in a complete circle:

Father/Mother:

May our God, who is mother and father to us all, bless us and all people everywhere and make us one family under his care, forever and ever.

All:

Amen.

Concluding Song

One step forward...

If there's one thing we've learned since the beginning of the renewal, it's that renewal is never a smooth continuous flow of progress. Renewal has to do with *people* primarily, and people have a way of growing that is, oh, so very human.

We need only watch the first steps of a child, those first unsteady, daring moves that are so hard to relate to the four-minute mile. There is sweat and tears, and predictably, some blood of scraped knees and stubbed toes.

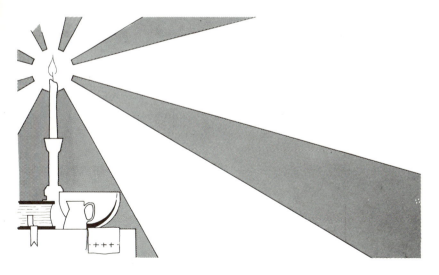

But the adventure of stepping out, springing from an inner drive, sooner or later leads each child to venture up on tottering limbs and out of mother's or father's arms. The movement to the reality that there is life beyond mother/father is a step into the reality that God is that life.

The formation of a Baptismal Team will be very much like those first steps. For every two steps taken in a forward direction, we can expect to fall one step back. It is important that those involved in "creative movement" in the Church have the vision to look back and forward far enough not to get discouraged by the inevitable third step backwards.

There is a children's song titled "Backwards Again" which celebrates the repetitious nature of shoes appearing on the wrong foot. But despite the fact that the syndrome may seem to go on forever, lo and behold, each child does learn to distinguish right from left.

So we must launch into the Baptism Team preparation with all the enthusiasm, zeal, determination, resourcefulness, and faith of a child in discovery. For new possibilities await us — and we are part of them all!

The progress is, then, predictably, two steps forward and one step back. After an initial movement in which people are invited, a team is set up and begins to be involved, there will be a backstep. Perhaps, some members of the team move away or drop out;

perhaps there is too much work for too few; perhaps there are personality clashes between members of the team or the Director and members. It sounds like Christian community, alright!

The test of ministry is our readiness to minister to others when things are more down than up. If we involve ourselves in Christian service only in so far as it is "total joy" to ourselves, there is something lacking.

For we are in service not to a program, or to the parish priest, or even to the family alone, but we are ministering on behalf of the community of Jesus Christ. We will be moved by what the Lord will do through our efforts, for the grace of a new child is a time of special openness, a time of new possibility that provides a setting for God to break through in his own way and in his own time.

We may caution ourselves in looking for results too quickly or too externally. There *will* be families who return to participation in parish life but let us not keep a head count. Our attitude must be one of openness that leaves the results in God's hands where they will rest well. Certainly, if the parish is not making efforts to respond more effectively to the responsibility of welcoming new members into the community, then, we should be ill at ease for there is no standing still in community life any more than there is a time when we can say "I have arrived" in our life of faith.

THE SINGLE END

"The Church wishes to serve this single end: that each person may be able to find Christ, in order that Christ may walk with each person the path of life.

"Jesus Christ becomes, in a way, newly present, in spite of all his apparent absences, in spite of all the limitations of the presence and of the institutional activity of the Church. Jesus Christ becomes present with the power of the truth and the love that are expressed in him with unique unrepeatable fullness."

Redemptor Hominis, encyclical by John Paul II.

Our conviction has become clearer and firmer that solutions to many of the problems we face will be found only when family members accept the ministry of bringing the good news to their own situations. You are called by God to build up the Kingdom by fulfilling responsibilities that are uniquely yours. This flows from your vocation as lay people...

We feel that we can go forward with you in further discovery of the truth and the beauty of marriage and the family which make women and men participants in God's work of creation. Each family's response to Christ's call to holiness stems from the ordinary situations of daily life. Families don't find their sanctity some place else, but right in the midst of what they live through day by day.

From Message to Families, October 24, 1980. Canadian delegation to Synod on the family.

35

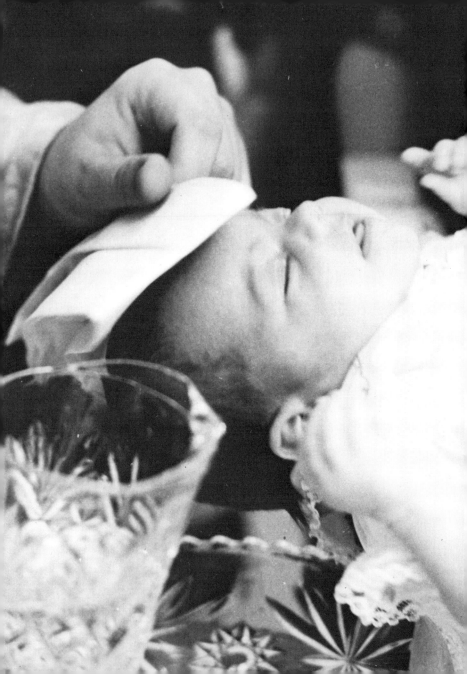

Prayer for a newly baptized child

We do not pray that you will experience no pain and sorrow, but that these will deepen your compassion for others.

We do not pray that you will never be treated unjustly, but that injustice will find in you a lifelong defender.

We do not pray that you will commit no sin, but that your sin will teach you to say "I'm sorry."

We do not pray that you won't be misunderstood, but that misunderstanding will lead you to desire to do only what God wills.

We do not pray that your life will be easy, but that your labors will be borne with deep conviction.

We do not pray that you will not be exposed to hypocrisy and sham, but that you will not become bitter or disillusioned with life.

We do not pray that you will never fail, but that you will have the courage to carry on.

We do not pray that you will never doubt, but that your doubts will lead you to depend on God.

We do not pray that you will be spared aggression, but that you will be able to mold it into peace.

We do not pray that your life will be long; we pray only that you will live life to the full.

In this way, you will live the mystery of the gospel, and the kingdom of heaven is yours.

Ann and Gerry Van Regan, 1974.

Parish Information Sheet

Family Name of Child   Given Names   Home Telephone Number

Address   Postal Code   Parent's Work Number

Date of Birth   Place of Birth

Father's Name   Religion / Denomination

Mother's Name (Maiden)   Religion / Denomination

Marital Status   Place of Marriage

Initial Contact (how, what, when)

Baptism Team Members

Names of Sponsors

Names of Other Children and Ages

Previous Baptism Preparation   Church Participation
   (when, where)

Suggested Place, Date, and Time of Baptism   Celebrant

Please use other side of sheet for other remarks.

Music Suggestions

And I Will Follow	CBW II, 691
At the Lamb's High Feast	CBW II, 563
Baptism Prayer	NALR (Glory and Praise, Vol. 1, #7)
Blessing (round)	CBW II, 722
Blessing (Living with Christ)	Novalis
Child of the Universe	NALR (Song Prayers) 35
I Have Loved You	NALR (Songs of Praise, Vol. 2)
Song of Baptism	NALR (Songs of Praise, Vol. 1, #104)

ENTRANCE

Be Not Afraid	CBW II, 714
Come to Me	CBW II, 693
Come to the Water	NALR (Glory and Praise, Vol. 2, #92)
Do not be afraid	CBW II, 713
I Have Decided	SOLW, 78
I Want to Walk as a Child	SOLW, 34
I Am the Resurrection	CBW II, 551
Song of the Holy Spirit	CBW II, 526

ACCLAMATIONS AFTER BAPTISM

Alleluia, Give Thanks	CBW II, 496
Alleluia (round)	CBW II, 663
New Life	NALR (Glory and Praise, Vol. 2, #124)
Oh How Good Is the Lord	SOLW (traditional) 6
Rejoice in the Lord Always	SOLW (traditional) 10
This Is the Day	SOLW, 6
You Have Been Baptized in Christ	CBW II, 593

COMMUNION

Help Us to Help	CBW II, 712
I Will Never Forget You	CBW II, 708
On Eagle's Wings	NALR (Glory and Praise, Vol. 2, #126)
The Lord Jesus	CBW II, 562
Yahweh, I Know	CBW II, 669

MISSIONING

Before the Sun Burned Bright	NALR (Glory and Praise, Vol. 2, #86)
For You Are My God	CBW II, 635
In Him We Live	NALR (Glory and Praise, Vol. 1, #27)
Glory and Praise to Our God	NALR (Song Prayers) 84
Forth in the Peace	CBW II, 550
They'll Know We are Christians	CBW II, 694

CBW II: Catholic Book of Worship II, 1980, Concacan Inc., Ottawa, Ontario. K1N 7B1

NOVALIS: (Living with Christ), P.O. Box 9700, Terminal, Ottawa, Ont. K1G 4B4

NALR: North American Liturgy Resources, Song Prayers, and Glory and Praise, Vol. I and II, 10802 North 23rd Ave., Phoenix, Arizona. 85029

SOLW: Songs of Living Water, Hodderlands Stoughton, Toronto, Ont., 1977.

Various Resources

And Their Eyes Were Opened, Michael Scanlan and Ann Therese Shields. 1976, Servant Publications, P.O. Box 8617, 840 Airport Blvd., Ann Arbor, MI 48107

Book of Blessings. 1981, CCCB Publications, 90 Parent Ave., Ottawa, Ont. K1N 7B1

Christian Sacraments and Christian Growth, Charles Keating. 1976, Twenty-Third Pub., P.O. Box 180, Mystic, CT 06355

Christening: The Making of Christians, Mark Searle. 1981, Liturgical Press, Engle Blvd., Collegeville, MN 56321

The Easter Passage: The RCIA Experience, Mary Pierre Ellebracht. 1983, Winston Press, 430 Oak Grove, Minneapolis, MN 55403

Infant Baptism Today, James Dullen. 1979, Pastoral Arts Association, 4744 West Country Gables Drive, Glendale, AZ 85306

A New Look at the Sacraments, William Bausch. 1977, Fides Publications, 333 N. Lafayette, South Bend, IN 46601

The Sacraments and Your Everyday Life, Bernard Haring, CSsR. 1976, Liguori Pub., 1 Liguori Dr., Liguori, MO 63057

The Shape of Baptism, Aidan Kavanagh. 1978, Pueblo Publications, 1860 Broadway, New York, NY 10023

Signs of Love: The Sacraments of Christ, Leonard Foley, OFM. 1976, St. Anthony Messenger Press, 1615 Republic St., Cincinnati, OH 45210

Teaching the Church Today, Carl Pfeifer. 1978, Twenty-third Publications, P.O. Box 180, Mystic, CT 06355

Theology of Baptism, Lorna Brockett, RSCJ. 1971, Fides Publications, 333 N. Lafayette, South Bend, IN 46601

BAPTISM PREPARATION

Written by:

Gerry van Regan,
pastoral minister,
St. Joseph's Parish, Ottawa.

Edited by:

Jerome Herauf

Layout:

Jan Gough, Gilles Lépine

Photography:

Cover: Reb Materi, O.M.I.;
p. 2: Jonas Abromaitis;
p. 9, 11, 12, 25, 36: Roman Matwijejko;
p. 22: Sheila Sturley, RSCJ;
p. 28: Miller Services Ltd.:
p. 31: Paul Hamel

Illustrations:

Cover 1, cover 4
and all inside illustrations:
Lee Thirlwall

*"... for anyone who is in Christ,
there is a new creation."*

(2 Corinthians 5: 17)

Winston Press
430 Oak Grove
Minneapolis, Minnesota 55403

ISBN: 0-86683-732-9

First Eucharist, Reconciliation, Confirmation

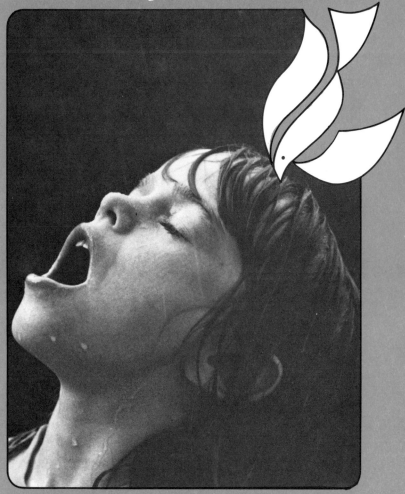

New Parish Ministries

WINSTON PRESS

Contents

New Parish Ministries was originally published by Novalis, Saint Paul University, Ottawa, Canada. This edition is published by Winston Press, Inc., by arrangement with Novalis, Saint Paul University. Copyright © 1982, Novalis. Copyright © 1983, Winston Press. All rights reserved. No part of this book may be reproduced in any form without written permission from the publisher.

ISBN: 0-86683-733-7 (previously ISBN: 2-89088-080-X)

Printed in Canada

5   4   3   2   1

Winston Press, Inc., 430 Oak Grove, Minneapolis, MN 55403

A Guide for the Parish Coordinator

Introduction and Pastoral Notes

The sacraments are approached here from the ordinary pastoral situation, and in the order in which — for better or for worse — they are usually celebrated.

Catechesis of reconciliation is an integral part of catechesis of the eucharist. Since these two sacraments seem linked in the minds of Catholics, and in pastoral practice, that link is preserved here.

Baptism, Confirmation, Eucharist is the traditional sequence of the initiation process, School-age children are rarely catechised for or celebrate the sacraments in this order. Confirmation, therefore, is placed at the end of the process, where, in practice, it is usually celebrated.

A Word from the Coordinator

What is our task?

Initiating children into the sacramental life of the Church is a complex and joyous task that cannot take place without the cooperation of many people — parents, children, priests, parishioners, catechists, liturgists, Catholic school community; and parents, children, and catechists working outside the Catholic school system.

All of these people make up the community into which the child is being initiated. The Coordinator is the person who helps everyone make sense of their respective roles in this community task of initiation.

What is the main task of the Coordinator?

The main task of the coordinator is to ensure that the sacramental initiation of children is a community event.

How is this to be done?

Form a team — choose a representative from each segment of the community involved in the particular sacrament.

The remainder of this booklet will outline the tasks and thoughts of such a team over a year's preparation for each sacrament.

Who Initiates?

A Word about Initiation

Sacramental preparation in the recent past has tended to concentrate primarily on *things you need to know before...*

Today, Sacramental initiation concentrates primarily on growing and ongoing entry into the believing, celebrating community. This means that the emphasis is not solely on the children, but on all of us who make up the community.

As we look at the life of our parish, our vision of our task takes shape something like this:

The sacraments are the high points in the life of this community; they are not private events, but key events in our personal lives celebrated in the heart of the community.

The Eucharist is the cornerstone of our community — it is appreciated by many older people daily, celebrated joyfully by young families; it is a source of strength and unity to older families, and constantly being discovered anew by young adults in their quest for life.

All these riches of the Eucharist we must learn to share with the next generation.

Reconciliation celebrates our constant striving. As a community, as individuals, we struggle, fall, are negligent, sometimes cruel, often uncaring, but the promise and experience of Reconciliation is constantly held out to us by the Church.

This promise, this experience, we must share with the next generation.

Confirmation is the celebration of the presence of the Spirit in our parish. Each of us is engaged in preparing a community where the new generation of confirmed will find a place where they can begin to grow into the fullness of Christ.

This is the vision we wish to share with the children.

Where do we start?

We start by assembling a team of community members who share this vision.

When do we start?

As early as possible in September (or earlier) — for two reasons:

● Our lives — for better or worse — are bounded by the school year. New energies abound at the start of this "new" year.

● Catechetical preparation for Eucharist, Reconciliation. Confirmation, is woven throughout the entire year. All those involved need to know the nature and content of the catechesis right from the start of the year, so that they can accompany their children along this important journey. This, of course, applies in a very special way to those families immediately involved.

Roles and Tasks
in Sacramental Initiation

Roles

For convenience, we intend to speak of just three roles:

Parents and families

Pope John Paul II speaks of the "Church of the home," and adds that "family catechesis... precedes, accompanies and enriches all other forms of catechesis" (Catechesi Tradendae, No. 68).

Catechists

They will provide a "catechesis that gives meaning to the sacraments, but at the same time receives from the experience of the sacraments a living dimension that keeps it from remaining merely doctrinal... it communicates to the child the joy of being a witness to Christ in ordinary life" (Catechesi Tradendae, No. 37).

Priests and Parish

The parish "must rediscover its vocation which is to be a fraternal and welcoming family home, where those who have been baptized and confirmed become aware of forming the people of God. In that home, the bread of good doctrine and the eucharistic bread are broken for them in abundance, in the setting of one act of worship; from that home they are sent out day by day to their apostolic mission in all the centers of activity of the life of the world" (Catechesi Tradendae, No. 67).

Tasks

Team planning:

If possible, before the end of August, the planning team should meet to coordinate those three roles, and to plan for the entire year. Many parishes plan for three sets of meetings for each sacrament — the first set in September, the second set just before Lent, and the third set some time (perhaps four weeks) before the celebration of the sacrament.

• Parents, as the Church has so often repeated, are the main teachers of their children. But, as Pope John Paul reminds us, this teaching is often without words, but rather in a day-to-day living of the Christian life (Cat. Trad. No. 68).

• Parents educate by providing the "stuff" of Christian family life, with all its dynamism of growth, celebration, failure, forgiveness, support and love. The catechist uses this life experience of the child as the jumping-off point for catechesis. The further task of the parent, then, is to be aware of the nature and content of the catechesis, and to build bridges for the child between school, home and parish.

• Some "bridgeable" moments for each sacrament

Eucharist: meals, friends, bread, birthdays, anniversaries, gifts. *Reconciliation:* struggles, apologies, communication, failures, family reunions, making up after a fight. *Confirmation:* growth, dreams, "what I will be...", service, identity.

Catechists

• The main task of the catechist is to accompany the children, as *privileged representatives of the community* on their journeys toward Eucharist, Reconciliation and Confirmation.

• No two parishes in this country are alike. The task of the catechist is to provide the best possible catechesis, given all the variables in any particular parish. *Sharing the Light of Faith,* The National Catechetical Directory, offers practical guidelines to accomplish this task.

• As well as being representative of the community it will sometimes be the catechist's task to suggest — from his/her experience with a particular age-group — appropriate changes to a parish regarding content of catechesis; style of celebrating or time of celebrating, depending on the readiness of the children. This dialogue includes, of course, the parents.

• Sacraments are celebrations of the parish community. The pastor along with the Pastoral Team, then, as leader of the community, has overall concern for all that pertains to the preparation for and celebration of the sacraments. His specific role, however, has more to do with the celebration than with the preparation. The pastor must be kept informed at all times about the nature, course and content of the catechesis and, whenever possible, be present at the meetings.

• Since the revision of the sacraments and the renewal of catechetical process, there are likely to be some profound differences between the manner in which parents have been prepared for and experience the sacraments, and the way their children are being catechised. The constant flow of liturgical life in a parish can go a long way towards making parishioners aware of these differences, but occasional homilies on each of the sacraments may also be necessary. This is especially so with Eucharist, Reconciliation and Confirmation, so that parents and teachers and children and pastors will be using the same language.

• In the whole process of religious education perhaps the leader's most important role is to be seen by the children as a friend. His presence in the schoolyard and in the homes of the children may ultimately be much more important than his presence in the classroom.

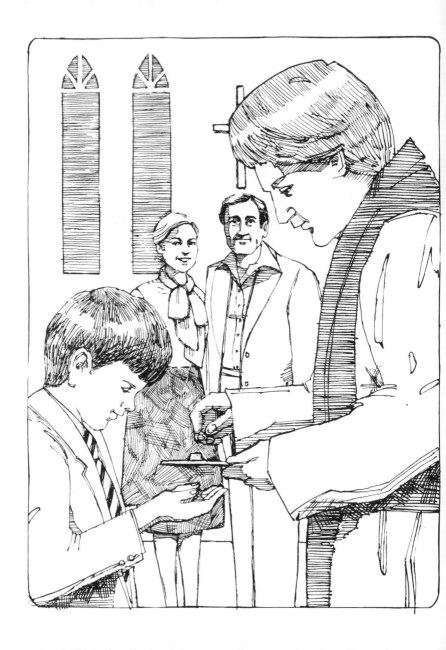

The Eucharistic Community

The initiation of new members into the Eucharistic community is a continuing process. In a very real sense, everything we do as a parish is preparation and initiation. The recurring high points of the liturgical year, parish festivities, personal and group prayer, parish ministries of service, healing and caring — all flow from the Eucharist and find their meaning and strength there.

> *Each community is responsible for the credibility of the Eucharistic proclamation of faith.*

We have chosen two aspects of specific preparation

a) the parish community as a whole

b) the families involved

The parish community

Each community needs to be made aware of its young members preparing for Eucharist. One graphic way of accomplishing this would be to hold a public inscription of candidates for admission to First Eucharist at one or more of the Sunday liturgies (see **Resources,** p. 32).

The families

To simplify the procedure, we give here the outline of three possible meetings during the year:

Meeting One:

Who? Parents should be an integral part of their children's catechesis.

When? As early in the school year as possible. A meeting held very shortly before the celebration of First Eucharist shows little respect for the role of parents in the process.

Goal: To make parents aware of the nature and content of the whole process of Eucharistic initiation, so that all involved may be clear about their respective roles.

Where? In the parish hall, if possible. This is a parish event. All involved should be invited, i.e., all children, catechists, parents, priests.

11

Tentative Outline

7.30 p.m.   Welcome... by Pastor.

7.35 p.m.   Coordinator (introduced by pastor) explains process of evening. Few words on communal nature of initiation process.

7.45 p.m.   Private reflection: individual written responses to such questions as: *What are your memories of your own First Communion? What has changed in your celebration of the Eucharist? What would you like to pass along to your child?*

8.00 p.m.   Sharing in groups of three-four.

8.15 p.m.   General feedback.

8.30 p.m.   Presentation on the general nature of Eucharistic catechesis as e.g., in *Sharing the Light of Faith*, the National Catechetical Directory; link between family experiences and school catechesis; pivotal experiences of friendship and celebration; not just First Communion but eucharistic way of life.

8.50 p.m.   Presentation by parent. Some specific points: Mass attendance, family preparation, prayer.

9.10 p.m.   Closing prayer — a Word Service celebration.

9.20 p.m.   Announcements.

9.30 p.m.   Refreshments, Book Display, etc.

Meeting Two:

When? Just before Lent.

Goal: To share with parents and all involved the specific content of the catechesis of the Eucharist. Meeting should include: time for private reflection, group sharing, plenary session for questions, presentation preferably by Grade II teacher, group prayer, some access to further resources.

See p. 23 for content of catechesis.

Meeting Three:

When? About four weeks before the solemn celebration of First Eucharist (see p. 28).

Goal: To plan the celebration, and include as many as possible in the preparation.

This meeting should result in clear, specific directions regarding times, dates, dress, local customs, nature of the celebration, photography, etc.

Conclude with some liturgical celebration of thanksgiving and a word of congratulations to all those involved.

The Reconciled Community

The Sacrament of Reconciliation is a privileged moment in a Christian life. It is a process that includes our relationship with ourselves, with each other, with God.

The celebration of the sacrament is not an isolated act in the life of a Christian, but part of a process of being reconciled — a moment on our journey from darkness to light, from isolation to community, from selfishness to service. This is the case for the seven, eight, nine and ninety-nine year old Christian. For this reason, the catechesis of reconciliation is interwoven with our lives, especially with our eucharistic lives.

In the child's catechetical program, we speak of reconciliation when we speak of friendship (and isolation), of light (and darkness), of happiness (and loneliness), of success (and failure), of obedience (and disobedience).

Preparation for the celebration of the Sacrament of Reconciliation has been going on since the parents first kissed away the tears of an infant — the first experience for the child of the Christian proclamation of a loving and merciful God, and the reconciling event of Jesus Christ.

However, as the conscious grappling with personal and group sin begins to occur in the life of the child, it is essential that the catechesis, experience and celebration of reconciliation become more and more consciously expressed.

The celebration of "First Confession" takes place at varied times, under varied forms, and for varied reasons across the country.

Traditionally, the Sacrament of Reconciliation has never been an integral part of the sacraments of initiation — baptism, eucharist, confirmation.

The only possible norm then would indicate that (a) Catechesis of reconciliation begin hand in hand with the start of formal catechesis (see *Sharing the Light of Faith*, the National Catechetical Directory, # 126), and (b) Celebration of the sacrament be determined by parent, priest, teacher, according to the readiness of the child.

Three Sample Meetings

Here, again, for convenience, we have chosen to outline three possible parish meetings.

Meeting One

When? As early in September as possible.

Goal: To allow everyone involved in the process to become aware of the nature and content of the catechesis of reconciliation.

Outline of meeting: In general, the five-part format as described in the section on First Eucharist seems to work well (see p. 11).

Part 1 Welcome, Introductions.

Part 2 *Telling personal and group stories* — memories of my First Confession; why I stopped going to Confession; how I celebrate forgiveness of sin in my life; my changing experience of sin; how I know what is right and wrong...

Part 3 *Telling the Christian story* — the gospel message of forgiveness, history of the Sacrament of Reconciliation, exploring the new Rites of Reconciliation.

Several different approaches are possible, but this section should always build on a heightened personal and group awareness of where I stand.

Part 4 *Interaction of the two stories* — my personal story/the Christian story. Group discussion, question and answer period, sample case studies, etc.

Part 5 *Closing celebration. A* gathering up of the fears, prayers, hopes of the assembly; a proclamation of the Christian message and call to conversion; a prayer of response; a gesture; a closing hymn.

Again, many formats are possible — the simpler the better. But this celebration should be seen as an essential part of the evening, and not as a mere Christian flourish.

Meeting Two and Meeting Three

When? Shortly before Lent, and some weeks before the actual celebration.

Goal: To acquaint parents and all concerned with the content of the catechesis of reconciliation (see page 25).

Note: There is a great deal of confusion in the Catholic community in general concerning the Sacrament of Reconciliation, and a widespread lack of familiarity with the new rites.

Most parish coordinators discover that this second meeting can profitably be spent almost entirely on a renewed adult look at the sacrament. The areas of conscience, moral development, personal and social sin, as well as personal and social repentance need to be covered. This is necessary groundwork before the nature of the children's catechesis can be effectively dealt with in the third meeting.

The problems for which sacramental penance is a solution come up very seldom in the lives of young children, and an overuse of the sacrament might indicate scrupulosity or unrealistic guilt. Grade school children are so little in command of their own lives and persons, so prone to misinterpreting their own experience ... Their faith is a participation in that of adults, their response to events and persons is intense, total and emotional, their responsibility is flawed, their feelings of guilt ... flowing from the discrepancies between rule and behavior rather than from conscious reflection on genuine sin. Therefore, religious educators should aim primarily at predisposing them to a favorable experience of the sacrament, predisposing them to a genuine relationship with the forgiving Christ, and the forgiving, ritualizing Church. Beyond that, we should proceed with caution.

(Elizabeth McMahon Jeep, *The Rite of Penance, Commentaries, Vol. II*, The Liturgical Conference, Washington, 1976.)

The Confirmed Community

In the past decade, the Rite of Confirmation has been revised so that "the intimate connection which this sacrament has with the whole of Christian initiation should be more lucidly set forth" (Sac. Conc. 71).

Quite simply, then, a good catechesis of Baptism is a good catechesis of Confirmation. Or to put it negatively, any catechesis of Confirmation which is not built upon the theology of Baptism is not a sound catechesis.

What is Confirmation?

● It is the celebration of the fullness of the presence of the Spirit in this particular parish — a Spirit given in all its fullness in Baptism.
● Confirmation is the annual recognition and celebration of the signs of the Spirit in our parish, one of the major signs being the class, for example, of 1990.
● Confirmation is the celebration of the confirmed community as it acknowledges the continued graceful presence of the Spirit in its members, in this new class of young Christians who are choosing this community as the place of their growth as Christians.

Once again, we see that we are describing a celebration of the whole community for the whole community — a local parish community initiating its young members more fully.

Once again, we choose to describe three parish meetings — without repeating the same general comments about time of meetings, format, or purpose. However, we would like to suggest some more specific approaches.

Three Sample Meetings

Meeting One

We suggest a first meeting only for parents to re-affirm the importance of their role and to offer them support.

Part 1 Welcome, introductions, etc.

Part 2 Biography writing. Lead parents to write a sketchy biography of the child who is preparing for Confirmation. Such questions as these will help:

• Do you remember the day of your child's birth? Jot down some

of your feelings, fears, hopes, joys.

• What stands out about the personality of your child?

• Do you remember the first day at school? First Communion?

• What are your child's gifts?

• What will your child have most difficulty with?

• What are your fears? hopes? now for your child?

Part 3 Allow parents time to share — first husband and wife, then in groups of couples.

Part 4 *Resource person:* Gather together the stories. Identify the presence of the Spirit in these lives. Lead the group to an explanation of Confirmation as the celebration of the fullness of the Spirit already given and, as just seen, already at work in the lives of parents and children.

Meeting Two

A celebration for parents and children in preparation for Confirmation.

___The celebration could follow this format _____

- Invitation to prayer
- Opening song
- Opening prayer
- Reading from 1 Corinthians 12:1-7
- Response to Reading: Parents, on sheets provided, finish this sentence: *What I pray for you most of all is...*
  Children, on sheets provided, finish this sentence: *What I thank you most of all for is...*
  Parents and children then exchange sheets.
- Gospel — John 13:34-35, 14:23-26.
- Brief homily
- Parents light candles from the Paschal Candle, and pass on the light to the next generation.
- Blessing
- Closing song

Meeting Three

If possible, this should be a gathering of parents, children and sponsors. It should take place about six weeks before Confirmation. Since the formal catechesis for Confirmation has been going on all year, the simplest format for this meeting would be an explanation of the Rite of Confirmation, supported, if possible, by suitable audio-visuals (see Resources, p. 32). This could be followed by a rehearsal.

Two concluding thoughts

1. The practice of having sponsors at Confirmation is a "left-over" from the time when adult Baptism/Confirmation/Eucharist was the norm. The sponsor was the link to the community and the companion along the journey of faith. In our present practice of celebrating the sacraments, the parents obviously fill this role. It is probably preferable, then, to treat sponsors as community representatives, rather than build an improbable picture of the sponsor as a future major influence in the life of the child. (In many places, the sponsor is one or both of the godparents.) For a more accurate description of sponsors, see the Rite of Confirmation.

2. The Bishop is the usual main celebrant of Confirmation. If at all possible, there should be some communication with the presiding Bishop on matters of catechesis, format of ceremony, nature of preparation, age of candidates, etc., to ensure as ordered and joyful a celebration as possible.

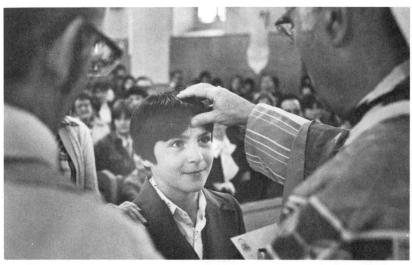

Catechesis of Initiation

Eucharist

1. A catechesis of the Eucharist for seven- and eight-year-old children must initiate children into the full complexity, richness, and yet simplicity of the Eucharist. It must be a real initiation — that is, a full incorporation of a person into the mystery of Christ. In other words, we do not prepare children for First Communion as though it were an isolated event.

2. We approach the Eucharist as assembly, as meal, as sacrifice, as memorial, as celebration, as sacrament of thanksgiving, as sharing of Word and breaking of Bread.

3. The process of the catechesis is from *experience* to *reflection* on experience in the light of the Word, to *response*.

4. *Experience:* Throughout the year, the experience of friendship is pivotal. All the dynamics of friendship link the year together — desire for friends, invitations and responses, communication between friends, remembering, sharing of life and love, gifts, thanksgiving, celebration.

5. *Reflection:* The child's experience is "illuminated" by looking at the life of Jesus with his friends, by listening to his words: "Come, follow me," "You are my friends," story of the Last Supper, "I have come so that you may have life," "I am the light of the world"...

As we saw with the parent sessions, the child's "story" is illuminated and transformed by reflecting on the story of Jesus and the Christian story. The catechesis is leading them to "put on the mind of Christ" which for the seven-year old, as for the adult, is a journey.

6. *Response:* The specific focus for the response of the young disciple in this year's catechesis is life in the Eucharistic community, and specifically, initiation into the liturgical celebration of the Eucharist. The process can be illustrated as follows:

Experience	Reflection	Response
Getting to know you	"You are my friends"	The Mass in general Entrance Rites
Communication	"I am the light…"	Liturgy of the Word
Sharing a meal	The Last Supper	Meal aspects of Eucharist
Gifts — sharing life	"I have come that you may have life."	Offering, sacrifice aspects of the Eucharist
Listening to each other	Mary, Mother of Jesus	Listening to the Word
Failures and difficulties of friendship	"What I command you is to love one another"	Penitential Rite, Our Father, Sign of Peace

Reconciliation

1. The process — experience, reflection, response — will be similar to the one just described for Eucharist. It will be noted that catechesis on reconciliation is an integral part of Eucharistic catechesis. For this reason, we intend simply to add a few comments.

2. About six weeks before the celebration of First Reconciliation, more specific catechesis should take place. The content and process of this catechesis may be found in *Sharing The Light of Faith*, the National Catechetical Directory, # 126.

3. It is important that a five-fold movement toward repentance and reconciliation be seen clearly:

• Personal experience of a relationship with God.

• Knowledge and experience of the demands of this relationship (many of these will be known to the children from their earliest moments: "don't fight... share your toys... tell the truth, obey... everybody, say your prayers".) They must now be experienced as demands that are in the context of the Christian relationship with God.

• The experience of failure, struggle, temptation.

• The articulation of failure, expressed in response to the constant proclamation of God's forgiveness.

• The celebration of conversion and reconciliation.

4. Having children go through the motions of going to Confession because "it is good for them" is not a true initiation into a life and sacrament of reconciliation. Dialogue between parent and teacher, parent and priest, parent and child will enable the parents to discern when their children are ready. This is the right and privilege of the parents.

Confirmation

1. The age at which Confirmation is celebrated will determine the form of catechesis.

2. First, three *cautions:*

• Catechesis for Confirmation should not be in the context of "becoming mature Christians," or "becoming adults in the Church."

• The students should never be left with the impression that this is the end of their religious education. Too much emphasis on "knowing the truths of faith before you're confirmed" often leaves this unfortunate impression. Some synthesis of faith suited to the student is of course expected, but a synthesis of faith for a young person does not sustain one throughout adulthood.

• All catechesis that makes Baptism seem deficient is distorted. Confirmation does not finish something left undone by Baptism, nor does it exclusively bestow the Spirit. Confirmation is a celebration of the fullness of the Spirit already bestowed.

3. An immediate preparation for Confirmation should include:

• Knowledge and experience of the Holy Spirit present in their lives

• A reliance on the Holy Spirit as a guide for the future

• An experience of the Holy Spirit active in the community

• An apprenticeship in the works of the Spirit — service to God's people

• An attitude of thanksgiving towards Creation and humanity blessed by the presence of the Spirit

• Some conscious expression of faith in Jesus Christ

• A recognition and acceptance of the fact that the Spirit is given to the community... a love of the Church

4. One or two homilies to the whole parish community would help to include them in this community celebration of the active presence of the Spirit in their midst.

Celebrating Initiation

Sacramental celebrations are celebrations of the whole Christian community — occasions when the parish tries to throw light on the present by remembering the past and looking towards the future. The Eucharistic proclamation of faith — Christ has died, Christ is risen, Christ will come again — is the central proclamation of every Christian celebration. In a Christian liturgical celebration, the true colors of our lives are for a moment revealed so that we may know who we are. In the Eucharist, the answer to our hungers and thirsts is revealed to us; in Reconciliation, the fact of our profound union with God and one another is revealed; in Confirmation, the all-embracing gracefulness of our humanity gifted with the fullness of the Spirit is called to mind and celebrated.

It is into this sacramental life that we are initiating our children — a life of discovering, experiencing and celebrating the presence of God in the gathered community, in a spirit of thanksgiving (Eucharist), reconciliation and promise (Confirmation).

We will add just a few notes on each sacramental celebration.

Eucharist

1. As far as possible, the celebration of First Eucharist will be a parish celebration, and not a school event, or series of school events.

2. Many formats have been found helpful:

• individual celebrations (as each family chooses) according to the readiness of the child, followed by one large parish celebration;

• small groups of four or five families celebrating First Eucharist together on Saturdays throughout the year, again followed by a solemn First Eucharist for the whole parish. In both of these, the advantages of intimacy and community witness are maintained.

3. The Eucharistic Prayers for children and other permissible liturgical adaptations should be utilized. Care should be taken, however, not to use children as readers, etc., for their "cute" effect, but for the effective performance of the ministry in question.

4. Songs, prayers, homily should be geared to the children, though not exclusively. The Eucharistic liturgy is never a spectator event.

5. A parish party after the liturgy will add to the festivity of the occasion.

Reconciliation

1. An abundance of possibilities exists here. Children will be celebrating Reconciliation under some or all of the following conditions:

• privately with parents, according to readiness

• at parish celebrations, particularly during Advent and Lent

• at school celebrations, during Advent and Lent, but also at the beginning and end of the school year

• in classroom celebrations occasionally during the year, some of which may not be sacramental

2. It seems appropriate to have a general parish celebration of Reconciliation for children somewhere during the Lent of Grade III.

3. Experience suggests that the first celebration of the sacrament for children should be with a priest who is known as a friend. It seems most appropriate to celebrate Form II (communal celebration with individual confession and absolution) with children because it combines effectively both the personal and communal dimensions of the sacrament. Whatever form is chosen, care should be taken that this is a genuine celebration of conversion, in an atmosphere of joy and hope.

Confirmation

1. Many parishes have found a Confirmation retreat, held a few days before Confirmation, to be an excellent form of celebration for the students. Usually, during Confirmation preparation, so many demands are made on the students that they lose sight of the joy of celebrating the gift of the Spirit in their lives. A day devoted to affirmation of the students as persons can help restore some balance.

2. The bishop, as main celebrant, should be made aware of the nature of the preparation the students have undergone. If at all possible, the bishop should meet the students before the celebration.

3. The parish community should be involved as much as possible, e.g.,

in the public welcome of the Bishop.

4. The size of the Confirmation class should be such as will keep the celebration to an appropriate length.

5. Students chosen to perform any liturgical ministries — lector, reading of General Intercessions, procession at Preparation of the Gifts — should be well prepared to perform their ministry as a service to the community. These ministries should not be seen as rewards for good students.

6. Again, a party after the celebration will add to the festivity of the occasion, and give all another chance to meet the bishop.

In Conclusion

Each parish community has its own customs, expectations, spirit and dynamics. These must be recognized and articulated, because it is into one particular parish community that each generation initiates its children. On the other hand, the impulse toward renewal and conversion in any parish community is linked to the ever-recurring celebration of the sacraments of life in its midst. A careful celebration of initiation can be a profound source of new life for a parish and, year by year, offers a rich catechetical resource.

In the revised Rite of Christian Initiation for Adults it is pointed out that the whole community grows into a fuller understanding of the mysteries of Christ, as the sacraments are explained anew and celebrated anew each year. The vision of a new Church given us in this Rite can be approached step by step.

Finally, the work of initiating new Christians into constantly renewing parishes needs the visible and consistent exercise of all the ministries. Only then can we cooperate in growing "in all ways into Christ, who is the head by whom the whole body is fitted and joined together, every joint adding its own strength, for each separate part to work according to its function. So the body grows until it has built itself up, in love" (Eph. 4:16).

Resources

An abundance of texts available on the market for each of the three sacraments we have been discussing.

The Redemptorist publication *Your Faith* (Student text and Leader's Guide) will provide a valuable summary of the Catholic faith for the more mature Confirmation student (Liguori Publications, 1978).

Arbour. Basil, *With Hearts Renewed*, 1982, Novalis, P.O. Box 9700, Terminal, Ottawa, Canada   K1G 4B4

Beaulac, Jules, *The Lord Invites Me to His Table*, 1980, Novalis

Becoming a Catholic Christian. 1979, A Symposium on Christian Initiation. Sadlier, 11 Park Place, New York, N.Y.   10007

Bitney, James, *All Things New: A Celebration of Forgiveness*. 1982, Winston Press

Bitney, James, *Come to Communion; It's All about Celebration; Go in Peace; Walking Together Again; Sabbath* (filmstrip on Sunday Assembly), Winston Press

Bitney, James, *First Communion: A Parish Celebration*. 1982, Winston Press

Brusselmans, Christianne, *We Celebrate Reconciliation*. 1975, Silver Burdett Company.

Buckley, Francis, *Children and God: Communion, Confession and Confirmation*. 1970, Corpus Papers, New York

Catechesi Tradendae, On Catechesis in our Time, Pope John Paul II. 1979, Canadian Conference of Catholic Bishops, 90 Parent Ave., Ottawa, Canada   K1N 7B1

Coady, Patricia; Griffin, Deborah; Jette, Theresa, *In the Breaking of the Bread*. 1982, Novalis

De Gidio, Sandra, *Sharing Faith in the Family*. 1980, Twenty-Third Publications, P.O. Box 180, Mystic, CT 06355

Kenny, Bernadette, *Children's Liturgies*. 1977, Paulist Press, 545 Island Rd., Ramsey, NJ 07446

Neville, Gwen and Westerhoff, John H. III, *Learning Through Liturgy*. 1978, Seabury Press, 815 Second Ave., New York, NY 10017

Rite of Christian Initiation of Adults. 1974, Canadian Conference of Catholic Bishops, 90 Parent Ave., Ottawa, Canada   K1N 7B1

The Rites. 1976, Pueblo Publishing Company, Inc., 1860 Broadway, New York, N.Y. 10023

**FIRST EUCHARIST, RECONCILIATION,
CONFIRMATION PREPARATION**

Written by:

Mary Malone,
catechetics professor at
Toronto School of Theology

Edited by:

Jerome Herauf

Layout:

Jan Gough, Gilles Lépine

Photography:

Cover: Mia et Klaus;
p. 5: "Vivants univers"; p. 6: Ken Harris; p. 13,
24: Roman Matwijejko; p. 20: Miller Services Ltd.;
p. 22: Karoli Dombi; p. 27: Gilles Lafrance

Illustrations:

Cover 1 and cover 4: Lee Thirlwall;
inside illustrations: Krista Johnston

*"Make your home in me,
as I make mine in you."*

(John 15: 4)

Winston Press
430 Oak Grove
Minneapolis, Minnesota 55403

ISBN: 0-86683-733-7

Marriage Preparation

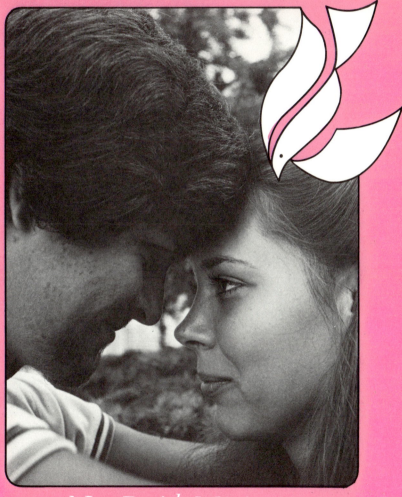

New Parish Ministries

WINSTON PRESS

Contents

New Parish Ministries *was originally published by Novalis, Saint Paul University, Ottawa, Canada. This edition is published by Winston Press, Inc., by arrangement with Novalis, Saint Paul University. Copyright © 1982, Novalis. Copyright © 1983, Winston Press. All rights reserved. No part of this book may be reproduced in any form without written permission from the publisher.*

ISBN: 0-86683-734-5 (previously ISBN: 2-89088-081-8)

Printed in Canada

5   4   3   2   1

Winston Press, Inc., 430 Oak Grove, Minneapolis, MN 55403

Introduction

The marriage of a couple is a concern of the whole Church, not only because marriage is a sacrament, but because the whole community (family, friends, neighbors) is affected by this sign and by the life of each couple. The Church is well aware that the period of engagement is crucial to the commitment to marry. It is at this time that a couple begins and develops the processes of communication which will influence the rest of their lives.

When we are speaking here of the Church, we are not referring only to bishops and priests. The Church is all of us gathered together in faith and common concern. Therefore, in the area of married life, it is vital that married men and women also address the couples from their own experiences. There can be no better sign for an engaged couple than to see and hear the witness of husbands and wives who are committed to continually growing in their own marriage.

It is important for married couples to join with pastors in offering engaged couples the opportunity to explore and develop their own relationships. This can become a very unique occasion for the whole Church to say to the couples that their marriage is special; that they are important to all of us; that they do not journey alone.

How to Get Started

• Contact your parish priest and learn about local needs.

• After you have spoken to a priest and other couples who share the same interests, together seek assistance from trained persons who can guide you in developing your own program and in developing the methods for effective presentation.

• Within most dioceses there are usually three services available:

1. Regional Programs run by a Diocesan Centre (sometimes called: Catholic Information Centre or Family Life Office). There you will find personnel, trained to present courses, and available to train others in the preparation and presentation of marriage courses.

2. Parishes which have taken a leadership role in marriage preparation. They too would have persons trained to conduct marriage courses. From them you could learn about the stages, techniques and materials you need to assist you in developing your own program.

3. Engaged Encounter, which has grown from Marriage Encounter, offers a program for engaged couples.

Information about any of these or about individual diocesan programs is usually available through your Diocesan Centre or parish priest. It is always best to explore all the options and then choose the one which best meets the needs of the couples in your parish.

It is essential that:

• You seek help from established groups.

• You do not try to do your "own thing", especially if all of you are new to this ministry. (After all, the program is for the couples and not simply to meet your needs as minister.)

• You take into account both well-established practices and new approaches.

After you have done all this, you can then add your own personal dimension to the program. However, always keep in mind that this is the work of the whole Church and not "your" mission alone.

Although you may not necessarily be always working with priests, it is vital to be constantly in touch with them about what you are doing. They should, at the very least, be available from time to time to speak to the couples — especially about the sacramental part of marriage and the wedding day itself. This will make clear one of the main objectives of ministries: that we have **co-responsibility** with bishops and priests in serving the needs of our communities.

Note: If your parish is small and you have only a few marriages each year, you might join with other parishes in your region to prepare and present a course. Each parish could take a turn hosting the sessions.

Group preparation of engaged couples

Group preparation of engaged couples is heavily favored in marriage preparation programs. This allows for variety in the presentations and for small group discussions on the various topics.

Other positive points concerning group preparation

● It creates an atmosphere for the sharing of common goals and concerns.

● It shows that problems which may arise during the engagement period are normal and natural in any growing love relationship.

● It brings out questions one or another couple may not consider or may even avoid discussing.

● It stresses that the whole community has an interest in the marriage of each couple.

● It emphasizes that each couple, and so each marriage, is unique and special.

● It allows a reasonable time frame for meeting the needs of engaged couples within the parish or region. (In large parishes, there may be more than 50 marriages a year. If the program consists of 5-7 sessions, think of the number of persons and hours needed to serve each couple on an individual basis.)

● It allows many friendships to form among the couples, which may remain with them throughout their married lives. These friendships can be an important source of support.

Preparation of individual couples

In smaller parishes or in special cases, it may be best to prepare couples on an individual basis. This can be done by the priest alone or in conjunction with one or two other couples. For these circumstances, we suggest the revised MOSAIC (1981 edition, Novalis, St. Paul University) with its Leader's Guide and five Couple's Booklets. The Booklets contain activity sheets, designed for the couple to complete together on their own. These activity sheets can become the basis for dialogue between the couple and the priest/married couples.

Lead couples

There are two ways in which lead couples may be involved in the preparation and presentation of the course content:

1. Those who prepare and make the main presentations of the themes of the program. It would be wise to have at least two couples who are prepared to handle each topic. This will avoid any break in the course if, for any of a dozen reasons, one couple is unable to attend. As the couples alternate in their turns to present the materials on a given theme, they will be able to get another viewpoint on the same topic and therefore enrich their own presentation.

2. Those who do not wish to make presentations to large groups but would feel more comfortable working with small groups of couples. This is just as important to a marriage course — dealing with the questions and issues raised in the presentations. However, this group should be well-versed in the various techniques of group dynamics and be generally well-read on all the topics considered in the marriage program.

God said,

*"Let us make humans in the likeness of ourselves,
and let them be stewards of the fish of the sea,
the birds of heaven
and all animals and reptiles that crawl upon the earth."*

*God created humans in his own likeness,
God created them male and female.*

*God blessed them, saying,
"Be fruitful, fill the earth.
Be stewards of the fish of the sea, the birds of heaven
and all the animals of the earth."*

*God looked at all he had made,
and indeed it was very good.*

*adapted from Genesis 1:26-28, 31
(from choice of readings for celebrating
the Marriage liturgy)*

A note of caution!

As lead couples prepare to present their view of marriage, they should beware of pretending to have "all the answers". Each person (and so each marriage) is unique. The goal of the ministry to engaged couples is to point to the possibilities that each person has for learning, growing and sharing through the mystery of the Sacrament.

It is truly an awesome responsibility to direct others. Those who come to prepare themselves will examine not only the words and vision, but will use the experiences shared to decide how they will live their own married lives. Those who would minister to others should approach their own part with humility and in a spirit of prayer and openness, committing themselves to growing alongside the couples they serve.

You are invited to share your faith and joy in your own marriage with those who have come to prepare themselves for the Sacrament. A sense of humor will assist you in reaching the couples. After all, marriage is an adventure, filled with surprises and mystery.

Preparing the course

Prior to the presentation of a marriage course, it is essential that the lead couples take sufficient time to do their homework and get to know one another. This will insure a quality program with built-in continuity.

In order to achieve good results, there should be at least *two preliminary meetings* of the course leader, the parish priest and the lead couples.

The *first meeting* should include a general information session and a sharing of expertise and strengths. Various parts of the program should be assigned. Any related audio-visual materials should be ordered for preview so that they may be well-integrated into the presentations.

Between meetings the lead couples should decide on how much material they can reasonably give in their session, and how they will adapt this material to their own style of presentation and the format of the session.

The *second meeting* should bring *all* the lead couples together. Each group should give an overview and a brief written summary of the topic assigned. This will allow the members to establish continuity among the various topics.

Hints for presenting the topics

- Pedagogy teaches that a person's attention span is somehow linked to the seat of the pants. In most cases, *talking at length* loses your audience. Break up your session with an activity and/or audio-visual materials. Try to have some fun along with the serious elements of the course. As you pay attention to these details, your score as a communicator will go up.

- A good concise summary given at the end of each session will help to keep you on topic. It will also help clear up the occasional puzzled look you may get during your session.

- If the couples will receive handout materials related to the topic, you can refer to them during the presentation and they can be reference points for you.

- Follow-up is an essential to good communication. It is always wise to begin your own topic with references to what has gone before.

Prayer of lead couples

Father,
We come to share our presence
as "salt" and "light".
Help us to listen
as well as to talk;
To be open to growing ourselves;
To be patient with those
who have differences of opinion.

But most of all,
let us bring to those you have given us
A sense of joy and hope.
We ask this with the confidence
Of our Lord and brother, Jesus.
Amen.

(reprinted from MOSAIC, Novalis, 1981 edition)

Course Content

The following approach has been used effectively. You may, however, want to adapt the suggestions to meet the needs of your own parish program. The content of the *seven evenings* was developed on the advice and from the experience of several persons who work in major centres for marriage preparation in both Canada and the United States. Even if you combine some of the topics in presenting your course, it is strongly suggested that you include *all* the topics presented here.

Session 1

Introductory Evening

This first evening is crucial to the whole program. The atmosphere should be comfortable, informal and yet show that all has been thoughtfully planned. There should not be a pupil-teacher, or "us" and "you" feeling. Rather the couples should experience a sense that we are all in this together.

Introduction should be made of those who will present the content of the program; time should be allotted for the engaged couples to talk informally with one another. This can be set up by showing and discussing a good film on communication; a sharing of why the couples have come to the course; or by using a questionnaire that allows them to state their expectations of this course.

Take some time for an informal coffee break and have the lead couples mix with the group.

At the end of the first session, set out the criteria for completing the program — attendance, participation in the groups, the reading that is expected, etc.

Session 2

Communication

Needless to say, everything we do in life is a form of communication. It is considered here as an independent theme to allow the couples to explore their styles and methods of communicating. How they relate

13

now will affect not only their marriage preparation but their growth throughout the years to come.

Invite them to explore:

● **family backgrounds** and how they contribute to their own communication. The factors will be: size of family, religious background, parental authority and how it was exercised, roles in the family, how emotions were expressed, etc.

● **how the other person expresses strong feelings:** joy, sorrow, but especially anger and frustration. It is essential that a couple learn to express anger without being destructive; that is, learn to "fight fairly".

● **dreams and hopes:** What is

behind strong feelings about family, home, children, work, God? If there are major differences in expectations, couples should seek positive methods of resolving them.

● how their communication affirms the **personal worth and talents** of each other.

● **areas of possible conflict:** The couples must be honest and not put off discussing issues, either hoping they will go away or that things will change after their wedding. There is danger in not dealing with present issues that will affect later life.

● **the notion of commitment:** Is there any reservation about the other person, such as the attitude: "I can always get out of this!" This will invalidate the marriage and is at best a lack of trust.

Session 3

Sexuality

In the not-too-distant past, the topic of sexuality was used almost exclusively to talk about male and female anatomy. It was also for many a source of embarrassment and was presented in a very clinical way. Since our sexuality is our maleness and femaleness and is a creation of God, it should be dealt with in as natural a way as the other topics.

Any presentation should explore:

● the biological structure of the male and female
● social images of sexuality as presented by the media

● sexual myths
● feelings about the act of sexual intercourse
● how and where sexual language is learned
● the act of intercourse itself as communication
● the act of sexual intercourse as the most intimate gift a man and woman can offer to each other.

This topic is often linked to the topic of children and their place in marriage. However, before couples can intelligently discuss creating new life, they should be aware of the implications of their own sex-

My dear people,
since God has loved us so much,
we too should love one another.
No one has ever seen God;
but as long as we love one another
God will live in us
and his love will be complete in us.

from the First Letter of John (4: 11-12)
(from choice of readings for celebrating
the Marriage liturgy)

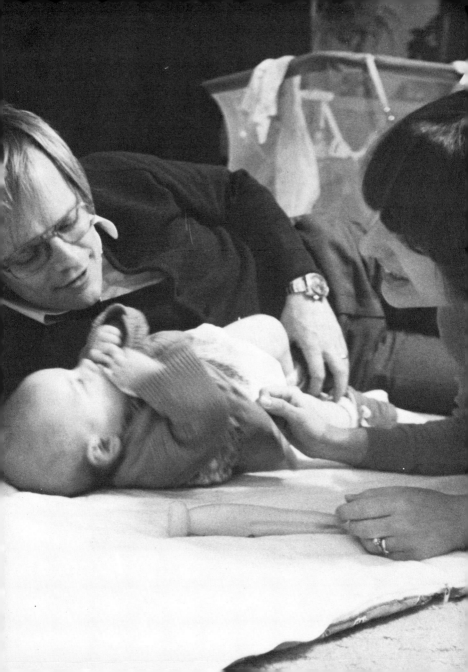

uality and sexual language. This will allow them the opportunity to reaffirm or redirect their self-image as sexual persons.

Session 4

Planning A Family

Of all the topics discussed in marriage programs, this is one of the most difficult to present. It has many emotional overtones — often mainly on the part of the leaders.

Cultural values have changed radically. With our experience of large populations, world poverty, educational opportunities, mobility, satellites and computers, we are more aware of and have to face many issues previously unknown or unquestioned. And in this world of instant gratification, it is difficult for many to face the long term commitment required to raise children.

Those who present this topic should be aware of the attitudes which bombard engaged couples; therefore they should present the materials with a very positive attitude, make sure that all the pertinent information is presented clearly, and leave a little room for the Holy Spirit to inform the consciences of the couples. It is very important that the topic of birth control be given objectively, stating clearly the Church's view in this matter and the options available.

Pertinent Information

- conception and development of the child in the womb
- the joy of creating new life and raising children
- various kinds of birth control and their implications
- the Church's view:
  a) the Encyclical, Humanae Vitae
  b) Paul VI, On the Development of Peoples
  c) Statements of Bishops' Conferences

Resources

Couples trained to deal with this topic may be found through your Diocesan Family Life Office. However, any couple with a positive attitude and well versed in Church teaching can effectively present this material.

Session 5

Finances

This is no topic for amateurs, especially in light of current economic trends — inflation, high interest rates, and society's expectations of a couple. Someone competent in the area of financial management and budgeting should be chosen to present practical methods for the couples to deal with:

a) *Budgeting* — how to, when to, income, kinds of income

b) *Savings* — practical steps to meet expectations of the couple

c) *Advertising* — the pros and cons of the kinds of messages given in the media

d) *Buying or Renting a home* —
when to, what to beware of, practical steps to plan for your home

e) *Insurance* — what kind, how much, being overinsured

f) *Credit* — wise and foolish uses of credit: loans and credit cards

g) *A Will* — practical reasons for looking after the future needs of both spouses; consequences of neglecting to make a will.

Many financial institutions have printed materials on all aspects of financial management. Your local bank is a good source. Today, many large firms have investment counselors to assist couples to plan wisely and avoid the many pitfalls in financial management.

Session 6

The Marriage Covenant

A Christian Marriage is a serious commitment, involving the whole Church. It is a covenant relationship in which the person Jesus commits himself, his Father, and the Holy Spirit to the couple.

From this union a "little Church" is formed, based on faith, hope, love, and the promise of new life.

This section of the course must take into account couples who will marry in the same faith and those who will enter an interfaith union.

For all couples:

● the meaning of Covenant and the part we play in it

● Marriage as Sacrament — sign of the life of the Church

● the Permanence of Marriage

● Fidelity in Marriage

For interfaith couples:

(This part could be handled by a couple sharing an interfaith marriage.)

- special challenges in an inter-faith marriage
- pressures on this kind of union, such as: roles, faith and prayer, religious practice, raising children, families.

In all of this, the couples should experience a Church ready and willing to assist them in creating a positive sign of what the Sacrament means and can mean in their lives.

Session 7

Final Evening

This seventh evening has many practical features for both the engaged couple and the ministers. It is time to *evaluate* the program for the future. Listening to the comments of the couples will insure that your program has an ongoing, growing quality and that it is in the service of others.

The session can be built around:

● a Eucharistic Celebration or Liturgy of the Word

● time for a written and confidential evaluation

● a social, in an informal setting, allowing the leaders to mix with the engaged couples on a one-to-one basis

● wine and cheese, potluck supper, music and singing.

Follow-up

This is one aspect of marriage preparation which is getting a long hard look. If we are serious about the couples we serve, our commitment doesn't end after seven weeks.

Within six months to a year, following these sessions, there should be a social and communications evening to which all the couples are invited. A discussion could be built around a good film, followed by coffee and time for sharing. The couples could be asked to evaluate the effectiveness of the course, based on their lived experience of marriage.

With such an evening, the couples will hear loud and clear that the Church continues to care for them and is serious about its continued commitment to each and every marriage.

Difficulties

With Engaged Couples

- person unwilling to participate in discussion
- couples who have been forced to take a marriage course

- couples who are under family pressures to get married

- persons who don't want to hear anything about religion

- marriage because of pregnancy

- conflicts between priests and a couple
- lack of good communication between the couples taking the course
- major psychological problems

Solutions

With Engaged Couples

- take some time to speak personally with each couple
- explain that, in spite of their situation, you will try to make the materials as relevant and interesting as possible
- get the couples to explore their motivations for getting married and insist that ultimately the responsibility for the commitment rests with them
- don't pull your punches on the issue of faith as key to any Christian marriage
- insist that because a happy marriage is free of many sexual restraints, pregnancy is no reason to get married
- talk to the couples and the priest about the need to be flexible
- point out that good communication is the basis for marriage

- refer the couples to qualified persons who can help with their situation

Difficulties

With Lead Couples

• take part not because they see value and hope in marriage but because they fear that marriage and the family in society are going downhill
• lead couples who talk a great deal but say nothing
• unable to relate to the couples' experiences
• not open to growing and learning
• have not read and carefully prepared their part
• think that since they are married they have all the answers.

Solutions

With Lead Couples

• screen out those who do not have a positive attitude toward encouraging the couples
• insist that those who take part, do their "homework"
• be kindly critical of one another's presentations
• challenge any who come with the attitude that they are the "experts" in marriage; furthermore, reinforce the notion that marriage is a continual call to growth
• take the time to pray together before each session and have an informal critique after the engaged couples have gone home.

Looking for results

It is nearly impossible to evaluate the results of a marriage program. The lead couples, in most cases, may never again see many of those who have come to participate in the course. But there are some positive signs to look for:

- couples who personally take the time to thank you
- being invited to share in the wedding day
- hearing from mutual acquaintances the couples' reactions
- the priest will also be confidant to many thoughts
- evaluation sheets will give many good indications
- friendships may form between the lead couples and some of the engaged couples.

For all those who seek to serve the Gospel, there will always be experiences of those who will refuse the gift. Jesus' life gives us many such examples. It was Jesus who, in his travels, spoke of the kinds of followers who would only sow, while others would reap the benefits. Unless we are willing to accept the risk, we may become disillusioned when we do not see tangible results.

Our prayer might be that we do our work for the sake of others and not for any transitory reward, remembering that the final results are in the Lord's keeping anyway.

They are happy, whose God is the Lord,
the people he has chosen as his own.
The Lord looks on those who revere him,
on those who hope in his love.

Our soul is waiting for the Lord;
the Lord is our help.
In him our hearts rejoice.
We trust in his holy name.

adapted from Psalm 33
(from choice of readings for
celebrating the Marriage liturgy)

What is a Christian Marriage?

A Christian marriage is a sacrament — a sign of God's active involvement in the life of a couple and a sign of the life of the whole Church. Marriage is built on the premise that it is strong, capable of everything, even of conquering death because it is built on love and faith in Jesus. His life and death are proof that love can overcome any obstacle.

When a couple enters into marriage, they are not doing a "one time thing". They are entering into a process of growth, discovery and learning together, believing that the love which animates Jesus lives in them also.

The love between a couple is the sign of the love of God made visible — a sacrament. Just as Jesus is made visible and tangible through the bread of the Eucharist, so too the life of the couple — the mutual love of husband and wife — makes God visible in his commitment to friendship with all persons.

Married Christians can claim to make Jesus' love visible to the world, precisely because Jesus extends the Covenant through them to the world around.

And so Christian marriage is a "gift" to the world in which God has called us to grow and love and be creative.

The Wedding Day

Be sure to take some time to talk with the couples about the wedding day and the ceremony itself. Remind them that the most important event of the day will be the wedding ceremony and the Exchange of Vows.

There are many optional Scripture texts, prayers and songs from which the couple may choose to express their love in a more personal way. Point out little booklets like, "Celebrating Our Love " (Novalis) which have been specially prepared to assist couples to make the day more meaningful.

Using the text, "The Rites" (Pueblo Publishing Co., p. 531 ff), go through the rite of marriage, giving practical examples of where in the rite the couple may take a more active part.

Advise the couples to spend some time with the parish priest, examining the readings, prayers and songs that speak to the couple of their love and marriage, and that are consistent with the meaning of the wedding ceremony.

Comments by lead couples

We have received more for ourselves as a couple than we have given. (Jim and Muriel)

We renewed our commitment to each other as we worked with the engaged couples. (Ralph and Claire)

The course reminded us that we ourselves had slipped from communicating many important things to each other. (Mike and Judy)

The openness of the engaged couples was an inspiration for me. (Al and Lynn)

I wish that more members of the parish could witness the honesty and faith of these young couples. (Ron and Mary)

We were nervous at first about expressing our marriage commitment in front of others. But we came away with a renewed sense of what marriage can be. (Joan and Des)

Comments by engaged couples

We enjoyed the positive, practical approach to marriage as a life commitment. (Guy and Sylvia)

It made us think about why we really wanted to get married. Our own commitment is stronger now. (Chris and Bonnie)

Although we began this course with our defenses up, we came away with a very positive understanding of "why" a marriage course. (Ron and Linda)

We were impressed with the sincerity and open-mindedness of those who made the presentations. (Maureen and Doug)

It was a great course — the highlight of our engagement. (Rob and Janice)

It helped us to see that we are not alone in our struggle to grow in our love and understanding of each other. (Ginette and Mike)

Blessing for engaged couples

*May your faith and hope blossom like the flowers
of Spring.
May your love nourish the dreams you share.
May your lives be long and filled with joy.
May you bathe in the love of your children
and their children.
May you come at last into the Kingdom of Love
Which the Lord in his goodness has prepared for you.
And may the blessing of God, Father,
Son and Holy Spirit,
animate your lives today and for all time. Amen.*

Resources

Mosaic: A complete Marriage Preparation Program with Leader's Guide. NOVALIS, Box 9700, Terminal, Ottawa, Ontario. K1G 4B4.

Celebrating Our Love: Preparing the Wedding Ceremony with Readings, Prayers and Songs. NOVALIS (as above).

Art of Loving (The) — Fromm. Harper and Row, Keystone Industrial Park, Scranton, PA. 18512.

Beginning Your Marriage — Thomas. Buckley Publications, 233 E. Erie St., Chicago, Il. 60611.

Dating and Marriage: A Christian Approach to Intimacy — Shimek. Winston Press, 430 Oak Grove, Minneapolis, MN 55403.

First Nine Months of Life — Flanagan. Heinemann, 59 Grosvenor St., London, England, W1X 9DA.

Humanae Vitae — Paul VI. Canadian Conference of Catholic Bishops, 90 Parent Ave., Ottawa, Canada, K1N 7B1.

Matrimonia Mixta — Paul VI. Canadian Conference of Catholic Bishops, 90 Parent Ave., Ottawa, Canada   K1N 7B1.

I Need to Have You Know Me — Larsen. Winston Press.

Permanent Love: Practical Steps to a Lasting Relationship — Ford, Englund. Winston Press.

Intimacy: The Essence of Male and Female — Luthman. Mehetabel and Company, 4340 Redwood Highway, San Rafael, CA. 94903.

Married In The Lord — Prieur, Cathechetical Communications, Bethlehem, PA. 18017.

Marriage for Life: A Handbook of Marriage Skills — Vath and O'Neill. 1982, Winston Press.

Mystery of Human Sexuality — Oraison. Andrews & McMeel, Inc., 4400 Johnson Dr., Fairway, KS. 66205.

Why Am I Afraid To Love — Powell. Argus. Allen, Texas. 75002.

Why Marriage? — Ford. Argus.

MARRIAGE PREPARATION

Written by:
Basil Arbour,
author of MOSAIC revision
and Novalis editor.

Edited by:
Jerome Herauf

Layout:
Jan Gough, Gilles Lépine

Photography:
Cover: Mia et Klaus; p. 2, 24: Mia et Klaus;
p. 5, 16,20: Roman Matwijejko;
p. 10-11: National Film Board of Canada;
p. 12: Sheila Sturley, RSCJ;
p. 27: "Vivants univers";
p. 31; Miller Services Ltd.

Illustrations:
Cover 1, cover 4, and inside: Lee Thirlwall

*"God is love, and anyone who lives
in love lives in God,
and God in him."*

(1 John 4:16)

Winston Press
430 Oak Grove
Minneapolis, Minnesota 55403

ISBN: 0-86683-734-5

Liturgy Planning

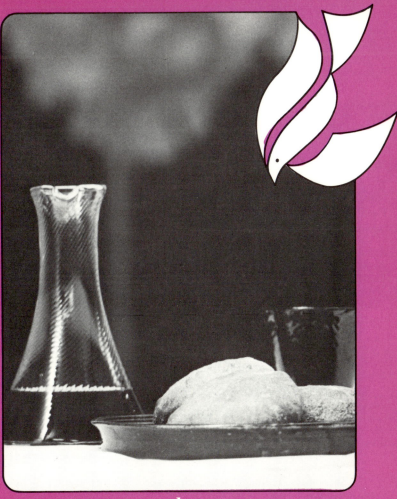

New Parish Ministries

WINSTON PRESS

Contents

New Parish Ministries was originally published by Novalis, Saint Paul University, Ottawa, Canada. This edition is published by Winston Press, Inc., by arrangement with Novalis, Saint Paul University. Copyright © 1982, Novalis. Copyright © 1983, Winston Press. All rights reserved. No part of this book may be reproduced in any form without written permission from the publisher.

ISBN: 0-86683-735-3 (previously ISBN: 2-89088-083-4)

Printed in Canada

5   4   3   2   1

Winston Press, Inc., 430 Oak Grove, Minneapolis, MN 55403

Welcome to the Ministry of Liturgy Planning

Few of us think of "getting ready" as ministry or as part of the celebration of a sacrament. Planning is usually thought of in terms of what you have to do before the important part — what has to get done before it "really happens."

Lately, however, we have begun to understand that planning for the Eucharist is intimately connected with its celebration. Those who do the planning are no less ministers than those who function more visibly on Sunday morning.

This booklet will hardly have all the answers. It does not even ask all the questions. It is intended to help planners, beginners and perhaps those more advanced, to look at this ministry, particularly as it serves the Sunday Eucharist. (Other celebrations are hinted at, but more in passing than in detail.)

Welcome to the ministry that serves the celebration by trying to "bring it all together."

Introduction

Scene One: It is 11:55 a.m. at St. Swithin's parish. The reader has not arrived, the servers are begging for instructions (someone has just told them there are baptisms today), the organist has just decided he cannot play the entrance hymn, and the cantor cannot decide which psalm refrain to use.

Scene Two: It is 10:30 a.m. at St. Cuthbert's parish. The procession leaves the sacristy to join the rest of the congregation in the entrance song. Everyone knows what to do, and does it.

Which one is good liturgy, which is bad? Or is it just a matter of organization? Each scene, each parish, is an overstatement. One seems to be total blunder; the other almost too good to be true. Reality will be somewhere in between — but we can try for the best, and that best often depends on good planning.

Liturgy is only as good as its planning

What is liturgy? The definitions can range from the profound-ly theological, such as those found in Pope Pius XII's encyclicals, to the very practical understanding of how you bring liturgy about. At its simplest, liturgy is what happens when Christians gather to celebrate the mystery of Christ — when they gather as Church to worship.

Liturgy then is at once a great mystery, the mystery of our relationship with God in worship, and a very practical task: that of worshipping well and carefully. And we can take that practical task to heart.

We plan liturgy because we care about it, because we understand that this activity brings us into particular contact with the Lord who reveals himself to us in a special way when we worship. Well-planned, well-tuned worship makes his presence clearer to us.

Liturgy is celebration at its best

Each of us understands that good planning is the key to successful celebration. Try a large dinner party without a plan! Sure, there is always "fast food," but the occasions that mean a great deal to us

3

demand more, they invite us to bring out the best, to feast, to party, to share — to celebrate.

It is not a matter of the minimum possible, but of the best desirable. What we almost take for granted in the important events of life should also take place in liturgy.

Rituals and shapes

We have standard opening and closing phrases for conversation; we follow a plan for getting up in the morning; we know how to celebrate birthdays and anniversaries. This is all "the stuff" of ritual, the ceremonial shape that we give things in order to communicate and share the events. Sometimes the rituals are personal ("the way I do things all the time"), but at other times they are shared and communicated.

The rituals of life can become oppressive, but their real function is to be helpful. They provide a shape and a framework for life.

Liturgy shares in this. The rituals that we use in liturgy allow us to participate with others; they enable us to communicate and share because we know what comes next. We do not have to know all or each of the details, but we can follow the flow.

Essentially, worship uses rituals to express itself. Liturgy planners are the ones who take the rituals of life and liturgy, the "given" things, and mold them into a shape for this celebration, for this action of worship.

Planners are the ones who mold this shape so that the community can celebrate well and prayerfully.

Shape means that this celebration has a flow — a beginning, middle and end. Its parts fit, its actions and decorations support, it "feels" right as well as makes sense. Building a shape that accomplishes all of this is what liturgy planning is all about.

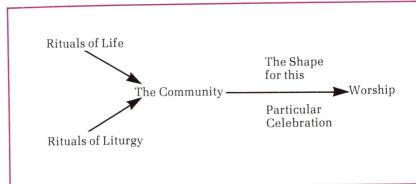

- What expectations do we have for this celebration?

- Can these expectations be brought about in this community, today?

- What resources are built into this feast in terms of history, meaning and texts? What aspect of the mystery of Christ are we celebrating in this week's liturgy?

- What does *this* congregation need to celebrate today? How does this relate to the specific mystery of Christ?

- What can the planners *do* to help this community worship in this way today? (What gestures can we use? what decorations? what songs?...)

The answers to these (and other) questions are the practical work of the planners who will build and "shape" the resources of the liturgy, including its rituals, into this community's act of worship.

Each liturgical celebration is the Church at prayer — the whole Church, here and now. The stimulation of prayer and worship is what planning is all about.

The place of celebration

No two church buildings are exactly the same. Some aspects, however, are essential. We are used to the visibility of the altar; now we add clearly defined places for the Word, presider, and musician-cantor. In addition, there are considerations such as the availability for other sacraments (e.g. baptism) as well as non-eucharistic celebrations. Above all, the church is a place that serves the community as a whole.

In past years everything had to be permanent; now we realize that mobility is a useful tool in design. To celebrate well, the good use of space is essential.

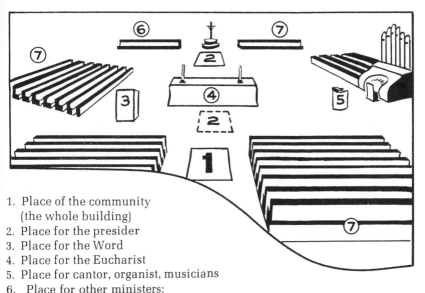

1. Place of the community (the whole building)
2. Place for the presider
3. Place for the Word
4. Place for the Eucharist
5. Place for cantor, organist, musicians
6. Place for other ministers: concelebrants, servers, etc.
7. Place for ushers, ministers of hospitality.

"Here you reveal your presence by sacramental signs, and make us one with you through the unseen bond of grace. Here you build your temple of living stones, and bring the Church to its full stature as the body of Christ throughout the world." (Dedication of a Church, Preface 1)

Levels of Planning

Walk into a church building on Good Friday — what do you see; how is it decorated; what does it "feel" like? Walk into the same building on Easter and it will surely provide a different sort of experience. Why does Christmas midnight mass seem to signify a whole tradition, rather than just a late evening celebration of the eucharist?

The liturgy begins long before any given celebration actually starts, but it is not simply a beginning in terms of planning. This beginning is atmosphere, tradition, prejudice, hope, and all sorts of other intensely human emotions. As liturgy planners, it is very important to understand and recognize, to build on as well as to work with, these emotions in planning the shape of the liturgy.

One simple question that should start any planning session might be: What are the strengths already present that we can build upon? Christmas, for example, offers some ready-made musical selections, even for a once-a-year congregation. (It also offers the challenge of reaching that occasional group.) People are well-disposed to the large feasts, and so it can become a time for planners to offer some challenge and insight.

Build on the inherent goodwill of the congregation at larger celebrations. It gives the planners a bit of a chance to relax, a chance to spend more time on the more difficult days — the "simple" Sunday celebration. It is possible to indulge in overkill, in so loading the already important events that they become exhausting for everyone. The Easter Triduum, for example, would generally benefit from simple, well-conducted celebrations.

Effective planning recognizes that there are limits — to this celebration, for this congregation, with this building, at this time — even with the resources of this group of planners. It means looking honestly at what will serve *this* congregation *now*. Education is a slow process and the liturgy is seldom served by exaggerated shock techniques.

"*Levels*" simply means recognizing and using two views of planning. The first we have already dealt with — congregations are at different stages at different times. Build upon the strengths — be gentle with the weaknesses. The sec-

8

"There are varieties of gifts,
but the same Spirit.
There are varieties of service,
but the same Lord.
There are many forms of work,
but ... the work of the same God."

[1 Cor. 12:4-6]

ond refers to the stages for planning any given celebration. There are layers to any event, any feast, any Eucharist. Where you start often controls where you finish up.

Physical

The first planning level considers the basic *physical* aspects of the building. The design of the sanctuary, the places of the ministers, and the location of essential furniture are controlled by architecture and structure. But even these can be modified somewhat.

What is the floor plan of the church — what is permanent and/or movable? Where are the essential ministers located; are they seen to be part of the worshipping community even if they are distinguished by function, seating and dress? Are they too prominent and a centre of attention, even when not functioning?

What does the congregation see: a place where the action of the liturgy is centered, or a remote and walled fortress; a pleasantly designed whole — one that reflects this community and this celebration — or a clutter of furniture with little design or purpose?

Concern for the physical extends to the simple matter of ventilation — is it too hot and stuffy in here? Is it too cold?

The basic physical plan of things is the first to greet people, and speaks to them before any decoration or individual. A little care here can make the other levels not only simpler, but more fruitful to deal with.

Physical ➤ Decorative

Decoration is one aspect of planning that has been with us for a long time. However, today's creative decoration has moved a long way from "ordering flowers for Easter." It is the part of the physical environment that is most easily controlled, changed and designed.

Banners, hangings, color and shape, plants, seasonal furniture (e.g., paschal candle), lighting, even the style of vestments: all come together to shape the celebration. Poor decoration (e.g., seasonal "leftovers" present weeks after their effective use) is to be feared more than no decoration at all.

Decoration need not be complicated to be effective. The size of most churches means that additions have to be large enough to be seen, but they must still not dominate the essential furniture. Two questions might help:

1) How does this decoration form a unit with what is being

celebrated; what does it say to and with the rest of the liturgy?

2) What does it look like, not just to the planners or on paper, but to those who will view it from the congregation? Decoration must be comprehensible and visually beautiful.

Physical ▸ Decorative ▸ Personal

From the physical we can move to the *personal,* or even the personnel. This is simply the "who" of the celebration, the involvement of congregation and ministers.

Today's liturgical celebrations involve a large number of people; in fact, they require them. This is not simply to help the action to move along (the strictly practical), but to demonstrate the diversity of ministry that comes together at this celebration.

Yes, it is possible to have one person fulfill many roles, but at some point parish groups have to decide their commitment to good liturgy and the number of people that this entails — and, therefore, scheduling, training, organization, follow-up, and evaluation.

Not everyone is suited to every task in life — or in liturgy. Recruiting and supervising those working at liturgical celebrations is an ongoing responsibility for the planning team, and it is one that must be taken very seriously. It is this one task that is perhaps the most critical for liturgy planners because it concerns the "how" of those who serve the community.

Physical ▸ Decorative ▸ Personal ▸ Conceptual

Finally, planners can (and are strongly encouraged to) enter into *content* planning — taking, discovering and shaping a concept for the liturgy. For particular eucharistic celebrations, or for non-eucharistic liturgies, this can extend even to the choice of prayers and readings. At the Sunday eucharist, content planning is more limited, since the readings and prayers are chosen in advance, but it still embraces any and all of the items which will help to clarify, expand and form what is taking place.

It is the responsibility of the planning team to offer commentary, program and bulletin notes, to work with the presider in his choice of texts that support the given material, and to help the musicians, artists and other ministers in their choice of expansive and supportive material. Texts are one matter, but the bringing of those texts to the here and now of this community and this celebration is the responsibility of the planner and the presider.

Again, *this* liturgy requires a shape, something that fits together as a whole. Each celebration is different: time, weather, daylight and darkness, season of the year, the abilities of this group — all have to be considered. An early morning eucharist cannot expect the same participation as a noon-time celebration. Planners have to be sensitive to what is possible, even as they have to encourage what is desirable. In the midst of their content planning, the committee members always need to have an awareness of the strengths and weaknesses of this community. That balance is at the heart of good liturgical planning.

The serving environment

By environment we mean the larger space in which the action of the assembly takes place. At its broadest, it is the setting of the building in its neighborhood, including outdoor spaces. More specifically, it means the character of a particular space and how it affects the action of the assembly. There are elements in the environment, therefore, which contribute to the overall experience, e.g., the seating arrangement, the placement of liturgical centres of action, temporary decoration, light, acoustics, spaciousness, etc. The environment is appropriate when it is beautiful, when it is hospitable, when it clearly invites and needs an assembly of people to complete it. Furthermore, it is appropriate when it brings people close together so that they can see and hear the entire liturgical action, when it helps people feel involved and become involved. Such an environment works with the liturgy, not against it.

Environment and Art, page 16.

What the faithful have received by faith and sacrament in the celebration of the Eucharist should have its effect on their way of life. They should seek to live joyfully and gratefully by the strength of this heavenly food, sharing in the death and resurrection of the Lord.

And so everyone who has participated in the Mass should be "eager to do good works, to please God, and to live honestly, devoted to the Church, putting into practice what he has learnt, and growing in piety."

1967 Instruction on Eucharistic Worship, National Bulletin on Liturgy, No. 13

Basic Information for Planners

To plan effectively, liturgy planners need to know something about the background and flow of the liturgy, about its structure and organization. The celebrations of liturgy, for example the Eucharist and other sacraments, move according to a certain plan or format. The Church Year moves along a well-thought-out scheme.

Knowledge of these schemes will not only make planning a far simpler exercise, but it will also enable planners to make use of a system that can be built upon and enhanced.

The next few pages of this booklet offer some general comments and guides to this background.

- The Church Year
- The Format of Eucharistic Liturgies
- The Parts of the Eucharist

CHRISTMAS CYCLE

Advent — 1 Sunday
2 Sunday
3 Sunday
4 Sunday

Christmas — Christmas day
Holy Family
Solemnity of Mary
Epiphany
Lord's Baptism

ORDINARY TIME
Part one

EASTER CYCLE

Lent — 1 Sunday
2 Sunday
3 Sunday
4 Sunday
5 Sunday
6 Sunday
(Passion or Palm Sunday)

Easter Triduum

Easter — 2 Sunday
3 Sunday
4 Sunday
5 Sunday
6 Sunday
Ascension Day
(7 Sunday)
Pentecost

ORDINARY TIME
Part two

Trinity Sunday   Corpus Christi   Christ the King (Last Sunday)

We find it immensely easier to order two bouquets of flowers than to plan something that will take time to construct. Oftentimes we become frightened by creativity, and we feel that we just don't have what it takes to be creative. We do this because we over-estimate the creative person. Creativity is largely a matter of good taste. It is largely a matter of understanding the restrictions and advantages of the place we want to decorate.

James Notebaart, *Modern Liturgy Handbook*, page 95.

Planning the liturgy, even at its simplest, certainly begins and ends with the Church Year. Even groups that will start their work with para-liturgical events (such as Thanksgiving Day or a parish anniversary) or concentrate on planning specific celebrations (Advent or Lenten reconciliation, first communion, confirmation), have to take into account the mood and flow of the Church's celebration of its life.

Knowing and understanding the character of the seasons of the Church's Year is as important as recognizing the character of the seasons of the natural year. For example, any day could well serve for a national Thanksgiving Day — but it is surely more significant in the autumn, surrounded as we are with the best that nature provides. Knowing the theological dimensions of the Church's seasons helps the planning of strong and fruitful liturgy.

The Church Year is divided up into three parts: Advent through Epiphany (Christmas cycle), Lent through Pentecost (Easter cycle — the most important of the three parts), and the days of Ordinary Time (the Sundays and weekdays outside the other two cycles).

Advent and Christmas

The Church Year begins with Advent. This season has two directions — it looks forward to the Lord's return at the end of time and, especially from December 17th to 24th, prepares for the memorial of the Lord's birth, Christmas Day. Advent is a season of joyful, although of spiritual expectation; it is not a time of penance nor a mini-Lent.

The Christmas Season extends from Christmas Day through the solemnity of the Lord's Baptism. It is a season of feasts — some directly connected with Christmas (such as Epiphany, Baptism, Solemnity of the Mother of God), and others that simply fall in the season, and therefore, must take on at least a bit of its character (e.g. St. John and St. Stephen).

Christmas is not the easiest of seasons in terms of liturgical planning. The "end times" character of Advent is often in peril because of the rush to plan early for December 25th. By the time Christmas appears and we can liturgically sing carols, congregations are tired of them. Finally, the feasts move so fast after Christmas that we scarcely have time to breathe, let alone re-decorate.

Some solutions? Learn new carols and revitalize the old ones with new accompaniment or choral touches. Explore the meaning of some of the other feasts and allow some of their richness to dominate. Let some of the Advent expectation permeate the entire season — even Christmas cannot merely look back.

This season is a good one for learning that you cannot do it all — or all at once. Planning has to be done early enough to allow the planners to celebrate too. Select

one idea, change it each year, allow it to dominate in terms of focus and decoration. Allow the natural feelings of the season to work for you as you try to increase people's awareness of new ideas of what the Lord's coming, past, present and future means.

Lent and Easter

Easter is the focal point of the year; the Easter Triduum (Holy Thursday evening through Easter Sunday) is the major statement of the Lord's redemptive activity.

For forty days of Lent those who are baptized prepare to recall their baptism, and in a special way those who are catechumens prepare for that event in their own lives. Through prayer and penance, the Church prepares for the Easter feast — which is not one day, but fifty days of celebration, continuing through Ascension Day and culminating with Pentecost.

Almost everything takes second place to this season; few feasts or solemnities are allowed to take precedence, or even appear. Holy Week and the Triduum bring special activities and rituals into play. Perhaps the most difficult aspect of Easter is the period after Easter Sunday. Lent seems to keep people's attention, even to increase it as the season progresses. The days after Easter Sunday often suffer from the exhaustion of the planner, the diminishing attention of the worshipper (penance we can understand, but celebration con-

fuses us). Added to this are the celebrations of First Communion, Confirmation, and other events annually scheduled for the Spring.

This is the Season that deserves our main planning attention. Its liturgies are rich — almost too rich — and need care and development. Even if there are no catechumens in a parish, Lent needs to be seen in terms of baptism if the Sunday readings are to have their fullest impact. The Sundays after Easter re-state and celebrate its message, and cannot simply fade away. Integrating the other sacraments of initiation (Confirmation and Eucharist) into the flow, rather than seeing them as events we happen to place here, will help keep the season alive.

Ordinary Time

The third period is made up of the remaining Sundays and weekdays. These 33 or 34 weeks (depending on the number of Sundays in the year) are split into the weeks between the Christmas season and Easter, and the weeks from Pentecost to the next Advent. Rather than being concerned with a specific feast-event, these Sundays are said to celebrate the fullness of the mystery of Christ as it unfolds in the gospels.

The readings focus on the gospel — a rather continuous reading of one of the gospels based on a three year cycle. Generally, the first reading (Old Testament) and psalm reflect the theme of the

21

gospel. The second reading is simply a continuous reading through the epistles — any immediate harmony with the gospel is somewhat coincidental. Through the readings, the Church seeks to reflect on the mystery that we preach, Sunday after Sunday.

It is during this period that we come to understand the importance of Sunday as the original feast day, the day on which the Church gathers to listen to the Word and to break the bread of the Eucharist.

Certain solemnities are built into the Season — the two Sundays immediately after the Easter Season are Trinity and Corpus Christi, the last Sunday of the year is Christ the King. At other times, there are feasts that may take precedence over a Sunday — Transfiguration, Assumption, etc.

While these days often interrupt the flow of the Year and can overpower the ordered presentation of the gospel (a negative side), they can (on the positive side) offer opportunities for focus and celebration in parishes that are just beginning to plan liturgy.

These Sundays often group together into units, brought about by the units in the gospel readings. These units can help planners focus their efforts. Sometimes, especially during the later Sundays of the year, the natural seasons offer some support (the end times combined with autumn's reflective moods).

A thorough knowledge of the Church Year, its rhythm and flow, as well as of the feasts and celebrations that are part of it all, is a must for the liturgical planners of any parish.

The focus of the Church Year

"*Holy Mother Church is conscious that she must celebrate the saving work of her divine Spouse by devoutly recalling it on certain days throughout the course of the year. Every week, on the day which she has called the Lord's day, she keeps the memory of His resurrection. In the supreme solemnity of Easter she also makes an annual commemoration of the resurrection, along with the Lord's blessed passion.*

"*Within the cycle of the year, moreover, she unfolds the whole mystery of Christ, not only from His incarnation and birth until His ascension, but also as reflected in the day of Pentecost, and the expectation of a blessed, hoped-for return of the Lord.*

"*Recalling thus the mysteries of redemption, the Church opens to the faithful the riches of the Lord's powers and mercies, so that these are in some way made present at all times, and the faithful are enabled to lay hold of them and become filled with saving grace.*"

Liturgy Constitution, par. 102.

What's in a symbol?

... just about everything.

Symbols are all around us, and they are largely unexplainable — more felt than understood. They seem to be part of us. We can "say it" with flowers, without offering any explanation. We can invite someone to a meal and the intent, the gesture of love, affection and friendship is simply obvious. Because of this intuitive character, the symbol is fragile. It is only as strong as we let it show itself.

To understand the liturgy is to understand the constant use it makes of the symbolic. To make effective use of liturgical symbols we have to allow them to speak to us. Planning teams need to be constantly aware of how symbols appear — how they look, how they sound, how they smell — in short, how they feel. Most important is the understanding that it is how the symbol appears to the congregation that counts. The planners may know what is meant, but if that is not communicated, if it is not readily sensed by those at worship, then the power of the symbol is lost.

For example — Incense is a symbol of prayer rising to God, something of sweet smell and cloud. A puff of smoke is not only a poor symbol, it is destructive of what is meant. Water sprinkled about, as a sign of Baptism, has to flow — someone has to get damp — not just fall silently on the carpet. Vestments have to be festive, well-cut, colorful; linens clean and suited to the environment; candles lit or removed.

Format of Eucharistic Liturgy

ENTRANCE RITE

Entrance Song
Greeting
  Sign of Cross
  Greeting
  Introduction
Penitential Rite
Hymn of Praise (Gloria)
Opening Prayer

When some other rite takes place at the start of the eucharist (blessing, sprinkling, special gesture) the penitential rite (as well as any further greeting) is omitted.

LITURGY OF THE WORD

First Reading
Responsorial Psalm
Second Reading
Gospel Acclamation
Gospel Reading
Homily
Profession of Faith
General Intercessions

A period of silence is important after each reading. It is especially important when there are only two readings — and, in this case, there should be a clear distinction between the Psalm and the Gospel Acclamation.

This is not simply the format of the "first part" of the celebration of the eucharist. It is the basic format for any celebration of the Word, even when there is no sacramental celebration included. For a "Word Liturgy," other songs and readings could be included and a gesture such as the sign of peace or something more directly connected with the nature of the liturgical celebration. After this gesture, the Concluding Rite would take place.

Celebrations of other events within the eucharist (weddings, ordination, religious profession, and so forth) usually take place after the homily and involve certain additions and omissions in the general plan.

LITURGY OF THE EUCHARIST

A. Preparation of the Gifts

Collection, procession, reception
Preparation of bread and wine
Invitation and Prayer over Gifts

The Prayer over the Gifts is the most important prayer here. The others need not be said out loud.

B. Eucharistic Prayer

Preface with its Dialogue and Acclamation (Holy, holy)
Prayer with Memorial Acclamation and the Great Amen.

There are currently nine Eucharistic Prayers in use, including those of Reconciliation and for Children.

C. Communion

Our Father
Sign of Peace
Breaking of Bread
Communion
Silent Prayer (Hymn or Psalm)
Prayer after Communion

Includes preparation of chalices for Communion under both kinds.

CONCLUDING RITE

(Announcements)
Greeting
Blessing
Dismissal

Brief, if at all. This rite is omitted if another action (procession, funeral liturgy, etc.) is to follow.

Larger liturgies, especially at important parish events, often include a number of concelebrants. Although they are associated with the main celebrant, they should not take over the sanctuary during the other rites and not perform the tasks that naturally belong to other ministers. During the Eucharistic Prayer, the concelebrants gather near the altar (taking care not to block the view). Their voices should never drown out the presider.

A knowledge of the Church Year helps the planner to understand the flow of the Seasons. An understanding of the basic format of the eucharist enables groups and individuals to see what is of greater and lesser importance, as they build the shape of the celebration.

Introductory rites

The parts which precede the reading of the Word — entrance song, greeting, introductory remarks, penitential rite, hymn of praise (Gloria), opening prayer — are meant to unify the community and attune it to the Word. Any one of these parts should be brief, concise, and to the point. Opening remarks, statements about the "theme" of the day, music (even on large feasts), and so forth, should never be so out of proportion to the other parts that one part takes over.

Sometimes certain parts are replaced by other rites (e.g., holy water blessing, Palm Sunday procession).

Liturgy of the Word

The scripture readings with their intervening chants are the major part of this liturgy. They are developed, expanded, and made contemporary in the homily, and intercessions.

Time is important. Nothing should hurry the proclamation of the Word and the community response in silence, psalm, and acclamation.

Readings from contemporary authors might be worked into the homily, but usually should not be included with the scriptures. Through the readings and the chants that accompany them — the meditative chant of the responsorial psalm and the praise of the gospel acclamation — we learn about and reflect on the One who calls us together. Time between the readings is essential to give the community a chance to reflect. Anything which disturbs or interrupts the "listening character" of this part of the liturgy has to be avoided.

The intercessions are general in their scope, but should reflect the scriptures of the day, the needs of this community, and the Church in general. They conclude the Word Liturgy.

Liturgy of the Eucharist

The Eucharistic Liturgy comprises the four actions expressed in Mark's gospel in which Jesus himself took, blessed, broke and shared bread and wine with his disciples (Mark 14:22-25). There are three sections to this part of the liturgy — the Eucharistic Prayer being the center and core.

1. Preparation. The preparation of the gifts of bread and wine (as well as the preparation of the altar and reception of other gifts, e.g. the collection) is simply that — a preparation. Various prayers and rites (some optional) surround this, but this rite must never become nor appear to be a major rite in itself.

Planners, therefore, should generally see that this part moves along as expeditiously as possible, suggesting that this be a more restful part for the community which has been very active to this point through the Word Liturgy (e.g. instrumental music rather than singing).

2. Eucharistic Prayer. This prayer is central to this liturgy. Led by the presider, the community fulfills the Lord's command to "do this" in his memory. The prayer follows in the tradition of the Jewish "blessing" prayers. The community participates with reverent and attentive silence and through acclamation and gesture.

The Eucharistic Prayer begins with praise of the Father for his saving work (the preface). After the preface, all unite in the first acclamation — Holy, holy, holy Lord... After a brief introduction or further development of salvation history, the Holy Spirit is invoked. The epiclesis prayer asks that the gifts we bring be transformed by the action of the Spirit into the Lord's body and blood. (The second half of the epiclesis, after the consecration, asks that we may share more fruitfully in the communion of the eucharist.) The narrative of institution of the eucharist (consecration) recalls Jesus' action of the Last Supper. A second acclamation (variable) is then sung (said) by all.

The part immediately after the consecration (the anamnesis or memorial) recalls the events of the Lord's saving work, projecting them through the present (this eucharist) into the future, as the Church unites with Jesus' offering to the Father. Finally, the Church which is made one by the eucharist, reflects upon its needs, in the intercessions.

The Eucharistic Prayer culminates in the closing doxology (praise of God) which is taken up by all the community in the great "Amen" acclamation.

The Eucharistic Prayer is a complex whole. The fact that so many of its parts have special names underlines this. Its parts flow together to produce the major prayer of the celebration. The people's acclamations are a part of that whole; they draw the prayer together and help develop what is being proclaimed.

Planners should be especially attentive to enhancing the people's participation through the acclamations, use of silence, background music, etc., thus rendering more active what is often a more passive moment for the congregation.

3. Communion. As Church, we have united with Jesus' gift as well as joined in his action of offering — we now share the gift we have offered. The Our Father along with its expansion (called the embolism) and acclamation ("For the Kingdom...") begins the Communion Rite.

Father,
we bring you these gifts;
we ask you to make them Holy
by the power of your Spirit...

Two gestures serve as a direct preparation for communion — gestures which emphasize the unity brought about and celebrated in the eucharist. All in the congregation exchange a greeting of peace, and the bread is broken in preparation to be received. The song, Lamb of God, is sung, as long as the breaking continues.

Finally the communion procession begins as the congregation comes forward to receive. After the altar is cleared, and there is a period of silent meditation, the rite concludes with a prayer.

Concluding rites

The eucharist concludes with a minimum of ceremony. Brief announcements, if any, take place at this point. After a final greeting and a blessing (sometimes expanded in solemn form), the congregation is sent forth to continue the Lord's work celebrated in this eucharist.

What's important

From the format scheme and from the paragraphs on the parts of the eucharist, it should be clear that there is not only an order in the celebration, but there is also a grading of importance. Certain parts of the liturgy are more important than others, and they must always appear so.

During the Liturgy of the Word, it is the readings that should predominate. General intercessions that are too wordy, even a homily that is too long, destroy the balance.

The entrance rite is particularly subject to distortion. A lengthy entrance hymn, Lord Have Mercy, and Gloria is simply too much music, even on a great feast. Opening remarks that become a homily weaken and distort the other parts. It is the opening prayer that climaxes the rite, and it needs to appear so.

Likewise, turning the Preparation of the Gifts into a major production might be fine to achieve a certain thrust (e.g., a large number of gifts for the poor, on a particular Sunday), but in general it is to be brief, concise, and unadorned. Music is encouraged here (especially instrumental), but the presider and the community should not have to wait for the song to end.

The acclamations during the Eucharistic Prayer are not interruptions; they are important to the Prayer's development. They lose something if merely recited. These short songs (Holy, holy; Mystery of faith; Amen) are among the most important parts of the eucharist.

During the Communion Rite, we are faced with a parallel to the Entrance — a series of short actions held together by a whole. Each must fit in. The breaking of bread is more important than the "Lord I am not worthy"; and the greeting of peace is a sign, not a community love-in. Communion itself should move reverently but well; a sufficient number of ministers will help the timing.

*From the format scheme and from the
paragraphs on the parts of the eucharist, it
should be clear that there is not only an order in
the celebration, but there is also a grading of
importance. Certain parts of the liturgy are
more important than others, and they must
always appear so.*

Finally, the Conclusion is brief and to the point — praise and dismissal. It is not a time to read the bulletin or cover the week's activities. Perhaps the possibility of a sharing after the eucharistic celebration is an important part of this rite yet to be discovered.

Priority scheme

RITES

- The Liturgy of the Word and Eucharistic Prayer

- Other "presidential" prayers: opening, over gifts, after communion

- Our Father, breaking of bread, communion

- Greeting, penitential rite, dismissal

- Preparation of gifts

MUSIC

Acclamations: Holy, holy; Memorial acclamation, Gospel acclamation, Great Amen

Responsorial Psalm, Entrance Hymn, Lamb of God

Communion song (during or after), Gloria

Other songs (preparation of gifts, recessional, incidental music)

(See the booklet "Musicians at Liturgy," also in this series.)

While no list can clearly establish the importance of rites and chants, there are some that are more important than others. Keeping an "order" in mind will help in understanding priorities and in putting planning time to best use.

Understanding makes a difference

Understanding the function of the parts of the eucharist makes a considerable difference in planning. For example, the entrance hymn of the liturgy is to be the actual start of the action of worship. It is not merely an accompanying song for the entrance or greeting of the ministers. Rather, it is the first formal action of the whole community.

Those groups that understand and study the real function of this song will not hesitate to choose it wisely, to encourage the organist to add strong accompaniment and variation, and to allow it its full time and development.

Who gets involved

Before it happens:
   Planning committee
   Sacristans, decorators, caretakers
   Individual planning and reflection, by each minister and by the congregation

The point of it all:
   The good celebration of this parish community

As it begins:
   Ushers and ministers of hospitality
   Musicians (who set the mood)

The celebration:
   Presider, deacon, concelebrants
   Servers and ministers of the altar
   Readers
   Musicians, cantor, organist, other instrumentalists
   Ministers of Communion
   Assistants for collection, gift bearers
   Other functions as needed

Afterwards:
   Preparation for the next celebration
   Remove decorations unique to this celebration

At the heart of it all:
   the celebrating community.

Today's celebrations, even the smaller ones, require a large number of people to minister, support, and strengthen the whole community. The service of each builds the whole.

"In this house you realize the mystery of your dwelling among us: for in shaping us here as your holy temple you enrich your whole Church." (Rite of Dedication of a Church)

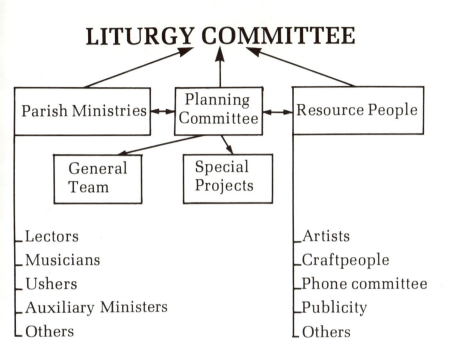

LITURGY COMMITTEE

Parish Ministries ↔ Planning Committee ↔ Resource People

General Team

Special Projects

- Lectors
- Musicians
- Ushers
- Auxiliary Ministers
- Others

- Artists
- Craftpeople
- Phone committee
- Publicity
- Others

*Since each one of you
has received a special gift,
you must place yourselves
at the service of others.*

*So that in all things
God may receive the glory,
through Jesus Christ. Amen.*

(adapted from 1 Peter 4:10-11)

The Planning Committee in Action

The material in this booklet is directed to a group of people whose concern will be the planning of good liturgy in a parish setting. Everything to this point has been directed at the "what" of liturgy planning — this section must try to tackle the "how" of it all, the people who will do the work.

The planning committee has a very special function. As a special branch or subcommittee of the main Liturgy Committee it must create the kind of atmosphere in which the resources of the larger group, the parish community, can thrive and flourish.

One person *can* plan liturgy, and a few people *can* direct liturgy, but their personal resources will soon be overtaxed and strained as they either try to cover everything thinly or find themselves underchallenged by the preparation of only a few events.

The planning group has to begin with a conviction and a dedication — good liturgy, the parish celebration, is the focus of effort. This is not just another service group; it is the team that works to mold the worship of the parish community into what it should be.

A committee at its best is a cooperative enterprise — individuals of different talents and expertise who work together to a common goal. To achieve its goal, the Liturgy Committee has to plan to operate as an effective, goal-centered group. Tasks are shared out, with a commitment to accomplishing them on time and a trust that they will be. Information has to be readily available and shared, including material that is critical of what the group might be trying to accomplish. Rules of order are imperative for clear direction and effective meetings.

Where to start?

How the group starts is perhaps not as important as actually getting started. Some people will naturally be involved — e.g. the leaders of musicians, readers, and other liturgical ministers, but the planning committee is not just the amalgamation of other parish groups. Phone calls to individuals with specific talents — e.g. people who can sew (they may never have even thought about wallhangings or vestments) — will involve a wider circle. Advertisements in the parish bulletin, invitations from the pulpit and by word of mouth, will round out the initial organization.

The first group meeting may, in fact, be a little large, but it can serve as an information and sharing event — who we are, why we think we are here. Some people may simply wish to put their talents "on file" for future contact on a particular project.

Some basic steps

1. Organization. Select a chairperson, someone who can direct the efforts of the group. Find out about interests and expertise. Discuss the involvement of individuals in the parish (readers, ushers, ministers of communion) to find out their needs. Set up smaller committees around the interests of individuals or along the lines of the planning levels (physical, decorative, personal, conceptual, cf. page 8 ff.).

Above all, even at a first meeting, make a decision to start planning for a specific day, not too far off, to get the committee working on a real project. Even if the planning is simple in its scope (e.g. some basic decoration), it will get the group started.

In the midst of the initial organization, find out who are missing and decide on how to have them present.

Keep it simple! Liturgy planning is always a long-range opera-

tion, and even a few things accomplished in the opening weeks will be a step forward.

2. Committees. Planning groups work with other liturgical ministers, and particularly under the umbrella of the main Liturgy Committee. For example, planners work with the musicians to create the mood of the day; they do not pick the hymns. Planners work to coordinate the various ministries; they do not pick readers for a given celebration. Planners are concerned with the decoration of the church; they do not make the wall-hangings.

Through committees, the planning team can involve more members in the effort, while keeping the size and number of meetings to a minimum. Committees can be formed along the four planning levels — e.g. concern with physical, decoration, personnel, and ideas; then, using the levels as guides for action, they can be further grouped around smaller units — e.g. the various ministries within the liturgy personnel.

3. Celebration. Planning teams are working groups, not only discussion groups. Knowledge of the why and how of liturgy is certainly necessary, but the action of putting it together is even more critical.

Dividing the team by days of celebration (e.g. a Sunday team, feasts, etc.) can be counter-productive simply because the members of the various groups lose continuity with the whole. It may certainly be easier to begin with one or two "festivals" to get the group launched, but the Sunday liturgy is where the planning must eventually reap its results. The work done must always benefit *the* weekly gathering of the local Church.

4. Evaluation. A planning team has to be sensitive to evaluation. Actually, evaluation of the liturgy in the parish may well be where it starts. Evaluation is a positive tool, not a complaint session; it is the activity of working through what went right as well as what went wrong.

Note: The Sample Meetings for long and short-range planning meetings may serve as effective evaluation guides (pp. 43, 45).

Communication between the various groups will make evaluation easier, because it will be an activity of cooperation, not self criticism. Remember — the parish is where it all comes about. Any planning team needs to remember that its major role is to be of service to its parish. One simple test of this service is: How does it look from the pew?

5. Tools. Meetings need guides to be successful. Each team will want to design "planning sheets" for focus and recording (see pages 43 and 45). Before each larger meeting, the chairperson or a small coordinating group can sketch out the general goals and concerns. This should be on paper. It will then be easier for the larger group to add comments.

For example, in a long-range planning session for Advent, the following might be offered —

Sample meeting — Long-range planning

Advent to Epiphany (19___)

Feasts:
1. Advent: four Sundays
2. Christmas: falls on — —.
3. Epiphany: falls on January — — (right after New Year)
4. Feasts: December 8; other feasts fall on — —.
5. Reconciliation celebrations.

General goals and concerns
Last year:

What did we do? (schedule)
What was successful? why? unsuccessful? why?
This year:

Goals — to assist our parish to worship and celebrate
as a community through planning liturgies.
(See also "Questions", p. 5)
Concerns — e.g. should we do something about celebrating
December 8?/when will the celebration of
Reconciliation take place. What planning required?

How to achieve goals
1) Overall Planning Session: see model for an individual planning meeting (p. 45). This dynamic may be applied to the planning of a Season as for an individual Sunday or feast. The Overall Session may take place during an evening; or a Saturday Workshop may be considered.

2) Organizing Teams for "Levels of Planning" (see page 8 ff.):

Physical: e.g. cold weather; parking; large numbers in the congregation over Season

Decorative: e.g. Advent wreath (visible?); decorations that can last for the whole Season

Personal: e.g. music — when to sing carols? extra help for distributing communion (ministers)? hospitality?

Conceptual: What is our theme? (derived from meeting — see meeting model, page 43).

Special ideas: e.g. use of artistic expression (audio-visual, dance, etc.)

Committee members ——————— Tasks———————

——————— ———————

——————— ———————

Next meeting date ————————————————————

Agenda items ——————————————————————

As a result of the meeting, groups and smaller teams could start their efforts and begin to enlist others to help. Christmas and Epiphany should flow out of the Advent initiatives as well as give some direction to them.

Rather than looking to individual Sundays, the committee looks at the whole design. The individual days need far less attention when the larger design is in place. Eventually, the individual days receive their own planning sheets.

6. Time. Yes, planning takes time — and the liturgy deserves it. Advance planning (Advent, for example, should be under way in September) and an approach that understands that "less is often more" will help the time factor.

While the larger committee may not have to meet weekly, involvement in smaller groups would likely involve a few hours each week.

To keep going — "Learn-understand-meet"

Three items will help the committee to stay strong and vital:

1) **Learn** — start reading about liturgy, about celebration in general, about a particular interest (decoration, design, music, etc.). Look carefully at your own parish Sunday liturgy, with a fair but critical eye. Find out what is going well, and what needs improvement.

2) **Understand** the needs and expertise of others. Working with the "professional" members of the liturgy personnel (cantors, organist, etc.) and with those who have been functioning for some time, without training (lectors, ministers of communion), as well as with those who simply have always helped (flower arrangers, cleaning volunteers) — requires care, understanding, and tact. Always!

3) **Meet:**

Sample meeting — planning one Sunday liturgy

First Sunday of Advent

Note: This meeting will be most effective if held at least three to four weeks in advance of the actual celebration.

Dynamics of the meeting:

• Begin with a short period of *prayer*, giving some time for recollection.

- Share a) **thoughts** and b) **feelings of individuals** in the group, based on the following or similar questions (Note: it is assumed that each member has thought and prayed about these prior to the meeting):

1) What does the Word Liturgy of this Sunday say to our world?
2) What does the Word Liturgy of this Sunday say to our parish community?
3) What does the Word Liturgy of this Sunday say to me, personally?

(Note: these questions may be reversed or taken in another order.)

- Come to a **group consensus** about these thoughts and feelings. What are the common (more than individual) thoughts and feelings? The consensus indicates a particular *theme* and *mood* for the Sunday liturgy.

- Keeping the overall goals in mind (p. 43), carry out a **Liturgy Brainstorming** session. To do this effectively, the group must now put into practice the information contained in the previous pages of this booklet. Accurate information about the following topics in particular must be utilized: Levels of Planning (p. 8); the Church Year (p. 17); Format of Eucharistic Liturgy (p. 26); Parts of the Eucharist (p. 28); Long-Range Planning (p. 43). With this information in mind, the group now begins to brainstorm all the *possibilities* for the liturgy of this Sunday. At this session, absolutely all suggestions are accepted!

- Conduct a **Liturgy-Decision** session: With the conclusion of the brainstorming, the group now moves from the "possible" to the "actual." The committee now decides, in very practical terms, what it suggests will be done in the various parts of the liturgy.

Note: It will be helpful to use a schema such as the Format of the Eucharistic Liturgy (p. 26-27) as a guide, at this point, for drawing up a *Celebration Sheet* for this particular liturgy.

Upon completion, the Celebration Sheet should be checked against the Priorities Schema (page 34) to see that all the important parts of the liturgy are being highlighted. It is also important that there be a *cadence* of highpoints and periods of rest throughout the liturgy.

This sheet should then be circulated, at least to each liturgical ministry involved in this celebration (e.g. readers, presiders, musicians, et al) so that all have a record of the planning. Better than this is to accompany the sheet with verbal explanation. And, still better, is that the individual ministers or representatives of each ministry participate at the planning meeting itself.

In each section of the meeting, a *record of notes* may be taken by each member of the committee, or by a secretary. It helps to keep track of the discussion.

Evaluation of the liturgy celebration itself should take place at a meeting following this particular Sunday. Basic questions, such as the following, may be asked: — Did this liturgy achieve our overall goal of assisting our parish to worship and celebrate as a community? How, or how not? Why, or why not? — What can we do to improve?

Evaluation of the meetings can take place at the same meeting as above, at the end of the Advent Season and/or at the end of the year. Questions like these may be asked

— Were we *affective*? did we listen, support, challenge one another as a loving community of faith? how? why or why not? how can we improve?

— Were we *effective*? did we accomplish a plan that represented the planning group? were we successful in each section of the meeting(s)? how? why or why not? how can we improve?

— Do we continue to *learn* about our parish community, our world, liturgical ministry, liturgy? how can we improve?

*No Christian community can be built up
unless it has as its basis and pivot
the celebration of the holy Eucharist.
It is from this therefore
that any attempt to form a community
must begin.*

*The 1967 Instruction on Eucharistic Worship,
National Bulletin on Liturgy, No. 13*

What do we plan

A. Sunday Liturgy

• The Sundays of the Major Seasons (Advent to Epiphany, Lent to Pentecost), but with care and attention to the weekly Sunday celebration.

• "Ordinary Time," grouping of Sundays can be a help.

B. Feast Days

• Days of special interest and celebration for the parish

• Word liturgies

Liturgical Calendar Days

Special Feasts during the Advent-Christmas-Epiphany Cycle:
Immaculate Conception, Holy Family, Lord's Baptism

Special Feasts during the Lent-Easter-Pentecost Cycle:
Ash Wednesday, Ascension

Trinity Sunday
Corpus Christi (or a day of eucharistic devotion)
Assumption
Christ the King
All Saints — All Souls

Related Celebrations

New Year's Day
Canada Day
Labor Day
Thanksgiving Day
Memorial Day

Parish Feast Days:

Patron saint or mystery (titular feast)
Anniversary of church dedication

Mission Day
National (patronal) feasts of parish ethnic groups
Diocesan celebrations

C. Special Celebrations:

Days that have significance to special groups or have a definite "group" or "seasonal" character.

General Parish Reconciliation — Advent, Lent
First Communion
Confirmation

D. Special Group Interests:

For ongoing consideration by special teams.

Baptisms
Weddings
Ministry to the Sick
Wake, Funeral, Rites for the Dying

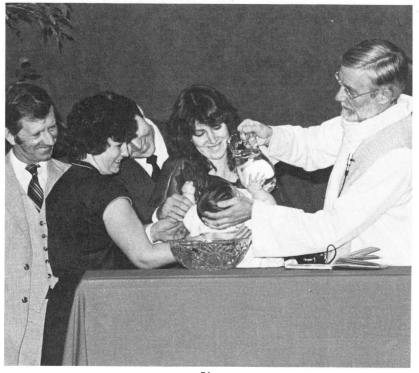

Afterwards, we continually remind each other of these things. And those who have possessions come to the aid of those who are poor; and we are always one with each other. For everything that has been given to our use, we praise the Creator of all through His Son Jesus Christ and through the Holy Spirit.

On the day which is dedicated to the sun, all those who live in the cities or who dwell in the countryside gather in a common meeting, and for as long as there is time the Memoirs of the Apostles or the writings of the prophets are read. Then, when the reader is finished, the president verbally gives a warning and appeal for the imitation of these good examples.

Then we all rise together and offer prayers, and, as we said before, when our prayer is ended, bread is brought forward along with wine and water, and the president likewise gives thanks to the best of his ability, and the people call out their assent, saying the Amen.

Then there is the distribution to each and the participation in the Eucharistic elements, which also are sent with the deacons to those who are absent. Those who are wealthy and who wish to do so, contribute whatever they themselves care to give; and the collection is placed with the president, who aids the orphans and the widows, and those who through sickness or any other cause are in need, and those who are imprisoned, and the strangers who are sojourning with us — and, in short, he takes care of all who are in need.

The Day of the Sun is the day on which we all gather in a common meeting, because it is the first day, the day on which God, changing darkness and matter, created the world; and it is the day on which Jesus Christ our Savior rose from the dead. For He was crucified on the day before that of Kronos; and on the day after that of Kronos, which is the day of the Sun, He appeared to His Apostles and disciples, and taught them these things which we have also submitted to you for your consideration.

St. Justin the Martyr, *First Apology* (ca. 148-155 AD.); taken from *The Faith of the Early Fathers*, William A. Jurgens, The Liturgical Press, Collegeville, 1970, p. 55-56.

Resources

There are many excellent books on liturgy — background, planning, resources. The following are offered by way of beginning. Although hardly a complete list, groups may find these a useful place to start. The other booklets in the New Ministries series will also offer resources, as well as being practical starting places in themselves.

Background

General information and background in liturgy

The Constitution on the Sacred Liturgy (Vatican II)
The General Instruction on the New Roman Missal (1969)
General Norms for the Liturgical Year (1969)
Directory for Masses with Children (1973)
Environment and Art in Catholic Worship (National Conference of Catholic Bishops, 1978)

Background books

Bouyer, Louis. *Life and Liturgy.* Andrews & McMeel, Inc., 4400 Johnson Dr., Fairway, KS. 66205.

Cooke, Bernard. *Ministry to Word and Sacraments.* 1977, History and Theology, Fortress Press, 2900 Queen Lane, Philadelphia, PA. 19129.

Duffy, Regis, O.F.M. *Real Presence.* 1982, Harper and Row, Keystone Industrial Park, Scranton, PA. 18512.

Gelineau, Joseph. *The Liturgy Today and Tomorrow.* 1978, Darton, Longman and Todd, 89 Lillée Rd., London, SW6 1UD.

Hovda, Robert, *Dry Bones.* 1978, Living Worship Guides, The Liturgical Conference, 810 Rhode Island Ave., N.E., Washington, D.C. 20018.

Seasoltz, R. Kevin. *New Liturgy, New Laws.* 1980, The Liturgical Press, 74 Engle Blvd., Collegeville, MN. 56321.

The Mystery of Faith: A Study of the Structural Elements of the Order of Mass. Federation of Diocesan Liturgical Commissions, 1200 New Hampshire Ave. N.W., Suite 320, Washington, D.C. 20036.

Truit, Gordon E. *Introduction to Parish Liturgy.* 1979, Celebration Books, P.O. Box 281, Kansas City, MO. 64141.

Liturgy Planning

Certain, Stephanie and Marty Meyer. *Goal Setting for Liturgy Committees*. 1981, Liturgy Training Publications, 155 East Superior St., Chicago, Il. 60611.

The Liturgy Documents: A Parish Resource. 1980, Liturgy Training Program, Chicago, Il.

Liturgy with Style and Grace. 1978, Liturgy Training Program, Chicago, Il.

Mossi, John P. *Modern Liturgy Handbook*. 1976, Paulist Press, 545 Island Rd., Ramsey, NJ. 07446.

In addition, each of the new rites for the sacraments was drawn up with an extensive introduction and set of guidelines. (Individual countries and local areas often have added their own suggestions and directives as well.) These should be consulted as background to liturgies. The notes on Baptism, for example, would be not only necessary when planning Baptisms (especially when they take place at the Eucharist); they would also offer background for a Sunday whose readings and theme are directed towards the notion of Baptism.

The books *Rites* (of the Catholic Church) I and II published by Pueblo, 1860 Broadway, New York (1976, 1979) contain the introductions as well as the rites of celebration. Basic resources for any group planning Sunday liturgies remain the *Sacramentary* and the *Lectionary*.

Practical Level — Eucharist

Ainslie, John. *Making the Most of the Missal*. 1976, Geoffrey Chapman, 35 Red Lion Square, London, WC1R 4SG.

Coady, Patricia; Griffin Deborah; Jette, Theresa. *Great Things are Happening!* 1981, NOVALIS, Box 9700, Terminal, Ottawa, Ontario. K1G 4B4.

Touchstones for Liturgical Ministries. 1978, The Liturgical Conference, 810 Rhode Island Ave., N.E., Washington, D.C. 20018.

Walsh, Eugene A. *The Order of Mass: Guidelines*. 1979, Pastoral Arts Associates of North America, 4744 West Country Gables Drive, Glendale, AZ. 85306.

Walsh, Eugene A. *Practical Suggestions for Celebrating Sunday Mass*. Part of a series that includes *The Theology of Celebration* and *The Ministry of the Celebrating Community*. Pastoral Arts Associates of North America, 4744 West Country Gables Drive, Glendale, AZ 85306.

Liturgical Year

Adam, Adolph. *The Liturgical Year*. Liturgical Press, 74 Engle Blvd., Collegeville, MN. 56321.

Bitney, James. *Bright Intervals: Prayers for Paschal People*. Winston Press, 430 Oak Grove, Minneapolis, MN. 55403.

Ellebracht, Mary Pierre. *The Easter Passage: The RCIA Experience.* 1983, Winston Press.

From Ashes to Easter. The Liturgical Conference, Washington, D.C. Revised 1979.

Hartgen, W. E. *Planning Guide for Lent and Holy Week.* 1979, Pastoral Arts Associates of North America, 4744 West Country Gables Drive, Glendale, AZ 85306.

Huck, Gabe. *The Three Days.* 1981, Liturgy Training Program, Chicago, Il.

Keeping Advent. The Liturgical Conference, Washington, D.C. Revised 1979.

Montgomery, Herb and Mary. *Easter is Coming.* 1982, Winston Press.

Nocent, Adrien. *The Liturgical Year.* (4 Vols.) 1977, The Liturgical Press, St. John's Abbey, Collegeville, MN. 56321.

Ryan, Vincent. *Advent to Epiphany,* 1977. *Lent and Holy Week,* 1976. *Pasch to Pentecost,* 1977. Veritas Publications, 7-8 Lower Abbey St., Dublin 1, Irish Republic.

Periodicals on Liturgy

Periodicals provide a concise and practical way to keep new material available for planners. Often they deal with individual seasons and Sundays, providing solid and practical suggestions for discussion and even implementation.

Assembly (Notre Dame Center for Pastoral Liturgy, Box 81, Notre Dame, IN.) Explores the tradition, meaning, and practice of some aspect of the liturgy.

Celebration (Box 281, Kansas City, MO.) A general creative worship service.

Homiletic Service. (Novalis, Box 9700, Terminal, Ottawa, Canada) A fine resource offering liturgy suggestions as well as scriptural materials and homilies.

Liturgy. (The Liturgical Conference, 810 Rhode Island Avenue, N.E., Washington, D.C. 20018.)

Liturgy 80. (Liturgy Training Publications, 155 East Superior St., Chicago, Il.) Articles and insightful approaches.

Modern Liturgy. (Resources Publications, 7291 Coronado Dr., San Jose, CA.) Creative suggestions on feasts, seasons, and para-liturgical celebrations.

National Bulletin on Liturgy. (Publications Service, 90 Parent Ave., Ottawa, Canada.) Has devoted individual numbers to history of eucharist, Sunday celebration, sacraments, and committees.

Worship. (St. John's Abbey, Collegeville, Minnesota.) Scholarly review concerned with liturgical renewal.

Teams should also consult the local "ordo" or yearly planning book for indications of national celebrations, dates of feasts, and the general calendar, *Liturgical Calendar,* Publications Office, United States Catholic Conference, 1312 Massachusetts Ave., N.W., Washington, D.C. 20005. In Canada, *Guidelines for Pastoral Liturgy,* Publications Service, 90 Parent Ave., Ottawa, Canada.

LITURGY PLANNING

Written by:

Kenneth Pearce
St. Mary's Church, Brampton, Ontario

Edited by:

Jerome Herauf

Layout:

Jan Gough, Gilles Lépine

Photography:

Cover: Jonas Abromaitis;
p. 2, 6, 12, 15, 51, 52: Jonas Abromaitis;
p. 9: Joyce Harpell;
p. 18: Jean Roch Veilleux
p. 20: Paul Hamel;
p. 23, 45: Mary Kibblewhite;
p. 30-31: Ellen Eff;
p. 35: Roman Matwijejko;
p. 38: "Vivant univers";
p. 42: Anne McLaughlin, GSIC;
p. 44: Mary Kibblewhite
p. 46: Pat Onofrio

Illustrations:

p. 7: John Lewis;
p. 16 and 24, cover 1 and cover 4: Lee Thirlwall

"... place yourselves
at the service of others; so that in all things God may
receive the glory."

(from 1 Peter 4: 10-11)

Winston Press
430 Oak Grove
Minneapolis, Minnesota 55403

ISBN: 0-86683-735-3

Readers at Liturgy

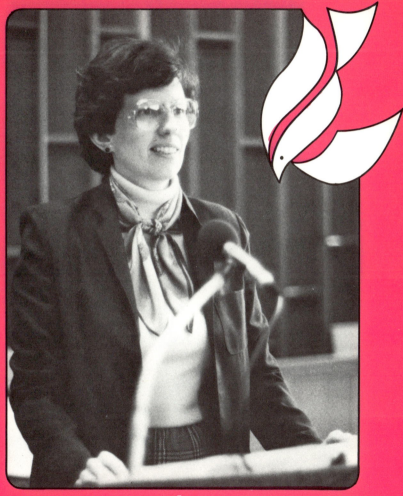

New Parish Ministries

WINSTON PRESS

Contents

New Parish Ministries was originally published by Novalis. Saint Paul University. Ottawa. Canada. This edition is published by Winston Press. Inc.. by arrangement with Novalis. Saint Paul University. Copyright ' 1982. Novalis. Copyright ' 1983. Winston Press. All rights reserved. No part of this book may be reproduced in any form without written permission from the publisher.

ISBN: 0-86683-736-1 (previously ISBN: 2-89088-082-6)

Printed in Canada

5 4 3 2 1

Winston Press. Inc.. 430 Oak Grove. Minneapolis. MN 55403

Friends...
this booklet is for you if:

You are already a liturgical reader.

Maybe you've been reading for years, as I have, but we all need evaluation periodically:
— How am I doing?
— Can I improve? How?
— Am I truly proclaiming God's Word?
— Or is it just a good sight reading?

You are an aspiring reader.

I've always wanted to be a Liturgical Reader, but:
— What would that involve?
— Have I the necessary qualifications?
— How can I get rid of my nervousness?

You are in charge of the readers in your parish.

— What guidelines do I follow?
— What helpful suggestions can I offer to those with specific problems?

You are concerned that the word of God be proclaimed well.

— What is this Ministry of Reader all about?
— How has this Ministry evolved over the years?

To all of you: these pages are dedicated in love and in service.

Molly

1

Ministry of Reader

Many of you "long-time" Readers probably started as I did, with little or no training, just "to help Father on Sunday." Did you know that lay people in the early Church proclaimed God's Word in the liturgical assemblies? Gradually, this responsibility became one of the minor orders conferred on men in training for ordination. So, laypeople were no longer permitted to function in this capacity until Vatican II came along, challenging all of us to reassess our baptismal role. God calls us by name to go forth and bear fruit that lasts (Jn. 15:16). Reading became one way in which I could publicly witness to my faith, in answer to my baptismal call. However, if I were going to "witness to my faith," then my reading would have to be much more than just a good sight reading. It would have to be a true proclamation.

Spotting the difference was easy. When I truly proclaimed, people would say afterwards, "Your reading touched me today. It certainly meant a lot to you, didn't it?" In assessing the difference, I realized that, before truly proclaiming, I had prayed for an understanding of the text and the ability to read it well. Before, by good sight reading, I had merely glanced over it hurriedly, forgetting to prepare prayerfully.

The Bible is God's Word, and Jesus is the Word made Flesh. Just as Mary gave flesh to the Infant Christ, so too do Readers give flesh to the Word Who is Christ. We are his mouthpieces. Christ is present, of course, regardless of our style as Reader, but the REALITY of his presence is strengthened and increased when his Reader proclaims with faith and skill.

Along about this time, much was being written and spoken about "new ministries" or "lay ministries" in the Church. Liturgical Reader could not really be classed as a "new" ministry because it has existed since the very early Church. What is new is the recent refocusing of liturgical reading as strictly a lay function * — a function that ministers to, or serves, the people of God.

So, in a sense, my experience over the past ten years is really a bird's-eye view of how the Ministry of Reader has evolved from an ancient lay function in the early Church, to a clerical minor order,

3

to post Vatican II just-helping-Father-out-on-Sunday, to truly proclaiming the Word, to effecting the presence of Christ within the worshipping assembly and, finally, to an awareness of how Liturgical Reader is truly a ministry serving God's people.

A role-model for this ministry? JESUS, of course! The gospel of Luke tells us that Jesus said, "Yet here am I among you as one who serves!" (Lk. 22:27) Jesus preached the Good News by healing the sick (Lk. 4:18). That is the mission we as Liturgical Readers are asked to share in, through baptism, by proclaiming the Good News well.

"It was your Word, Lord, which heals all things." (Wis. 16:12)

What qualities did Jesus bring to his ministry? He was always compassionate, concerned, loving. His ministry was, very clearly, two-directional: vertical, in praising his Father, and horizontal, in serving his Father's people.

Jesus, then, is our role-model, and the theme of our ministry must be, as his was: *Love and service* — praising the Father, through lovingly serving his people.

* Vatican II Documents:
Constitution on Sacred Liturgy: General Instructions on Roman Missal: #34 and 66.

4

Motivation and Misgivings

What motivates me to become a Reader?

● My desire to witness to my Christian faith.

● My concern that the Word of God be proclaimed well.

● My awareness that any reading talents I might have are not for myself alone but for the good of the whole community.

In baptism God calls me by name and gives me the strength to stand up and be counted as one of his followers. In confirmation, the Holy Spirit gives me the courage to witness boldly for Christ.

God speaks to his people *now*, through his Word, and calls them to action.

Paul speaks of the gifting of the Spirit as a prelude to ministry. These spiritual gifts or charisms (from the word "charis" meaning "love") Paul also calls services or ministries: ways of using one's energies for the good of the community. (I Cor. 12:3-7)

What causes the great fear I feel?

Usually I feel nervous about reading in front of people because I am afraid I might make a mistake or lose my place or forget what to do at what time. I am too *self-conscious*, afraid of looking foolish.

How can I overcome this great fear?

This nervous tension or fear is an *emotion*. It is good as long as it is channelled properly. I find it consoling to know that 70% of all people who stand before assemblies experience nervousness, which causes a chemical change in the blood.

SYMPTOMS?

- your mouth becomes dry
- your voice becomes shrill and high
- your hands perspire
- your knees begin to tremble
- you have "butterflies" or maybe even "eagles" in your stomach.

Sound familiar? Well, this nervous tension can work positively for you, if you will let it, because you are at your physical and mental best when you are keyed up this way. You look more poised and confident, and perceive the text more keenly. Besides, a Reader who is not the least bit nervous will never move the assembly to a full meaning of the Word of God. So, let's channel that good emotion of fear positively by:

- Prayer
- Concentrating on the Word of God and on
- the Assembly more than on yourself
- Proper preparing*
- Acting confidently*
- Relaxing*
- Proper breathing*

*These will be discussed more fully in the section on Preparation.

"I said, 'Ah, Lord Yahweh, look, I do not know how to speak: I am a child!' " But Yahweh replied, "Do not say, 'I am a child.' " Then Yahweh put out his hand and touched my mouth and said to me: "There! I am putting my words into your mouth."

(Jer. 1:6, 7a, 9.)

Preparation

Liturgical Setting of Ministry:

The Word of God is proclaimed by the Reader during all Word liturgies: Mass, the Sacraments, para-liturgical services. Most frequently, the Reader proclaims at the Sunday Eucharist.

In the early Church, the taking, blessing, breaking and sharing of bread, the four actions of the first Eucharist were re-enacted, re-created by the early Christians, and celebrated along with an agape meal — a meal of love. Gradually, however, this was not felt to be a true sign of Christian love, because many brought much food, but ate it to the exclusion of others in the community. So, the agape meal was dissociated from the Eucharist.

Then, it was felt that the four actions alone: the taking, blessing, breaking, and sharing of bread constituted too short a service. So the Sabbath synagogue prayer service — consisting of a reading from the Old Testament, a psalm, instruction by the rabbi and communal prayer — was borrowed. With the addition of readings from the New Testament, a Gospel acclamation, and the Creed, this became our present Liturgy of the Word.

FIFTH SUNDAY OF LENT A (34)

SECOND READING   *If the Spirit of him who raised Jesus from the dead*
is living in you
then he will give life to your own mortal bodies.

A reading from the letter of Paul to the Romans   *Rom 8:8-11*

People who are interested only in unspiritual things can never be pleasing to God. Your interests, however, are not in the unspiritual, but in the spiritual, since the Spirit of God has made his home in you. In fact, unless you possessed the Spirit of Christ you would not belong to him.

7

While the Bible contains the whole inspired Word, the Lectionary used at Mass contains only portions of it. These selected sections of the Bible are set up in the Lectionary on a three-year cycle: Cycle A, Cycle B, and Cycle C. So, while we may be very familiar with the passage we are proclaiming, because of our prayerful preparation, the people in the pew are hearing it only once every three years.

A missalette is a very useful tool for personal meditation on God's Word. However, the Word is proclaimed from the Lectionary, so it is an advantage to practise from it beforehand. See if your parish can provide small study editions of the Lectionary for readers to use.

Because the theme of the liturgy is taken from the Gospel, it is good to read the Gospel first, even though this will be proclaimed by a deacon or priest, rather than a lay Reader. Knowing this theme helps the Reader to understand the readings he/she will be proclaiming.

Next, we suggest studying the First Reading, which is usually taken from the Old Testament. It has been selected because it relates to the Gospel theme. Then, read the Psalm, which also should touch on the Gospel theme. Finally read the Second Reading from the New Testament. Only on special feasts is this second reading chosen to relate to the Gospel. Usually it is an ongoing reading from one of Paul's letters.

STEPS TO FOLLOW

1 *Pray for understanding*
2 *Locate Readings in study Lectionary*
3 *Read Gospel first for theme*
4 *Read First Reading from Old Testament relate to Gospel theme*
5 *Read Psalm*
6 *Read Second Reading — usually an ongoing reading from Paul*

The Bible is really a whole library of books. As such, it contains many different literary styles: history, laws, prophecy, wisdom, poetry, letters, travelogues, parables and miracles. Since the Reader is at- tempting to communicate mood and meaning, as well as words, it is important to recognize these different styles in the various books from which Word Liturgy readings are taken.

Old Testament Literary Styles

How to proclaim them

History: A written record to preserve the past for future generations. (E.g. Ex. 12 — Passover — Lect. #40)

Requires the Reader to be a story-teller par excellence — describing vividly, with much animation, but not over-dramatization.

Laws: Guidelines or moral codes to help one live a good life. (Ten Commandments: Ex. 20: 12-17; Lect. #29B)

Should be spoken with authority: *"It is the Lord who speaks."*

Prophecy: Words given by God to his people — through a chosen individual — to comfort, sustain, strengthen and uplift the Christian community. (Isaiah 61:1-3, 6, 8-9. This text is fulfilled in the gospel — Lk. 4:16-21; Lect. #39)

A prophet is one who is speaking for God. These texts must be proclaimed with authority, animation, and clarity.

Wisdom: Wise sayings to help the individual to live a good life. (Wis. 6:12-16; Lect. #155A)

Read them with a tone of admonition and hope.

Psalm: The psalms are Israelite poems put to music. They could possibly be considered the Jewish hymnal hit-parade of 750 B.C. Covering every human emotion: joy, sadness, anger, grief, thanksgiving, etc., they can basically be divided into two categories: praise (e.g., Ps 150); lament (e.g., Ps. 38).

Being able to determine the mood of the psalm can help the Reader to put the proper meaning and feeling into his/her proclamation.

9

New Testament Literary Styles

How to proclaim them

Letter: Sent by one of the apostles to one of the early Christian communities. (E.g. 1 Cor 1:1-3; Lect. #65A)

An important letter has arrived, and I have been chosen to read it to the members of my Christian community.

Travelogue: An account of a missionary journey with all its trials and tribulations. (Acts 14:21-27; Lect. #55C)

I am recounting a trip friends have taken. It was exciting for them and I want to convey that excitement to the assembly.

Parables: Jesus used these short stories to attract the curiosity and attention of his listeners, and to clarify his teachings. These parables instruct by comparison. (Mt. 13:44-52; Lect. #110A)

If the Reader creates a mental image of that comparison, he/she will be more able to help the listeners to visualize it as well.

Miracles: These usually include:

1) Jesus meeting the sick person
2) A description of the sickness
3) The healing
4) Proof of the healing
5) Awe and wonder in those present. (Mk. 5:21-43; Lect. #99B)

Much expression must be put into the reading of these miracle accounts, especially to convey the wonder people felt when faced with Jesus' healing power.

The Scripture passage for any Word liturgy may be very short and difficult to understand out of context. Several intervening verses may be omitted from the passage. For example, the reading might be Philippians 1:4-6, 8-11 (Lect. #6C). To help me come to a better understanding of God's Word, it could be helpful to locate this passage in the Bible.

Some Bibles have a summary of each particular book: who the writer was; when and where he wrote; the conditions or problems existing which might have prompted him to write it. Possibly reading a bit before and after the designated passage might clarify the reading for me. Certainly it could help if I were to read the missing verses.

If, after all this, I still have not really understood what the passage is saying, a commentary on the Scripture readings might provide more insight. A number of these commentaries are listed in the bibliography.

Questions I can ask myself to help me understand the text

1 Does this passage tell me something about God?

2 Does it tell me something about God's plan for humankind?

3 What does it mean for ME TODAY?

Answers:

1 God is steadfast, persevering, all-knowing, all-loving.

2 God's plan is that we share in spreading the Good News of his great love for us, lovingly, as Jesus did.

3 Love is the way I must follow to be prepared for Judgment Day.

STEPS TO FOLLOW

minimum

1 Pray for understanding
2 Locate passage in Bible
3 Read a bit before and a bit after it, plus any missing intervening verses

optimum

4 Read any background notes on the sacred writer and book
5 Consult a commentary for further insight.

Surveys have shown that proper preparation can help to eliminate 25% of one's nervousness in front of an Assembly. It would increase the Reader's confidence, if he/she is well prepared.

Have you had the experience, as I have, of arriving at church, only to have Father say, "Our scheduled Reader hasn't shown up yet. Would you mind doing the readings today?" Whether or not you are actually scheduled to read at next Sunday's Mass, it is a good idea to glance over the readings for that Sunday, at least once. Then you are not completely unprepared if, unexpectedly, you are asked to read.

However, when you are scheduled to read, here are some helpful hints: *Pages on which each step is covered in depth are notated. Some Readers like to spend ten minutes a day in preparation, beginning on the Monday before they will proclaim. Others prefer to spend a longer period of time preparing, closer to their Sunday proclamation.*

STEPS TO FOLLOW

At home
1. Pray for guidance
2. Locate assigned texts (see Lect. "Introduction" and "Index
3. Read silently for comprehension
4. Look up any difficult words in dictionary
5. Check pronunciation of names (Lect. pgs. 524-29)
6. Follow Liturgical Preparation (p. 8)
7. Follow Scriptural Preparation (p. 12)
8. Read texts aloud
9. Read texts aloud before a mirror
10. Practise deep-breathing and relaxation (pgs. 14-17)

At Church
11. Be at church well ahead of time
12. Use some of this time to deep-breathe yourself into a relaxed, calm, poised attitude
13. Check out what the other liturgical team members expect of you (p. 33)
14. Pray that all members of the liturgical team may carry out their ministry well
15. "Let go and let God." The Spirit will sustain you.

Breathing Techniques: Symptoms, Solutions, Exercises

1. Philip sounds so nervous when he reads that listening to him makes me uncomfortable. What causes his problem?... Much of Philip's nervousness is caused because he is not breathing properly. If he were breathing deeply from the diaphragm, rather than shallowly from the chest, he would be more relaxed, and would not sound so nervous... A good *exercise* to help Philip promote deep abdominal breathing and to eliminate shallow breathing is to exhale completely. Then, as Philip inhales, he should check to make sure that his shoulders do not rise. He should place his hand on his diaphragm, which is situated just below his rib cage. His hand should go out as he inhales, and in as he exhales.

Inhale

Exhale

Another method of checking to see whether he is *breathing deeply from the abdomen* is to lie on the floor and place a book just below the rib cage. If the book rises as Philip inhales, and falls as he exhales, he is breathing properly.

Inhale

Exhale

2. Susan never seems to have enough breath to finish sentences when she is reading. What can she do about it? ... Susan's problem would be much improved if she could learn improved *breath control*. Here is a good *exercise*. Inhale. Then, as she exhales, Susan should slowly count to five. As she practises this exercise, she should gradually be able to work that count up to ten. It is not so important how much breath she inhales. It is more important how she controls it as she exhales. Practising this once or twice a day will quickly help Susan to achieve better breath control, and will help her to have enough breath in reserve to complete her sentences when reading.

Inhale

Exhale

When Ted reads, his voice is jerky, and seems to stick in his throat. What causes this? ... Ted's voice is jerky because he is not exhaling his breath properly. The exercise described above (#2) could help his problem. Our voice seems to stick in our throat when the throat muscles are all tightened up. Relaxing through *abdominal breathing* (#1) can help prevent this. *Yawning* (not in front of your Assembly, of course), and *humming* also loosen throat muscles.

4. Jane's voice is so weak when she reads, we scarcely can hear her, and we are afraid she is going to faint before she finishes. What should she do?... *Deep breathing* described in #1 can help Jane. This will relax her, help her to be less nervous. By relaxing her throat muscles, her voice will sound stronger. Hearing her own strong voice will then give her extra confidence. Her extra confidence will convey itself to the Assembly and they will feel more comfortable.

5. Peter's voice always sounds so tired. Can you help him?... *Inertia* on the part of the Reader helps put the Assembly to sleep. Peter's problem stems from poor breathing habits. If he will stand erect, evenly balanced on both feet, head up, chin in, shoulders back, his body will have more room for *deep breathing*, which can help to overcome his problem. His strong clear voice will then help him to sound vital and alive in his proclamation.

6. When George reads, his voice has such an unpleasant *nasal sound* to it. What could he do to overcome that? ... *Erect posture* (#5), *deep breathing* (#1), and *proper breath control* (#2) can help to relax. This, in turn, will counteract his problem. Our voices are less shrill and nasal, when we are relaxed. We see this first thing in the morning. Our voices are lower pitched, more relaxed, but as the day wears on and we become more tense, our voices become shriller and higher pitched.

7. Julia mumbles when she reads, and we cannot understand her. What can she do?... First of all, Julia needs to *relax*. The breathing exercises described in #1 and #2 can help that. Then, Julia needs to practise the exercise described on p. 21 to give more flexibility to the lip and jaw muscles. Finally, an exercise that can further help to overcome Julia's problem is to take all the long-vowel sounds, chanting them such as:
"AY-AY-AY-AY-AY-AY-AY
EE-EE-EE-EE-EE-EE-EE
EYE-EYE-EYE-EYE-EYE-
OH-OH-OH-OH-OH-OH-OH
YOU-YOU-YOU-YOU-YOU-"

Comprehension

True communication is not just a matter of mouthing words correctly. It also involves transferring the mood and meaning of the message from my mind to the mind of the listener. Since this is so, I must have some comprehension, some understanding, of the mood and meaning of the text I will be proclaiming.

Reading the text over several times, silently and then aloud, can help me to determine the mood and tone. Is it joyful or solemn? petition or pure praise? Mentally establishing the mood and tone will help me to incorporate that feeling into my proclamation.

When reading the text, did I understand all the words? Do I need to consult a dictionary or pronunciation guide?

In reading aloud, have I been able to establish a good cadence or rhythm that is suitable to the meaning of the text? Is it possible for me to write the basic meaning of this text in one sentence? If so, I have some comprehension of it.

EXERCISE: from Baruch 3:9-13

Listen, Israel, to commands that bring life;
hear, and learn what knowledge means.
Why, Israel, why are you in the country of your enemies,
growing older and older in an alien land,
sharing defilement with the dead,
reckoned with those who go to Sheol?
Because you have forsaken the fountain of wisdom.
Had you walked in the way of God,
you would have lived in peace for ever.

I read it silently several times. What does the word "defilement" mean? I look it up in the dictionary. It means "uncleanness" or "corruption." I read the text aloud. How do you pronounce "Sheol"? I look it up in the pronunciation guide at the back of my study edition of the Sunday Lectionary. It is pronounced "Shē-ōle."

What is the meaning of this text in one sentence? "Walk with God and you will walk in peace!" Reading it aloud again, I carefully note the punctuation, and work on establishing a good cadence and rhythm. This text sounds solemn and authoritative to me. I must put solemnity and authority into my proclamation of it.

Punctuation

Punctuation is the use of periods, commas, question marks, quotation marks, colons, semi-colons, and exclamation points, to help make the meaning of the message clearer. They are written aids to the Reader to assist him/her in a good oral proclamation. Following these visual sign-posts can help one achieve better comprehension, speed, timing and expression.

EXERCISE: from Isaiah 52:14-53:1

1   As the crowds were appalled on seeing him
2   — so disfigured did he look
3   that he seemed no longer human —
4   so will the crowds be astonished at him,
5   and kings stand speechless before him;
6   for they shall see something never told
7   and witness something never heard before:
8   "Who could believe what we have heard,
9   and to whom has the power of the Lord been revealed?"

As you can see, the reading is broken up into good sense-lines. Each line expresses a thought. There is no punctuation mark at the end of line 1. However, the marks at the beginning of line 2 and end of line 3 act as brackets: This is an interjection added to explain line 1. It should be read in a lower voice than lines 1 and 4.

The colon after line 7 denotes a pause before proclaiming what was heard. Quotation marks enclosing lines 8 and 9 tell us this is to be proclaimed as conversation. Since it concludes with a question mark, our voice should also express a query by a raised inflection at the end.

Must I adhere strictly to written punctuation?... Written punctuation is merely an aid, a tool to help the Reader. One is not strictly held to it. If, after prayer and practice, one finds a different phrasing helps to convey the message more clearly, as he/she perceives it, then by all means feel free to use it.

Suggestion:

As a general guideline, the timing of pauses suggested by the different punctuation marks are as follows:

comma	silently count: 1
semi-colon	" ": 1-2
colon	" ": 1-2
bracket	" ": 1-2
period	" ": 1-2-3
question mark	" ": 1-2-3
exclamation point	" ": 1-2-3
end of paragraph	" ": 1-2-3-4

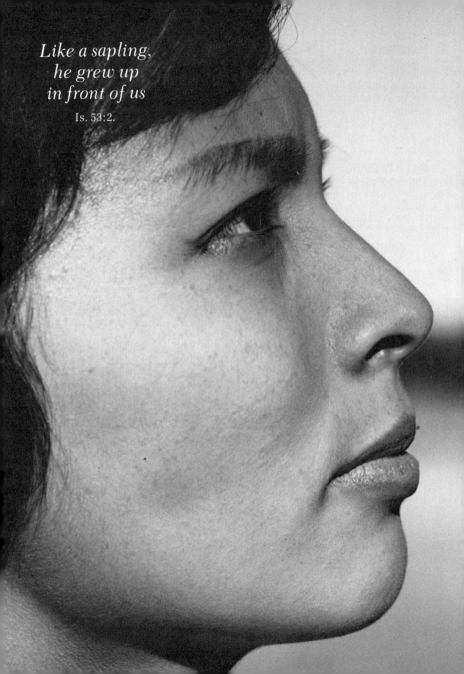

*Like a sapling,
he grew up
in front of us*

Is. 53:2.

Phrasing

Phrasing is a particular way in which a person expresses himself or herself in language. It is marking sentences into intelligible sections to convey more adequately the message intended. Acquiring the art of proper phrasing can enhance the quality of your proclamation.

It is usually attained only after trial and error, much practice and perseverance. Good phrasing makes the meaning more intelligible; poor phrasing can completely alter or destroy the message. *Example:* Isaiah 52:13.

Poor phrasing:

"See, my/servant will/prosper,
he shall be/lifted up, exalted,/rise
  to/great heights."

Good phrasing:

"See,/my servant will prosper,/
he shall be lifted up,/exalted,/rise
  to great heights./

Notice that the existing written punctuation suggests good phrasing. This is covered in depth on page 19.

How do I determine good phrasing?

It is necessary to practise out loud to truly determine good phrasing. Then, two senses are brought into play to help assess the situation: your sight and your hearing. It is important to hear the correct phrasing; your Assembly is hearing it, not seeing it.

EXERCISE:

Determining which word in each line should be stressed can help to decide proper phrasing.

Example: Isaiah 53:2

    LIKE a sapling/he grew up in front of us.

    Like a SAPLING/he grew up in front of us.

    Like a sapling/HE grew up/in front of us.

    Like a sapling/he GREW up/in front of us.

    Like a sapling/he grew UP/in front of us.

    Like a sapling/he grew up in FRONT/of us.

    Like a sapling he grew up in front of US.

Aloud, repeat each of these sentences, stressing the capitalized words. Let your ear tell you which one best conveys the meaning of the sentence as you perceive it.

21

Good phrasing can lead us to establish the proper cadence or rhythm of a particular reading. The Reader should be aware that the cadence used for reading either the Psalm or the New Testament is quite different from that required for a good proclamation of the Old Testament. Usually some comprehension (p. 18) of the meaning of the reading helps to suggest a suitable rhythm or cadence.

Voice Quality

Jesus came to tell us that God the Father loves us. He was an announcer, a herald of that Good News. As his mouthpieces, we must also be **heralds,** announcing, proclaiming his Good News with faith and feeling. Of utmost importance, then, is the quality of the voice with which we announce God's message to his people. Some areas we should consider carefully are those of expression, speed, volume, pitch, and diction.

Expression

If we are to put meaning and feeling into our proclamation, we cannot read in a monotone. This will quickly cause members of the Assembly to tune us out. The meaning of the message may be lost.

Remember: When we are conversing with a friend, we do not speak in a monotone. Sometimes we speak slowly and thoughtfully. At other times we get excited and speak more quickly. When we are really interested in what we are saying, we have an alive, energetic look on our face.

Suggestion: Practise reading out loud, preferably in front of a mirror. In this way, we see as well as hear ourselves in action. Following the punctuation and understanding what we are reading will help us to avoid speaking in a monotone. We usually end questions with a rising inflection in our voice (e.g. Mt. 11:9)

"Then what did you go out for? To see a prophet? Yes, I tell you, and much more than a prophet!"

Speed

You know what happens when you drive your car too fast? There is danger of losing control, isn't there? The same thing can happen when, through nervousness or habit, we read too quickly. We are in danger of losing control, of stumbling, of making mistakes. It is less likely that the Assembly will truly receive God's message. They may not be able to listen to that fast pace. It may tire them, and they may tune us out.

Remember: They are God's people, and deserve the best. Particularly do they deserve a well-paced proclamation for which to be thankful. Usually we read much more quickly than we think. Very rarely do we hear a Reader who speaks too slowly.

Suggestion: Recording a reading, then playing it back, can be helpful in assessing and adjusting our reading rate. Did you know that the difference between a too speedy proclamation and a well-timed one is really only a matter of a minute or so?

Volume

A key factor in any communication is volume. If the listener cannot hear the message, true communication does not take place. It is the responsibility of the Reader to make sure his/her volume is sufficient for the situation. Too little volume suggests timidity, nervousness, and makes the Assembly nervous too. Too much volume sets up a listening barrier, irritating the Assembly, because no one likes someone shouting.

Remember: Relaxation, deep breathing, and good posture are very important in maintaining good volume (see pgs. 14-17). Even when using a microphone, we must project our voice a bit to be easily heard (see Microphone Use, p. 29).

Suggestions:

1) Work on the buddy system. Have a friend or relative sitting in the back of the church give you a prearranged signal (hand over one ear) if you cannot be heard.

2) Pretend your voice is a ball. Throw it to the very back of the church, preferably to the farthest ceiling point. It will carry out over the heads of the Assembly and settle down over those in the very back row, so that all can hear.

Pitch

A low-pitched voice is fuller, more resonant, has greater carrying power, and is more easily listenable. Women, in particular, have problems with high-pitched voices. I had been reading for two years, doing very well, so I thought. One Sunday, after liturgy, my husband said, "Well, you've finally made it!" "What do you mean? Haven't I been doing a good job?" "Yes," he said, "but now you've finally relaxed enough to get your voice down to a good listening pitch." That taught me a good lesson. We do need periodic assessment by others so we don't begin to take our ministry for granted. No matter how expert we become, none of us is perfect, and there is always room for improvement.

Remember: You can lower the pitch of your voice mainly through relaxation and good breathing habits (pgs. 14-17).

Suggestion: One method I found helpful was to record my normal voice, then record the same text with a hand over one ear. Radio announcers do this often. It does help to lower the pitch of your voice. Feeling and hearing the difference in that pitch will acquaint you with how your voice and throat feel at a proper pitch. The lower the pitch, the more easily you will be heard.

Diction

Words are made up of vowels, consonants and syllables. All three are there for a purpose. A good Reader uses them well. The vowels make the music of our English language. Consonants break those vowel sounds neatly, and syllables separate words into distinct parts that help us in proper pronunciation. If we neglect to use any of these vowels, consonants or syllables, our proclamation can become indistinct and unintelligible.

Remember: We need to enunciate our vowels in full round tones, articulate our consonants clearly and distinctly, and include all the syllables (dropping word and sentence endings is definitely a "no-no"). God's people deserve to hear the full, majestic language of the Bible proclaimed well.

Suggestions:

1) A good *exercise* to help one enunciate *vowels* in full round tones is to repeat the sentence: *"How now brown cow"* a number of times, aloud and in front of a mirror. This also helps to counteract any problem one might have with lip-laziness, because it exercises the muscles of the lips and jaws.

2) A good *exercise* to help one articulate *consonants* clearly and distinctly, is to repeat the sentence: *"Peter Piper picked a peck of pickled peppers"* a number of times aloud and in front of a mirror. This also helps to counteract lip-laziness, which can make a reading mumbled and indistinct.

3) If one is enunciating vowels in full round tones, and articulating consonants clearly and distinctly, one usually includes all the syllables. However, it is a good idea to record yourself reading a text. During the play-back, concentrate particularly on whether you skip over or slur any syllables, words or sentence endings.

Caution

While it is important not to drop word or sentence endings, it is equally important not to add extra sounds or syllables known as *word whiskers:* e.g. "and-uh," "so-ah," "well-um." Word whiskers are sounds speakers use to fill the silence while determining the next word to speak. Most of us use them occasionally. Using too many of them can become distracting to your listeners and can destroy the meaning of the text. Being aware that they exist and that you do use them is the first step towards consciously eliminating them.

Body Language

People see us as well as hear us when we are at the lectern. Our dress, posture, gestures, non-verbals all speak volumes, even before we open our mouths.

What should I wear when I am reading?

What we wear as a Minister of the Word reflects the importance or dignity we attach to that Word, and should be in keeping with it.

Can I lean on the lectern, cross my legs, or keep my hands in my pockets?

The more casual our posture, the more casual the message appears. Posture should be erect and dignified, not just for appearance, but also for good breathing.

What about gestures, are they allowed?

Gestures that feel phoney to the Reader will look phoney to the Assembly. Too many gestures can become a distraction. Remember, this is a proclamation, not a theatrical dramatization.

What are non-verbals, and when can I use them?

Non-verbals are messages conveyed without the use of the spoken word, such as smiles, frowns, nodding the head up and down for affirmative emphasis, or back and forth sideways for negative emphasis. These can be used any time they will help your reading be a truer proclamation.

Eye contact

If we really want to get a message across to another person, how do we do it? Of course! We look them right in the eye! The eyes are the windows of the soul. Our witness is made believable to the people in the pews when they can see our faith in our eyes. So, good eye-contact is essential to a good proclamation. When people are truly receiving our message, they have intelligent, attentive, comprehending looks on their faces; they may also be leaning slightly forward in their seats. The listening silence of an attentive Assembly is an almost tangible feeling. We can't get that kind of "feedback" if we do not look at our Assembly at least once in a while.

Certainly we should be able to establish eye contact during our introduction, at the end of every paragraph (when we should be pausing anyway to let the Assembly reflect on what has just been read), and especially at the end when we say: "This is the Word of the Lord." What we are really saying is, 'All you people listening, what I have just read to you, I truly believe to be the inspired Word of God.' This is really our profession of faith, and is most effective when we are looking directly at them.

It is important that our eye contact not be centered on one person or section of our Assembly. If we never look to the far corners of the church, the people seated there could tune us out. Good eye-contact can help those listeners to operate more efficiently. If we look at them, they know we are aware of them, concerned about them hearing and understanding. They are less likely to pretend attention, or to become distracted.

Suggestion: Practising in front of a mirror is an excellent way of working on good eye-contact. Pretend your audience is in the mirror. Attempt to look at them as much as possible, while still maintaining a good flow in your proclamation. If you are afraid of losing your place while establishing eye contact, run one hand down the centre of the page in the area you are reading, and you will quickly locate your place again. It is important for good eye-contact that the reader have the lectionary at a good level so that a head-bobbing problem does not cause a distraction. Our eye contact should be an eye movement, not a head movement, down to the text and up out to the assembly. Many readers, tall ones in particular, find holding the book a help in this area (see p. 34).

Acoustics

A Reader can be truly proclaiming God's Word, and yet the full effect of the proclamation can be lost, if the acoustics are less than perfect and the Reader does nothing to deal with the situation.

Possible Problems

- Echoes

- Dead Spots

- Absorption of Sound

Possible Solutions

- Slow down your reading, not just sentences, but slow down words and syllables as well, while still keeping a smooth flow. Pause longer between sentences and paragraphs.

- We have one in our church. I have found it helpful to have a relative or friend sit there who will give me a pre-arranged signal (hand cupped over one ear) if I cannot be heard. I know that if I can be heard in the 'dead-spot' area, I can be heard anywhere in the church.

- The human body is one of the greatest absorbers of sound. If the church is filled to capacity, I will need more volume and voice projection than if it is half-empty.

Microphone Use

The hearing of the Word is a collective activity. God is calling his People together to address them as a body. His Word calls them to action. No action will be taken if the Word is not heard. In any communication, the greatest responsibility for accurate transmission of a message rests with the sender. In Word liturgies, that responsibility belongs to the Reader. An excellent proclamation can be ruined by improper use of the microphone.

Each microphone set-up is different. Therefore, it is advisable to have a practice session to familiarize yourself with the microphone you will be using. Being comfortable with it will add to your self-confidence.

During that practice session, bring along a helper. Practise how far away you can move from the microphone, both backwards and sideways, and still be heard by it. Your helper can quickly detect that for you.

Many people feel that with a microphone they need not project at all. This is not true. When you read in a large church filled to capacity, you still need to project well to be easily heard.

Where should I position the microphone to be heard well?

If the microphone is in a direct line between the nose and the mouth it is in a good position.

How far away from the microphone should I stand?

Twelve to eighteen inches is an average distance to stand from the microphone. However, this is better determined during your practice session, as most microphones are very individual.

Are there any problems I should avoid with a microphone?

Remember that if you are too far from it, you may not be heard. However, if you get too close, your voice may become garbled and indistinct; or a howling, reverberating sound may begin.

Since microphones are mechanical, there is always the danger that they may not work. On one occasion when I had been asked to speak at a World Day of Prayer Service, the microphone system began to pick up a country-music program. It was a case of either trying to project over that, or speaking without the microphone at all, which is what I opted to do. So don't become too dependent on microphones, and continually practise projecting well. This has been covered in detail on pages 22-24.

Remember: It is difficult to project adequately in a large area without a microphone and still maintain good voice quality and expression. This takes much practice.

Procedures

Each parish, because of the physical size and set-up of its church, celebrates the liturgy in its own unique way. The following comments, then, are merely to alert us to the fact that there may be acceptable alternatives to what we are presently doing. Since the main purpose of a community gathering together to celebrate is to praise God and to help create for everyone present an experience of him, then all liturgical procedures must necessarily be chosen to lead to this goal.

The *Lectionary*, the community's symbol for the Word of God, must be of sufficient size and decoration to be worthy of the Word of God. It is from this beautiful symbol of the Word that the Reader proclaims.

Sometimes, it can be helpful to have *more than one reader* proclaiming the Word at a single liturgy. Perhaps Mary's voice helps me to a deeper meditation, but John's voice does the same for my husband. Certainly it is inspiring to hear more than one reader, particularly on special celebrations, such as Good Friday or the Easter Vigil.

In the *Entrance Procession*, the Lectionary may be carried by the Deacon or Reader. Ideally, it should be held high enough so the community may see its symbol of the Word. (If the Reader is not comfortable with it in this position, it may be held in a dignified manner at chest level.) The Reader would walk in procession, directly behind the altar servers, and directly in front of the Ministers of Communion, Deacon and Presider. The Lectionary may then be placed on the lectern or ambo[1] provided for it, and the Reader takes his/her place.

[1] THE AMBO, OR PLACE FOR PROCLAIMING GOD'S WORD: *"The dignity of God's Word requires that some fitting place be provided whence it may be proclaimed; it should be a place on which the people would naturally concentrate their attention during the Liturgy of the Word. Normally this place should be a fixed ambo, not a mere portable lectern. As dictated by the shape of the church the ambo should be put where those who read from it can be easily heard and seen by all."* Documents of Vatican II, Constitution on Sacred Liturgy, VII, 272.

Many Readers *sit* in the sanctuary, proceeding to the lectern at the time of the reading. However, it is really a truer sign of lay participation in the liturgy if the

Reader sits with his/her family in the assembly, coming up at the necessary time. This procedure makes it possible for many qualified readers to participate in this ministry, where before they might have been torn between wanting to serve as reader, yet feeling they should be with their spouse and young children.

When Communion rails were still in vogue, there were three divisions in the church: the sanctuary, the body, and the vestibule. With the removal of these Communion rails, however, we now have only two divisions: the sanctuary and the vestibule. This means that everyone in the celebrating community is in the sanctuary. The tabernacle is acknowledged on our way in by a bow or genuflection, but does not distract from the focal point of the lectern during the Liturgy of the Word, or the altar during the Liturgy of the Eucharist. Readers, then, need not bow to the tabernacle or presider before beginning their reading. If a bow is felt necessary, it should be to the Word of God contained in the Lectionary.

Particularly after the readings, it can be helpful to make use of brief periods of *SILENCE*. When the reading is completed, the Reader should bow his/her head and lead the assembly in prayerful, meditative silence. Twenty to thirty seconds would be about right, allowing those gathered to turn inward and meditate on what the Word of God just proclaimed is saying to them. This procedure should be well explained to the Assembly before it is undertaken; otherwise, people will feel uncomfortable with it, thinking the reader has forgotten what comes next.

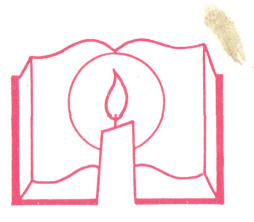

Liturgical Team Work

Being in church is not the same as *being church.*

The first can be very passive, while the second should be very active. During a liturgy, those present have been called by the Lord to praise him as Church, as his Body. Just as a chain is only as strong as its weakest link, so, too, the praise by a particular celebrating community is only as effective as the praise by each of its members.

We are all gathered to help create for one another an experience of God. This means that we are a team operating on the "one for all and all for one" theory. At all times, when we are not actually functioning as Ministers of the Word, we are, first and foremost, members of that celebrating community, alert to what is happening around us as well as within us. As such, we must be supporting all the other members of our liturgical team — presider, ministers of Communion, servers, musicians, choir, ushers, and members of the worshipping assembly — by our hospitality, by our awareness of them and concern for their comfort and well-being, by our strong, faith-filled responses, both said and sung.

This means, of course, that the necessary preparation for our prayerful proclamation will be done BEFOREHAND, not during the celebration, when other members of our liturgical team need not only our passive bodily presence, but our active cooperation as well.

McDonough, Patrick: "Being in Church",
Sign, Vol. 60, No. 1 (Sept. 80) p. 6.

Questions and Answers

● *Is it permissible to change or elaborate on the introduction to a reading?*

Rather than elaborating on the introduction, such as "Today's first reading for the second Sunday of Advent is a reading taken from the book of the prophet Isaiah," we suggest the introduction be exactly as given in the Lectionary: "A reading from the book of the prophet Isaiah." A lengthy preamble, such as in the first example, merely delays the start of a reading, and could possibly distract the listeners from the actual Word of God or cause them to tune out the Reader before he/she actually gets to the Word.

● *Should it be necessary to tell the assembly that this is the First or Second Reading?*

In the early "post Vatican II" era, many of us were so confused by the changes in the liturgy that we appreciated all the signposts telling us what was happening. Besides that, we are accustomed to being "told" what to do. However, most of the changes have been in effect for some time now, and we are being encouraged to be "adult" Christians, so we really should not have to be told which reading is being proclaimed. As Readers, we need to treat the people in the pew as mature enough to figure out which reading they are hearing.

● *Could you comment on the explanation in SMALL LETTERS at the top of the Lectionary readings? Not always is it read aloud, and I wonder why?*

Actually, the short explanation at the top of the Lectionary reading is there to help the Reader prepare well. It usually contains the theme of the reading in capsule form. However, it is suggested that it not be read aloud to the Assembly. The Word of God should be allowed to stand on its own merits.

● *Sometimes during my reading, the members of the Assembly all turn over the pages of the missalettes at the same time, causing a distraction. Is there anything I can do about it?*

If the quality of your proclamation is good enough, if you read with faith and feeling and skill, and thus convey the true meaning of God's Word, the Assembly will want to put down their missalettes in order to listen to your proclamation. If you notice a distraction over a period of Sundays, you may invite the Assembly to put down their missalettes during the reading.

● *Occasionally, in my nervousness or hurry, I make mistakes. What should I do about them?*

Don't forget your relaxation and deep breathing (pgs. 14-17) before you start, to help eliminate your nervousness and to slow your reading. We all make mistakes because we are human. The secret is to minimize them as much as possible, and the Assembly will, too. I remember once starting a reading at the wrong time. Father had to interrupt and carry on with the proper prayers. It was a humbling experience for me; made me more alert and cautious about my timing from then on, but nobody criticized me openly, or became irritated with me, and the floor didn't open up beneath me, although I wished it had.

Remember: If you make a mistake, minimize it. Don't interject "pardon me" or "excuse me." That will destroy the continuity and meaning of the text. If the reading is not understood, and the homilist arrives on the scene, having based his homily on the misunderstood reading, it is like a play with the first act missing.

● *I am a good sight reader. Is it not sufficient to read over the text silently in preparation?*

Have you never had the experience of finding that a word, which your eyes understood with no problem, proved to be a real tongue-twister when spoken aloud? Besides that, practising aloud helps one to establish good rhythm and timing, and acquaints one with the proper places to pause for breath without breaking the sense of the text.

● *Is it permissible to hold the Lectionary when reading, rather than leaving it stationary on the lectern?*

Yes, certainly, hold the lectionary. In fact, this makes the community's beautiful symbol of God's Word more visible. It also helps tall readers eliminate a possible distracting head-bobbing problem when they are trying to establish eye contact. By picking up the Lectionary, they can raise it to a more effective eye level. If you intend to hold the Lectionary, practise resting it comfortably in the palm of one hand, with the corner of it nestling in the bend of your arm for security. The other hand is then free to use as a place guide down the centre of the page, or to turn pages.

● *I have difficulty knowing when to begin my reading. Can you help me?*

When the Liturgy of the Word begins, and it is your turn to walk to the lectern, take your time. Find your place in the Lectionary. Look out over the Assembly. Use these few moments to deep-breathe yourself into relaxation. This will give the presider and the Assembly time to seat themselves comfortably. Your silence will call their attention to the focal point of the lectern. The deep-breathing will enable you to begin your proclamation in a clear, relaxed, effective voice. When you think you have paused long enough before starting, pause a bit longer — a slow count to 5. Your timing should be just about right.

• *I find it difficult to know when to pause for breath when reading from Paul. Many of his sentences go on for whole paragraphs without a break. What can I do about this?*

It is absolutely necessary to practise Paul's readings aloud, especially because of his run-on sentences, which you have described. By reading it aloud, you can experiment with where you can take breath pauses without breaking the meaning of the text at an awkward spot.

• *How can we maintain excellent quality in the Readers in our parish?*

Many parishes have regular meetings for their Liturgical Readers, scheduled weekly, monthly, or at least several times a year. These meetings are structured in various ways. Some consist of spiritual growth exercises (scripture reading and discussion, speaker, film, tape), individual reader assessment time, general discussion on existing reader procedures or possible changes to enhance the Liturgy of the Word. A close feeling of community is fostered among the Readers, enabling them to support and assist each other in maintaining high-quality proclamations, mainly through adequate preparation.

• *Can you give me a short formula to follow in preparing to proclaim God's Word?*

Just remember the 5 P's:

PRAY...

for guidance in preparing, and strength to proclaim well.

PREPARE...

well, and ahead of time:
Liturgically (p. 7-8)
Scripturally (p. 12)
Technically (p. 13-29)

PRACTISE...

silently and aloud, and preferably in front of a mirror.

PERSEVERE...

Rome wasn't built in a day, and one reading does not make a skillful Reader.

PROCLAIM...

with faith and skill, with meaning and feeling, so that your proclamation will touch the hearts of the listeners and move them to respond more fully to God's Word.

• *What is the difference between a good reading and a TRUE PROCLAMATION?*

Following are two quotations that may best answer this question:

"When God is my only concern, when God is the center of my interest, when all my prayers, my reading, my studying, my speaking, and writing serve only to know God better and to make him known bet-

I put my hope in your Word.

ter, then there is no basis for anxiety or stage fright. Then I can live in such a state of preparedness and trust that speaking from the heart is also speaking to the heart."[1]

"There is a story — I do not know its source — of an old man and a young man on the same platform before a vast audience of people. A special program was being presented. As a part of the program each was to repeat from memory the words of the Twenty-third Psalm. The young man, trained in the best speech technique and drama, gave... the words of the Psalm.

"The Lord is my shepherd..." When he had finished the audience clapped their hands and cheered, asking him for an encore so that they might hear again his wonderful voice.

Then the old gentleman, leaning heavily on his cane, stepped to the front of the same platform, and in feeble, shaking voice, repeated the same words — "The Lord is my shepherd..."

But when he was seated no sound came from the listeners. Folks seemed to pray. In the silence the young man stood to make the following statement: "Friends," he said, "I wish to make an explanation. You asked me to come back and repeat the Psalm, but you remained silent when my friend here was seated. The difference? I shall tell you. I know the Psalm, but he knows the Shepherd!"[2]

[1] Nouwen, Henri J. M. *The Genesee Diary. Report from a Trappist Monastery.* New York, Doubleday, 1981. P. 76.

[2] Allen, Charles: *The Healing of Mind and Soul in the Twenty-Third Psalm.* Foundation for Christian Living. Pawling, N.Y. p. 21-2.

Resources

Reference Books for Liturgical Readers

The Jerusalem Bible. Darton, Longman & Todd, Ltd. and Doubleday & Co., Inc., Garden City, New York, 1966. Reader Edition with Introduction and Notes.

Lectionary for Mass. 1970, Catholic Book Publishing Company, New York, N.Y.

Commentaries on the Lectionary

Celebration: A Creative Worship Service. P.O. Box 281, Kansas City, MO 64141

Homily Service. The Liturgical Conference Inc., 810 Rhode Island Ave., N.E. Washington, D.C. 20018

Discover the Bible. A weekly bulletin published by the Bible Centre of the Archdiocese of Montreal, 2000 Sherbrooke St., W., Mtl., P.Q., H2K 1B9.

Coughlan P. and Purdue P., *Commentary on the Sunday Lectionary,* 1970-72.3 vols. Liturgical Press, 74 Engle Blvd., Collegeville, MN. 56321

Crotty, R. and Manly G., *Commentaries on the Readings of the Lectionary,* 1975. Pueblo Publishing Co., 1860 Broadway, New York, N.Y. 10023

Fuller R., *Preaching the New Lectionary: the Word of God for the Church Today,* 1971-74. Liturgical Press, 74 Engle Blvd., Collegeville, MN. 56321

Maertens T. and Frisque J., *Guide for the Christian Assembly.* (Revised to conform to the new lectionary), 8 vols., Fides Publisher, 333 N. Lafayette, South Bend, IN. 46601

Sloyan G., *A Commentary on the New Lectionary,* 1975. Paulist Press, 1865 Broadway, New York, 10023

On the Ministry of Liturgical Reader

Ministers of the Word, a resource packet. The Commission on the Liturgy, P.O. Box 937, Green Bay, Wisconsin, 54305

Allen, H. (Editor) *The Reader as Minister,* 1980. The Liturgical Conference, 810 Rhode Island Avenue NE, Washington, D.C. 20018

Carr, W. M., *A Handbook for Lectors,* 1968. Paulist Press, 1865 Broadway Ave., New York, N.Y. 10023

Hardman, B. E., *Speech and Oral Reading Techniques* for Mass Lectors and Commentators, 1966. Liturgical Press, 74 Engle Blvd., Collegeville, MN. 56321

Harrison, G.B., and McCabe J., *Proclaiming the Word,* A Handbook for Church Speaking, 1973. Pueblo Publishing Company, 1860 Broadway, New York, N.Y. 11023

Staudacher, J. M., *Laymen Proclaim the Word.* Franciscan Herald Press, 1434 West 51st Street, Chicago, IL. 60609

Staudacher, J. M., *Lector's Guide to Biblical Pronunciations.* Our Sunday Visitor, 200 Noll Plaza, Huntington, IN. 46750

Tate, Judith, *Manual for Lectors.* Pflaum Press, 2451 East River Road, Suite 200, Dayton, Ohio, 45439.

On the Training of Liturgical Readers

Byrne, Rev. P., editor, *Training Readers,* Vol. 9, #56 of *The National Bulletin on Liturgy,* 1976. CCCB Publications, 90 Parent Avenue, Ottawa   K1N 7B1

Nordkamp, B., *Training Readers,* #5 of Training for Community Ministries. Collins Liturgical Publications, St. James Place, London, SW1A 1PS, England, 1978.

Wood, Geoffrey, et al. *The Lector's Guide: A Four-Week Training Program,* 1973. The Liturgical Conference, 810 Rhode Island Ave. N., Washington, D.C. 20018

READERS AT LITURGY

Written by:

Molly Callaghan,
C. W. Wright & Associates, "Effective Communications"

Edited by:

Jerome Herauf

Layout:

Jan Gough, Gilles Lépine

Photography:

Cover: Roman Matwijejko;
p. 2, 25, 28, 30: Roman Matwijejko;

p. 10: Socabi; p. 20: National Film Board of Canada;
p. 37: Mary Kibblewhite

Illustrations:

Cover 1 and cover 4: Lee Thirlwall;
inside illustrations: John E. Lewis

"Then Yahweh said to me:
'There! I am putting my words
into your mouth.' "

(from Jeremiah 1:9)

Winston Press
430 Oak Grove
Minneapolis, Minnesota 55403

ISBN: 0-86683-736-1

Musicians at Liturgy

New Parish Ministries

WINSTON PRESS

Contents

New Parish Ministries *was originally published by Novalis, Saint Paul University, Ottawa, Canada. This edition is published by Winston Press, Inc., by arrangement with Novalis, Saint Paul University. Copyright © 1982, Novalis. Copyright © 1983, Winston Press. All rights reserved. No part of this book may be reproduced in any form without written permission from the publisher.*

ISBN: 0-86683-737-x (previously ISBN: 2-89088-084-2)

Printed in Canada

5 4 3 2 1

Winston Press, Inc., 430 Oak Grove, Minneapolis, MN 55403

Prelude

Questions such as the following are often asked — by parish musicians, clergy, members of liturgy committees, and interested parishioners — about music in church:

What are we doing when we make music in church?

Why are we doing what we are doing?

What should we be doing?

What can we do?

It is already clear from this kind of questioning that there is more involved in parish music programs than getting the service planned, getting the folk group in shape, or playing the organ. Working with people, motivating people, and developing people in a common faith which expresses itself in worship is the heart of the matter.

We worship — in spirit and in truth.

We make music — that is spirited and true.

We sing — and we like it.

When all is said and done these statements summarize the spirit and direction of this little booklet. There is an inner logic behind its organization which runs something like this:

Persons make music.

Music is planned with persons in mind.

*Coordination and teamwork can greatly improve music
in parish worship.*

*The liturgy itself and the liturgical year offer
basic structures for planning.*

We think that this booklet will make a modest contribution by reviewing some fundamentals, and proposing concrete ways for developing and improving parish music programs that are "spirited and true."

1

*"all creation
sing out your joy..."*

Persons Develop Programs

It is always good to begin at the beginning. Good music programs in a parish come from persons who work hard at making good music happen. If they are happy with what they are doing and proud of it, you're off to a good start. Developing and building a spirit of teamwork, cooperation, and growth will be your ongoing challenge.

Bringing persons together to evaluate and assess a program can indeed be "touchy," but it is well worth the effort. It is essential to understand and deal practically with the uniqueness of a particular assembly, and with its leadership. Significant progress cannot be made apart from this kind of realism. Consider carefully the following persons and categories of persons. They all have their own contribution to make.

The musician or liturgist whom your parish has hired

If your parish has the means and the priorities to hire a music coordinator, an organist or a choir director, it stands to reason that this person will be involved in planning the music as well as being a member of the liturgy committee.

The person responsible for doing the music or making the music with the assembly should have a major role in the choices that are made. Even if a particular choice represents a compromise or is actually against his/her better judgment (e.g.: a Latin Gloria at Midnight Mass), he/she will at least understand the reasons behind the decision and be able to bring it to life with the assembly. In some cases, it is part of this person's contract to chair a music committee, although this is not necessarily the best approach. A chairperson with no "vested interests" can sometimes assure the smoothness of the meetings and see that all voices are heard.

Organists, folk group leaders, and cantors

These persons have direct experience with the local assembly at the various liturgies. Sometimes a cantor or folk group leader can tell "by the eyes of the congregation" whether the music is coming alive or not. The week-to-week experience of these persons is essential to realistic planning.

It is also a good idea to bring together musicians of various skills and backgrounds to form an overall planning team. Some parishes have worked at building a "core reper-

toire" which can be used with both the organ and the guitar so that the whole assembly is learning the same music and developing greater confidence and spontaneity in the singing. Very often the distinction between "folk" and "organ" selections is artificial and unimaginative. *Silent Night* and *Greensleeves* are by no means the only selections that can be arranged for everything from a single unaccompanied voice to a full symphony orchestra.

Members of the choir and folk groups

These persons have valuable experience to offer. They also have their own contacts with family and friends who offer ongoing feed-

back. Knowing what members think and involving them in the process of decision-making is also excellent for morale.

4

The parish liturgy committee

This group is responsible for giving a sense of direction to musicians and music planners in order to assure a common spirit and direction. It may be, for example, that the liturgy committee has settled upon a very quiet and reflective spirit for the Lenten Sundays, or has decided to make the ministry of hospitality central to the Advent and Christmas seasons. If parish musicians are kept in touch with these discussions and decisions, their contribution will be more helpful and effective as well as personally more rewarding.

The parish clergy

Good lines of communication between the priest celebrant, the musicians, and other ministers is essential for good worship. In some congregations, the pastor may even want to suggest a particular hymn, the text of which he will refer to in his homily; you wouldn't want him to look surprised or shocked when you pull out the Latin Gloria. Along with setting the tone for the whole celebration by his high profile, the pastor is also in a unique position to hear the comments and criticisms of the people, and may have some very helpful suggestions.

Interested members of the assembly

Persons not directly involved in parish music leadership can offer a perspective all their own. How opinions are gathered and evaluated, however, can be problematic. Even though asking for volunteer critics can often bring out chronic malcontents, an effort should be made to take the opinions and attitudes of the entire assembly into account, during the planning process.

5

The Music Committee

A good approach to the evaluation and development of a music program, at least in larger parishes, is the establishment of a music committee which brings these persons described above into an ongoing partnership. The success of such a committee, however, will largely depend on the tone and sense of direction which is taken from the beginning.

A good general rule might be: "THINK LITURGICAL YEAR." Since our "parish years" run from September to June, and the Liturgical Year begins with Advent, late September is a good time to get started, preparing for the Advent Season. By then people are already settled in and recovering from the many activities and new beginnings which September invariably brings. This provides plenty of lead time for the First Sunday of Advent, which falls in late November or early December.

Plan some long and some short meetings. A Saturday may be a good time for a longer session to review and evaluate last year's celebrations, read through new materials, etc. A weekday evening would allow plenty of time for a shorter session.

Organizing the year

Your agenda for the year may wind up looking something like this:

Late September

Getting Started

1. Evaluate Ordinary Time now in process, possibly making minor adjustments.

2. Review last year's Advent-Christmas-Epiphany cycle, and build on that experience. Look over the scripture readings for the Sundays and Feasts involved to determine if there is a particular emphasis, theme, or tone that emerges. Invite members to bring specific suggestions to the next meeting, and to remember to bring their music.

3. Make sure that someone consults with the Liturgy Committee or Liturgy Planning Committee, if your parish has one, so that efforts will be well coordinated.

4. Put the finishing touches on the fall feasts which you may want to highlight: liturgical feasts such as All Saints, All Souls, and Christ the King, as well as other special days such as Thanksgiving or Memorial Day.

Early October

Advent-Christmas-Epiphany Planning

1. Go around the room and hear the suggestions of each member of the group. Sing the musical possibilities together. Enjoy the music and one another.

2. Organize a musical program for the season. Be specific. Begin perhaps with Epiphany and work backwards.

3. Determine what, if any, special resources will be needed, e.g., a trumpet for the First Sunday of Advent, a flute for Christmas Eve. Assign specific persons for specific tasks, e.g., contacting the trumpet player, ordering the music, getting the necessary copyright permissions.

Early November

Advent-Christmas-Epiphany: Finishing Touches

1. Hear reports on assignments given at last meeting.

2. Complete plans, if you ran out of time at the last meeting.

3. Review the program and work out any final details so that you won't have to meet in December.

Late January

Advent-Christmas-Epiphany Evaluation
Lent-Easter-Pentecost Pre-planning

1. Reflect together on the season just completed. How do members feel about it? What worked? What didn't work? What did they enjoy most about the experience? Why? Be sure to have somebody write these things down so that you will have them for reference next October.

2. Look briefly at Ordinary Time now being celebrated. Make whatever minor adjustments seem necessary.

3. Review last Lent-Easter-Pentecost. What is most memorable about last year's experience? Is there a particular tone, spirit, or theme which emerges from the liturgy of the season? Again it is very important to coordinate these matters with the Liturgy Committee or Planning Committee. What kinds of plans are being made for the sacraments of Baptism, Confirmation, Eucharist, and Reconciliation? Brainstorm possibilities. Assign tasks for next meeting.

Early February

Lent-Easter-Pentecost Planning

1-3. as in early October

Late February

**Lent-Easter-Pentecost:
Finishing Touches**

1. Complete work of last meeting, if necessary.

2. Work out final details so that you won't have to meet again until April.

Mid-April

**Lent-Easter-Pentecost Evaluation;
Ordinary Time Pre-Planning**

1. Reflect on the Lent-Easter part of the cycle just completed, as you did with the Advent-Christmas-Epiphany cycle in January.

2. Look ahead to Ordinary Time and brainstorm possibilities. Don't forget also to evaluate the Sundays between Epiphany and the First Sunday of Lent.

May

**Lent-Easter-Pentecost:
Complete Evaluation
Ordinary Time:
Planning Overview**

1. Evaluate Pentecost celebration.

2. Make concrete plans for Ordinary Time, as you did previously with the major seasons.

3. Look back over the year. What were the high and low points? Why? Set goals for next year.

4. Have a "See you in September" Party.

"Sing to the Lord ...
a new song!"

Looking at meetings

With our agenda determined, we are now challenged to make our meetings productive and enjoyable. Meetings can be endless and futile; they can also be exciting and productive. It may be helpful at this point to look at music committees in terms of the life and energy of any group. Although our experience generally makes us aware only of the task at hand when we set out for a meeting, there's more involved than just "getting something done." Three headings can help us clarify what we're dealing with.

The task

The group has come together *to do something,* to plan the music for their parish. Most committees are primarily aware of this reason for coming together — and it is essential that something be actually accomplished. Progress is essential for the health of any group. If nothing is getting done, members soon lose heart. Good organization and efficiency in running the meetings is therefore very important.

The education of the members

Ongoing learning about liturgy and music, hearing about the experiences of other groups and parishes, and reading through new materials will not only be interesting to the members of the group, but will enhance their effectiveness as pastoral leaders. It is therefore helpful to circulate materials for people to read and discuss — even to invite a guest speaker — to keep the group fresh and alert to new possibilities.

Personal satisfaction

The work of planning for parish worship can be done effectively only when persons are taken seriously. This is particularly true in churches where the musicians are, for the most part, volunteers. The basic human need for recognition and affirmation, along with the satisfaction that comes from making a contribution to something that is considered important to the life of the community, is heightened when working with volunteers.

It is particularly important, therefore, that the level of motivation be taken seriously in working at developing a good spirit among parish musicians. Music is the common denominator which brings the group together, but music is not the ultimate goal of the committee. The goal must always be worship in spirit and in truth — always beyond voices and instruments.

Professional musicians, like other talented and energetic people, can be trapped by a spirit of competition and a preoccupation with performance. This often derives from their training and is also an aspect of the human condition. Others, who are not necessarily professionals, may not have experienced these dynamics to such an extent in their training, but they are not less susceptible to the human condition.

The difference between a church service, for example, and an organ recital is immense — as is the difference between a theatre and a sanctuary. Both call for excellence and artistry, but from very distinctive points of view.

Another matter to be aware of when working with committee members is that of the inevitability of differences in theological opinion and musical taste. These differences can be capitalized upon to provide variety and interest in the ways liturgy is celebrated.

Unless, however, there is care and sensitivity on all sides, such differences can be alienating and counter-productive.

The more adequately the committee can meet the needs of its members under all three of the above headings, the more mature and productive the group will become and the more enriching it will be to serve on it.

Finally — a note on the chairperson: If the whole process sounds complex and delicate, it's because it is! "Wherever two or three persons are gathered together, there is tension"! (Which Gospel did you read that in?) The chairperson need not be a universal expert in things liturgical and musical but should be well organized, sensitive, and a good listener, along with having a good sense of humor.

It may be a step in the right direction if the chairperson were to meet with one or the other member of the group after each meeting, to review the course of the session and reflect on what happened.

Was the meeting a good experience for all the members? Were all members welcomed and heard? Did members learn anything of value? Was anything tangible accomplished? Will members likely look forward to the next meeting?

How do we Know
what we're Doing is Right?

It's one thing to plan, either as an individual musician or as a member of a team or committee, but it's quite another to assess success as a *liturgical* musician or *minister* of music. A number of factors need to be taken into account in this process of planning and ongoing evaluation: the structure of the liturgy itself, the liturgical year, and the nature of the musical elements.

The Eucharistic liturgy has much in common with a piece of music. There is a way in which it can be considered an artistic whole. It has its own inner direction, balance, proportion and rhythm. It has elements which are emphasized, and elements which serve to support the major emphases.

The structure of the liturgy itself:
——————— Seeing it as a whole ———————

Even the simplest musical piece has at least a beginning and an end; but simply to play the piece from the beginning to the end, even if the notes are correct, is not to *make music.*

There are high points and low points, moments of intense energy, and moments of repose. A particular note or a particular phrase is played sensitively only when the musician is aware of the whole piece and interprets that note or phrase in light of the whole.

The Eucharistic Liturgy has much in common with a piece of music. There is a way in which it can be considered an artistic whole. It has its own inner direction, balance, proportion and rhythm. It has elements which are emphasized, and elements which serve to support the major emphases.

Much has already been written on the structure and flow of the liturgy. A few suggestions for further reading can be found at the back of this booklet.

The diagram on the next page attempts to bring a lot of this material together and to present three parallel views of the liturgical whole. The first column deals with what the assembly is *doing*; the second lists the ritual elements which give shape to the action; the third column attempts to prioritize — in terms of balance, proportion, and the flow of the rite — those elements which are sung.

The schema presumes a cantor or song leader and a priest celebrant who is able and willing to sing his parts on special occasions.

Planners would be safe in using the six star elements as the core upon which they build. Add five, four, three, two, and one star elements — in that order — for increasingly solemn or festive liturgies.

ACTIONS OF THE ASSEMBLY

ACTIONS OF THE ASSEMBLY	RITUAL STRUCTURE	SONG
WE GATHER AS A PEOPLE OF FAITH	Gathering Song Greeting Penitential Rite/Lord Have Mercy Glory to God Opening Prayer	
WE LISTEN TO GOD'S WORD AND RESPOND IN MIND AND HEART	First Reading Responsorial Psalm Second Reading Gospel Acclamation Gospel Homily Profession of Faith General Intercessions	
WE RESPOND IN ACTION		
Eucharistic Ritual: WE TAKE BREAD AND WINE	Preparation of Table and Gifts	
WE OFFER THANKS AND PRAISE	Eucharistic Prayer The Presidential Prayer The Acclamations of the People	
WE BREAK THE BREAD AND PREPARE THE CUP	Lord's Prayer Greeting of Peace Breaking of Bread (Lamb of God)	
WE COMMUNE IN THE BODY AND BLOOD OF THE LORD	Communion Communion Meditation Time	
Mission to the World: WE ARE SENT OUT	Blessing Dismissal Closing Song	

Overview of the liturgical year: Setting a context

Along with the internal rhythm of a given celebration, the way in which individual celebrations relate to one another and build on one another, during the year, is likewise significant. The liturgical year provides a framework for these connections and offers an overall direction. It will be helpful to take a brief look at the three major seasons of the Church Year with an eye to music planning.

The Lent-Easter-Pentecost Cycle centers on the sacraments of initiation, i.e., Baptism, Confirmation and Eucharist. Living persons are being welcomed into the Church during this time, while the community is being renewed in the energy and grace of these same sacraments. By design and purpose, at the Easter Vigil, the most solemn celebration of the dying and rising of the Lord and the celebration of Baptism, Confirmation and first Eucharist of catechumens take place. It is likewise by design that Confirmation should be celebrated with young people at one of the Sunday celebrations during the Easter Season or on Pentecost itself, and that the sacrament of Reconciliation is emphasized during Lent and often celebrated with children for the first time during that season.

The sacramental actions taking place within the community provide a natural human rhythm and a sense of direction for those involved in planning the celebrations. The energy and solemnity of the music is determined by the energy and solemnity of the liturgical action.

It is true that the readings of the individual Sundays provide direction for the choice of hymns as well as instrumental selections, but choices are best made when the season or cycle is viewed as a whole and when the sacramental actions being celebrated are planned for seriously.

The Advent-Christmas-Epiphany Cycle is quiet and reflective. In spite of the fact that there's a great deal of pre-Christmas bustle, there isn't a great deal of activity going on within the Church's liturgy. It is rather a time for deep meditation on the direction of the world in terms of its ultimate end and purpose, of wonder at the dignity and beauty of the created universe within which God willed to become flesh, and of reflection on the various ways in which the "Word" is manifested in history.

19

There is a tremendous amount of music available for this season, and wonderful opportunities for its use within the liturgy. It might not be a bad idea, however, for music planners to think twice about "gearing up for Christmas." Especially because of the rush which most people experience at this time of year, the liturgy could provide a moment of quiet stillness and contemplation. Why not take advantage of the weeks after Christmas when the busy world is hushed (or exhausted) to do something special with music. Too many planning groups concentrate on the Midnight Mass of Christmas, and then go on vacation.

Another suggestion might be to take full advantage of the assembly's readiness to sing during this season. Make sure you include a healthy repertoire of traditional materials, being careful not to become too predictable or trite.

Ordinary Time can more easily be dealt with on a Sunday-to-Sunday basis. The Gospel and First Reading are usually linked rather closely with a common theme echoed in the Responsorial Psalm. The Gospel sets the tone, and the First Reading with its Responsorial Psalm are related to it.

The Second Reading, however, follows its own sequence; so don't be surprised if you see no connection between it and the other two readings.

Music is chosen in light of the structure and flow of the liturgy itself, i.e., highlighting the more important elements of the liturgical action with song (cf. page 17). It is the main thematic content of the readings, however, which will be your best source of ideas, especially for the hymns.

The musical elements involved: Assembling the pieces

When it comes time to make the final musical choices, a good understanding of the basic types or genres of music involved in a sung liturgy will also be important. The most basic musical elements which involve the assembly are acclamations, refrains or antiphons, litanies, and hymns.

Acclamations

There are at least two places in the liturgy that call for the singing of acclamations: the Gospel is preceded by an acclamation, and the Eucharistic Prayer includes three acclamations (The Holy, Holy, Holy; the Memorial Acclamation; and the Great Amen).

These acclamations are strong and vibrant affirmations of faith. Each of them serves as a musical "yes" offered by the entire assembly to the presence and action of the Lord. They are best when sung almost spontaneously, without books, almost without thinking — by heart.

As with all liturgical music, the style of the acclamations will reflect their function. If they are to have a spontaneous, effortless quality, most congregations will probably be able to master only two or three sets — which makes the best choice very important. Leaders and Planners will want to choose acclamations that "wear well."

Ideally, the acclamations in the Eucharistic Prayer will have the same spirit and feel, be in the same key, and perhaps even be built upon the same musical theme. This will serve to unify the Eucharistic Prayer rather than disrupt it. Instrumental introductions, if necessary, should be very brief so that the singing itself flows out of the priest celebrant's invitation. A quiet "lead in" to the acclamations could even begin while the priest is still speaking — which would establish the key and make any further introduction unnecessary.

Many choirs in the past had grown accustomed to learning "new masses" and introducing them at the great feastdays. This no longer seems a good practice. Teach new acclamations during Ordinary Time so that by the time great feastdays come around, they will "sing themselves." And don't be afraid to stick with them for a while. With a little imagination, harmonies, descants, even brass parts can be added to dress them up.

Refrains or antiphons

Although often considered with acclamations, refrains or antiphons are really quite different in spirit and function. In the first place, there are many more of them and they vary a great deal. The lectionary provides a suggested antiphon with each responsorial psalm. Seasonal refrains are also provided, along with a great variety of responsorial music for the Communion Rite and other times of movement in the liturgy.

These refrains tend to be more meditative than acclamations, echoing and re-echoing the heart of a certain psalm, or the spirit of a particular moment in the liturgy. "Taste and see the goodness of the Lord," or "Where charity and love are, there is God", for example, have been extremely popular over the centuries at Communion time.

A refrain should be brief, musically attractive, and easily learned, although not necessarily as "explosive" or spontaneous as the acclamations. It will be up to the judgment of local leaders to determine how best to deal with refrains, but it would be wise to take note of which ones catch on and which ones don't, so that a good repertoire can be built.

If the assembly is weak on responsorial singing, it would be well to stay with the seasonal suggestions for the responsorial psalm, perhaps even repeating it at the Communion, and choosing musical settings that are rhythmically clear and strong.

Litanies

A litany is a form of prayer or song that builds through repetition. The litany of the saints is a more classical example, but even the rosary has something in common with a litany. The prayers blend into one another so that their verbal content becomes less important than the mood or atmosphere created.

During the Eucharistic Liturgy, there are three litanies: the Lord Have Mercy, the General Intercessions, and the Lamb of God. The present form of the Lord Have Mercy is a bit short to feel much like a litany, but the other two litanies have more musical potential than we usually give them.

If the General Intercessions are brief statements of petition (not mini-homilies), and are numerous enough to set up a good rhythm between the cantor and congregation, their singing can be very effective, especially during penitential times of the year. The Lamb of God is designed to be sung during the breaking of the bread and preparation of the cups for communion. It is repeated over and over until the action is completed, and can be very expressive of longing and anticipation.

Hymns

Hymns are poems set to music, usually with a steady, predictable rhythm. Often their texts are original compositions, but there are also many metered translations of the psalms and other biblical texts in hymn form.

Their use has been particularly important in Protestant churches where the rational or intellectual content of the church service is traditionally strong. The hymns, with their many verses, served not only as prayers but as ways of teaching and reinforcing doctrine and piety — the preacher often referring directly to a particular line or stanza.

Within the Roman Catholic tradition, hymns have played a secondary role. In the Latin Mass, for example, there were no metrical hymns. In our present liturgy, however, hymns can be very effective, if choices are made carefully. Many good hymnals, for example, have an index relating each hymn to its biblical inspiration — this can be very helpful in choosing a hymn which corresponds to a particular reading.

If the whole hymn is not sung, care must be taken in the choice of verses so that violence is not done to the text as a whole. The cantor and/or choir may wish to alternate verses with the congregation, or an interlude may be played between certain verses that lend themselves to a "pause."

At the beginning of the liturgy, a hymn can usually be an effective way of getting the assembly to its feet and doing something together. Another possibility, which has proven successful from time to time, is a hymn after the homily which gives the assembly an opportunity to affirm what was said, followed by the creed in question and answer form (as in the renewal of baptismal promises).

The assembly can also be invited to join in the singing of a hymn after Communion, followed by the prayer, blessing, dismissal, and organ recessional. In whatever ways hymns are used within the liturgical context, special care must be taken not to overload the liturgy but to maintain a good sense of balance and proportion.

Praise God in his temple on earth,
Praise him in his temple in heaven.

Praise him with trumpet blasts,
praise him with lyre and harp,
praise him with drums and dancing,
praise him with strings and reeds,
praise him with clashing cymbals!

Let everything that has breath praise the Lord!

Psalm 150

Programs Develop Persons

So far, we have discussed the value of teamwork among parish musicians, and have looked at the liturgy itself for some direction in establishing a solid parish music program. Our next task will be to attempt some practical application to the parish music program itself. This is not so much a question of establishing goals as establishing a sense of direction and a plan of development. Music at worship, like any art, never reaches a state of perfection.

There's always some place further to go. The areas for development briefly outlined here may give at least a clue to establishing priorities in the development of an overall approach to music in the parish.

Toward developing an assembly that sings better and enjoys it more

Is it not true that "the ears of God are not nearly as important as the hearts of people"?

There is something wonderful about a classroom full of Grade 1 children singing about flowers and birds — and the love of God — at the top of their voices. There's something wonderful too about the way a group sings "Happy Birthday" or "For He's a Jolly Good Fellow." We all experience this sort of thing from time to time, and even as onlookers in a restaurant or tavern we are struck by the singing and the relationships expressed in song — even though usually off-key and pitched too high!

Music in the liturgical assembly, as in the Grade 1 classroom or at a birthday party, expresses faith in life and in life's goodness. Feelings such as these have a depth and substance which are beyond merely rational concepts, even beyond the written or spoken word. The goal or direction at stake here is not merely getting the people to sing, but motivating the assembly to sing with spirit, to

experience their song, to experience one another in song, to support one another's faith through the vehicle of song.

The parish music ministers may want to consider the following questions which might suggest ways to help the assembly experience their own song and enjoy that experience.

Is the assembly free to sing?

People by nature tend to be shy and reticent about singing out, especially in a culture where people really don't get singing until the party is well along.

This is one of the reasons why hospitality is so important. Helping the people to know they are at home when they gather in church needs to be a top priority. How about inviting the people to introduce themselves to one another as part of the warm-up before the action of the liturgy begins? Why not occasionally rehearse a well-known hymn or refrain, inviting the assembly to sing with full heart and voice, helping them to *experience* just how good that feels? The more relaxed and at home the assembly is before the liturgy begins, the better they will sing, and the better they will feel about it.

Are there enough copies of the music to go around, and are there effective means of distributing them?

The kind of care that has plenty of copies readily available, and that has ushers or other ministers of hospitality handing them to people as they wish them a "good morning" and a welcome, does wonders in creating a good spirit. These kinds of actions tell the people that they are important and that their participation is essential.

Are people given a fair chance to learn the music?

A brief rehearsal, before the liturgy begins, tells the people that they are important and helps them to sing with ease and confidence. A long rehearsal with too much new music can turn people off.

It is up to planners to exercise discretion in organizing the introduction of new music and spreading it over weeks and months, so as not to discourage the spontaneous confidence which characterizes community song at its best.

A Protestant organist commented recently that it was her goal to introduce four new hymns to the congregation over the next year. Four new hymns in a community where hymn singing has been a part of the tradition for hundreds of years may seem a rather timid goal, but perhaps we need to stop and take notice of what we are doing. The temptation in Catholic parishes has been to teach at least a new refrain every Sunday. The seasonal refrains may be a better approach, together with a choice of hymns and acclamations that have a certain "staying power." If you make your selections carefully and the people like them and respond well, don't be embarrassed at sticking to them for a while. Confident, sturdy community song may be of greater value than a lot of variety. Here's where balance and good judgment come in.

Do you choose music with people in mind?

The melody, the range, the rhythm of the selection are all important components in a song that works with people. Another major component, however, is the text. Apart from its relationship to the scriptures of the day, does this text say anything that the community would want to say out loud, much less sing? A song leader can often tell when the assembly is caught up in what they are singing — and it is invariably when the melody, rhythm and text are well-integrated and have a content with which they can identify. All too many hymns reflect a world-view totally different from our own, even though the tune is attractive, even stirring.

There are texts set to music in the "folk idiom" where the ideas expressed are either shallow or where the level of community, friendship, and sharing are utterly beyond what is realistic for a parish assembly. It just doesn't ring true to life — people can't be expected to sing something which doesn't correspond to their inner need to sing. Be careful of the words you put into people's mouths. Obscure or inappropriate texts cannot be expected to "catch on."

What kind of introduction is given? Are numbers announced clearly? Are instrumental introductions long enough?

The assembly responds best to clear, concise directions. People need to hear or see the hymn number clearly and distinctly, and need time to find it. The organ or instrumental introduction establishes the spirit and rhythm of the selection, and should be long enough to give a real signal of what is expected. The leader of song and the instrumentalists work together to provide a real introduction and invitation to the assembly. Together they give the message to the assembly: "Please rise and sing." Improving the quality of the invitation improves the quality of response.

How are the acoustics in the building?

This is a question which must be taken into account, especially when church buildings are being constructed or refurbished. Heavy carpeting, drapes, pew cushions, and acoustical tile all work together to produce a quietness that can be deadly. In such an environment, individuals hear only themselves when they sing. They can't hear their voices coming back to them and blending with those around them. The sounds of the organ are swallowed up and not given a chance to fill the space.

It is often argued that carpets and cushions give warmth to a room, but it is probably the wrong kind of warmth. The kind of warmth that is called for in our church buildings comes from persons gathered in fellowship and prayer — doing things together in an environment that is conducive to and supportive of their common action.

It is true that compromises need to be made. If the acoustics are very lively, the reading and preaching tend to be muffled, but the musicians of the parish would be providing a real service to the assembly by insisting that acoustical questions be dealt with seriously and with the assembly in mind.

Toward developing the music ministry of the priest celebrant

It might seem odd to move, in our discussion, from the assembly right to the priest celebrant, but think about it just the same. As leader of prayer, he is also leader of song and holds a key position in making the music of the assembly come alive.

For example, his tone of voice, bodily gestures, and facial attitude at the end of the Preface can either call forth a good response from the community in the "Holy, holy, holy" or tell the people that it really doesn't matter.

At other points in the liturgy, the actions of the priest celebrant who picks up his hymnal and joins in the singing can be a powerful gesture of leadership — music ministry. If he enjoys his role of presiding over the liturgy and identifies with the assembly in a corporate act of listening, singing, sharing food, etc., his influence will be very powerful in encouraging heartfelt participation.

Toward developing the music ministry of the cantor

The cantor's traditional responsibilities lie in singing the verses of a psalm while the choir and congregation join in a refrain. The most effective procedure is to have the cantor sing the refrain once, asking the community to repeat it at the beginning of the psalm; and then by hand, voice and body inviting the community to repeat that refrain at various points throughout the psalm. The same procedure is followed at the Gospel Acclamation.

The Responsorial Psalm after the First Reading, and the Gospel Acclamation are the most familiar musical elements which the cantor leads. There are, however, other points in the rite where responsorial singing of psalms or other materials could be effective, such as during the entrance procession or during the communion. The cantor can also serve as leader of song and intone the litanies (Lord Have Mercy, and Lamb of God) as well as chant the General Intercessions. He/she can also lead the hymn singing and conduct a short rehearsal before the liturgy begins.

Because the ways in which a cantor serves are so many and so diverse, it is important that such a person have not only a good voice, but a welcoming presence, and a personable approach to the assembly. Organists and choir directors need to work closely with cantors to train them in the basic skills of music leadership and a style of singing that invites participation, not just listening. A person with a pleasant, straightforward voice is often more effective in this position than one with a great deal of color, drama, and "vibrato."

Toward developing the music ministry of the choir or folk group

When there is a choir present, the degree of solemnity is automatically heightened. The first and perhaps most important role of the choir is to add strength and leadership to the six and five star elements of the liturgy as indicated on page 17, perhaps even adding descants and harmonies to the acclamations and hymns.

The four and three star elements could be sung in dialogue with the congregation, consistent with the responsorial or litany forms.

The choir may even, on occasion, choose to render one or other of these elements on its own, e.g., the Lamb of God, or the psalm after the first reading.

Of the two or one star elements, an appropriate choral selection can often be very effective at the time of preparation of table and gifts, or after communion.

A note of caution may be in order. Care must always be taken that the choir or folk group does not place all its energies in choir selections and let the assembly shift for itself. At the same time, the choir's role as leader of community song and its potential in embellishing the song of the assembly is too often overlooked.

The secret of planning and building a good musical liturgy is found in keeping an eye (and an ear) open to the essentials, starting with them and building from them, always striving for good balance and proportion.

_____Toward building the music ministry_____
of the instrumentalists

The ability to provide definite and firm _leadership_ to the assembly is the most important skill required of an instrumentalist in the liturgy. For the organist, a bright though not overpowering registration should be chosen to lead community song. Articulation should be clean and crisp, tempo steady, even anticipating the congregation slightly to keep it from slowing down. As was mentioned before, introductions need to be long enough to allow the people to find their place, catch the spirit of the piece, and catch their breath before singing. This, however, is not true of the acclamations during the Eucharistic Prayer, which should flow right out of the priest's invitation. Sufficient volume should be used to lead and support the congregation.

The ability to _accompany_ is quite another skill. To be sensitive to a director or a cantor and to subordinate one's own interpretation to that of another person is essential. A good accompanist in psalm verses, for example, can be described as "not heard but _felt_."

In addition to the role of leader of song and accompanist, the instrumentalist makes a contribution in his/her own right, which is often overlooked in the liturgy. There are points in the service (beyond the prelude and postlude) where instrumental music can find a place of its own.

Instrumental music to provide a "breather" during the Preparation of the Gifts or as a meditation at Communion are ways in which the talents of instrumentalists can find good expression within the liturgy. What is required, however, in making such decisions is imagination and sensitivity to the direction of the liturgy and the spirit of the particular celebration at hand.

Finally, care must always be taken that musicians, especially organists, do not fall into the "piped-in music" syndrome. There are fine materials of various lengths and difficulty which can be used within the liturgy without resorting to just "filling in." This being said, opportunities for background music do exist at times such as when the Responsorial Psalm is being read antiphonally.

Postlude

To serve with music — such is the high calling of parish musicians. God is best served when people are served. People are best served when they are led to prayer and praise and service.

The liturgy of the Church offers a privileged moment for Christians to gather and rededicate themselves, in the Spirit of the risen Lord, to becoming what they sing. Let it be. Amen.

Official documents

General Instruction of the Roman Missal, found in the front of the Sacramentary.

Guidelines for Music in the Mass, in Catholic Book of Worship, choir edition, Nos. 80-103. 1980, Canadian Conference of Catholic Bishops, 90 Parent Ave., Ottawa, Canada K1N 7B1

Music in Catholic Worship, Bishops' Committee on the Liturgy. 1972, U.S. Catholic Conference, 1312 Massachusetts Ave., N.W., Washington, D.C., 20005

Books

Bauman, William A.; *The Ministry of Music* (1975, The Liturgical Conference, 810 Rhode Island Ave., N.E., Washington D.C. 20018.)

Deiss, Lucien; *Spirit and Song in the New Liturgy* (1970, World Library, 2145 Central Parkway, Cincinnati. OH 45214)

Hatchett, Marion J.; *A Manual for Clergy and Church Musicians* (New York: Church Hymnal Corporation, 1980).

Huck, Gabe; *Liturgy with Style and Grace* (1978, Liturgy Training Program, 155 East Superior St., Chicago IL 60611)

Huijbers, Bernard; *The Performing Audience* (1972, North American Liturgy Resources, 1082 North 23rd Ave., Phoenix, Arizona 65029)

Mitchell, Robert; *Ministry and Music* (1978, Westminster, 925 Chestnut St., Philadelphia, PA 19107.)

Walsh, Eugene, S.S.; *The Theology of Celebration,*
Ministry of the Celebrating Community,
Practical Guidelines for Sunday Mass,
(North American Liturgy Resources, 1082 North 23rd Ave., Phoenix, Arizona 65029)

Periodicals

National Bulletin on Liturgy (Canadian Conference of Catholic Bishops, 90 Parent Ave., Ottawa, Canada K1N 7B1)
Sunday Eucharist I, Bulletin 71 (November-December, 1979).
Sunday Eucharist II, Bulletin 77 (January-February, 1981).
Called to Sing His Praise, Bulletin 40 (September-October, 1973).
Music in Our Liturgy, Bulletin 72 (January-February, 1980).
Diocesan Commissions and Parish Committees, Bulletin 66 (November-December, 1978).
Planning our Year of Worship, Bulletin 67 (January-February, 1979).
Year of Praise, Bulletin 47 (January-February, 1975).
Steps to Better Liturgy, Bulletin 83 (March-April, 1982).

Pastoral Music (225 Sheridan St. N.W., Washington D.C. 20011)

NOTES

MUSICIANS AT LITURGY
Written by:

Corbin T. Eddy,
parish pastor, and professor
of liturgy and pastoral theology

Edited by:

Jerome Herauf

Layout:

Jan Gough, Gilles Lépine

Photography:

Cover: Bob Anderson;
p. 2: Gilles Lafrance;
p. 6, 18: Joyce Harpell;
p. 10-11: Frund;
p. 14, 34: Roman Matwijejko;
p. 21: Ellefsen Photo;
p. 26, 28, 31, 32: Jonas Abromaitis;
p. 36: Mia et Klaus;

Illustrations:

Cover 1 and cover 4: Lee Thirlwall

" . . . *sing to him, play to him,*
tell over all his marvels."

(Psalm 105: 2)

Winston Press
430 Oak Grove
Minneapolis, Minnesota 55403

ISBN: 0-86683-737-X

Lay Presiders at Liturgy

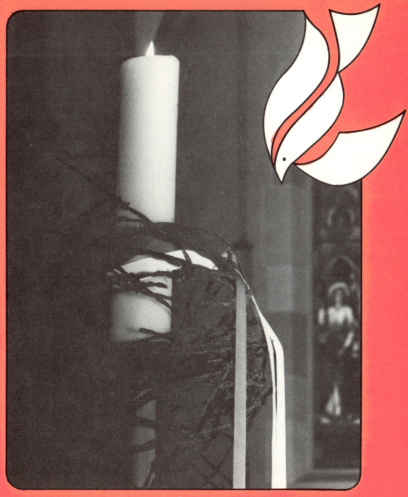

New Parish Ministries

WINSTON PRESS

Contents

New Parish Ministries *was originally published by Novalis, Saint Paul University, Ottawa, Canada. This edition is published by Winston Press, Inc., by arrangement with Novalis, Saint Paul University. Copyright © 1982, Novalis. Copyright © 1983, Winston Press. All rights reserved. No part of this book may be reproduced in any form without written permission from the publisher.*

ISBN: 0-86683-738-8 (previously ISBN: 2-89088-087)

Printed in Canada

5 4 3 2 1

Winston Press, Inc., 430 Oak Grove, Minneapolis, MN 55403

Foreword

"Father's been sick since yesterday. But, since you've all come here today, we're going to pray together, even though he can't be with us. There will be a Liturgy of the Word and then communion will be distributed" (a religious sister in Montreal, 1980).

"During the summer, since I'll be alone and I'll have to celebrate Mass at three different resort locations, I won't be able to preside over the Eucharist here every Sunday. In spite of this, when I can't be here, the president of the Parish Council will preside."

Fact: in the absence of their priests, Christian communities are gathering together, discovering a fresh meaning to their prayer and their responsibility to the Church.

Can "even though" and "in spite of that" bring with them advantages?

Meaning of the Lord's day:

This is the day when the Lord calls his people together to worship. United in the Spirit, we give thanks to our Father through Jesus Christ for the great gifts of love: God has made the world, and he has saved us through the life, death, and rising of our Lord. When a community cannot express this thanks by means of the Mass, it can still come together to hear God's word and reflect on it, to pray for the Church and the world, to sing his praises, and to encourage one another in the life of grace.

from *National Bulletin on Liturgy*, May-June 1981; page 102

"Lay Presiders at Liturgy" is designed for all those religious or lay pastoral animators who on occasion, or regularly, preside over or take part in liturgical celebrations in which no priest is present, for example:

• leaders of prayer groups and other religious movements;

• adults who work with adolescents' and/or children's groups;

• those who organize activities in nursing homes and senior citizens' residences.

A few basic principles are outlined but, more significantly, some concrete indications are given on how to build toward meaningful celebrations and make them a reality for your group.

This brochure is not a recipe book or a manual of instructions. Instead, it brings together practical suggestions and hints to help pastoral and liturgical teams better understand and fulfill their roles as animators in these celebrations.

The Church Gathers

The theme of Christians gathering together to worship has always been the core of any definition of the Church. For example, "The Church, the People of God" depicts the communion between the Lord and his community — a communion experienced particularly on Sundays when Christ, alive and present, dwells among his followers who proclaim his Word and bless and break the bread as he commanded them to do.

On this, the "day of the Lord," Christians gather to hear God's word that refreshes and gives new life to those who hear it. They assemble to celebrate the risen Messiah, to participate in his resurrection which is the source of their total renewal and re-creation. In coming together on the first day of the week, they welcome the Christ of Easter who promised to be with them until the end of time and who, even now, promises resurrection and eternal life to all who hear and follow. By faith, they receive him who came into the world "to make all things new." In faith, they respond to his call to work actively in his mission of world renewal.

Christians united by the Lord's call and in his name are the Church, the sacrament of salvation in the world. Even when they are not celebrating the Eucharist, their unity and togetherness is a gathering of the Church.

Gathering together as the Church

Gathering together as the Church implies opening oneself to Christ, present and acting in and through his Spirit. It certainly means to welcome the Word of God in faith, and to give it priority. Likewise, it means to create a climate in which those present can respond prayerfully to the proclaimed Word.

Christians do not meet simply

4

for a "get-together," to exchange pleasantries or take stock of their accomplishments. They come together to praise and worship the Father through Jesus Christ, in the Spirit. Yet, in this encounter with God, they are given a mission. They hear a message that urges them to go out into the world to witness to something they have perceived in their assembly: the coming of the Kingdom of God. Their gathering together finds meaning only in their being sent forth into the world to bear fruit.

A Church assembly can be seen to revolve around four actions:

WELCOME

- A people gathered together in the Lord's name

WORD

- A people called and challenged by the Good News

PRAISE and COMMUNION

- A people that remembers and renews its covenant with God

ACTIVE COMMITMENT

- A people sent on mission

Different types of gatherings

Even when there is no priest on hand, Christians should nevertheless convene on Sundays; this is the first type of gathering that comes to mind: the Sunday assembly of the Church, including within that celebration the distribution of communion.

There are other assemblies as well:

- A group of Christians, making their spiritual journey together, who do not feel quite ready for the celebration of the Eucharist;

- A group of Christians who, for reasons of poor health, can not participate in the Mass: e.g. senior citizens in an old age home;

- Others who find themselves a

considerable distance from a church (scouts on an overnight trip in the wilderness);

• Christians who, during the week, go to prayer meetings at the church or in their homes.

These are examples of gatherings from which a priest is occasionally absent. But since each Christian assembly is held in anticipation of the Eucharist — itself the foundation and focal point of the community — we must never lose sight of the vital link which the Eucharist has with these other group experiences of the Christian community, which can take place either before or some time after the Eucharist.

Christians can and should assemble even when a priest is not available. This can truly contribute to growth in the community. After all, it is a dimension of the Church's coming together. Still, the community must never forget that for it to be fully alive in the Spirit of the Lord, it must celebrate the Eucharist, which can never take place without a priest.

Sample invitations

In the absence of our pastor, you are cordially invited, this coming Sunday, to the gathering of our parish family for prayer together with the distribution of communion, to be presided over by myself. In the sacristy at 9:00 a.m. and in the church at 11:00 a.m. Everyone is welcome.

A.P., pastoral animator

In the absence of our pastor, this Christian community will convene next Sunday. The celebration will be led by our liturgy committee and will be presided over by_____, our pastoral animator.

Jack Johnson, President, Parish Council

In the name of the risen Lord, I invite you all to the Christian assembly next Sunday. In my absence, the liturgy will be conducted by our liturgy committee, and_____will preside over the celebration itself.

*"Let us give thanks
to the Lord our God,
for his love endures forever."*

The Work of a Team

Ministers of Christian assemblies, in the absence of a priest

Who should direct the gathering of Christians when the priest cannot be there? Not just anyone, — but there are those who, depending on the situation, might well be good choices.

Surely it must be someone who:

• is known and well accepted by the parish community or by a majority of those whom he or she will serve in this capacity;

• has an adequate background in the Christian faith enabling him or her to carry out this role meaningfully and competently;

• has, over a period of time, been actively engaged in community-oriented activities and who enjoys a good reputation within the community;

• has demonstrated an openness and availability to the working of the Spirit by respecting others and by a prayerful approach to life;

• has been selected by representatives of the particular community (Parish Council) with the approval of the pastor responsible for the parish;

• possesses basic communication skills;

• can and will work with others on a team or committee to plan liturgical services.

Simply because a particular person already has a position, such as President of the Parish Council, does not necessarily mean he or she is the best choice for this ministry. The mere fact that a Sister from a religious community happens to be available to accept the responsibility does not excuse a group from looking within itself to find persons more closely identified with and therefore more representative of the parish family.

In parishes where there are permanent deacons, it is obvious that the very nature of their ministry empowers them to preside over the Christian assembly in the absence of the priest. But most of them have the good fortune not to be alone in their efforts. Others who are both resourceful and competent are often willing to lend assistance.

A Christian assembly should be able to identify with its animators. Consequently, it is crucial that those responsible for animating do not dominate the group in such a way that others present would be uncomfortable participating. Yet it is equally important that they guide the celebration smoothly so that the contributions made by individuals are of a certain basic quality.

Depending upon the particular group, there may be several persons assisting at a celebration, including:

• *The presider* (male or female) who convenes the gathering and invites them to pray together. He is the one chiefly entrusted with calling the assembly together.

He does not do everything himself. He introduces and concludes the celebration and presides throughout it.

Normally, he will be located in a chair in the sanctuary, or elsewhere amidst the gathering, where he can be easily seen and can himself have direct visual contact with the others.

• *The readers* whose function it is to proclaim the Word of God.
• *The animators* or animator of the assembly who invite(s) those present to take part in various ways.

Others can be:
• singers and musicians
• those whose ministry is to welcome the congregation to the church or place of worship
• the commentator
• ministers of communion

Except for ordained ministers and permanent deacons, there is no real need for animators to be vested. In some parishes, where it has been a custom that they be vested, the presider and the ministers of communion will be gowned in albs.

Alone, or with others?

One person cannot and should not perform all the functions in the assembly no matter how talented, energetic or capable he or she may be. When the pastor is absent from the parish, an occasion is thereby presented to each person in the parish. It is an opportunity for the Church because *we* are the Church — we must all take responsibility for expressing our faith and educating others in that faith.

But if every person in the parish shifts the responsibility to others, whether they be ordained ministers or members of parish council, a real danger arises. That parish is running the risk of having its members become more and more distant from the life of the parish: the life of that community will suffer; less and less interest will be taken in the Eucharist or other liturgical celebrations; attendance will wane at the Mass because the members of the parish are not involved in the celebration.

The celebration team must bear this in mind in planning liturgical celebrations which will maximize the involvement of the congregation. The team itself should represent a true cross-section of the parish — not just those who always volunteer to help out or those who are frequently at church.

The team should also, if possible, arrange for workshops in specific areas where expertise can be of great assistance — such as in music or singing. Furthermore, the team should work in close collaboration with the parish priest. This applies also to planning celebrations when he will be unable to be present. This way, the team can draw upon his intuitions and experience as well as on his gifts as an animator, so that in organizing and giving thought to a particular liturgical service, the team has a better grasp of the aspirations of the parish, its needs, and the ways in which it feels comfortable in expressing these.

Do we start from "square one"?

Putting together a celebration requires drawing upon the planning team's resources and using the tools already available, all the while taking into account the particular adaptations which will be necessary to make the celebration meaningful for the community. Customs of the parish, in its forms of worship, should be remembered. The readings found in our Section on "Resources" — particularly The General Instruction of the Roman Missal, Living with Christ and the National Bulletin on Liturgy, are, in our opinion, fundamental materials. Here the team can find suggestions which can be modified for the celebration being planned.

Here are a few indications on how to adapt the materials:

● We pray with Jesus to God our Father.

● The plural "We" is used to indicate that prayer is a communal step toward the Father taken by all present.

● Try to avoid the practice of using standard "formula-prayers" taken from one of the books.

● Personalize the message or content of the prayers themselves so that they reflect the moods, concerns and wants of the community.

● Prayers reserved to the priest should, of course, be omitted so as to avoid confusion between celebrations when he is present and those when he is not (the blessing, the Eucharistic Prayer, the greeting of the congregation by the priest).

— For example, we can say: Let us take a moment to become silent and to become aware that the Lord is with us rather than to say "The Lord be with you!"

Choices to be made

Before the celebration

The animator prepares him or herself.

He or she prepares the outline for the celebration and communicates it to those involved.

During the celebration

The animator will conduct the celebration entirely or almost entirely by him or herself.

The participants listen and respond,
or
The participants carry out instructions.

After the celebration

The ceremony is forgotten,
or
The animator congratulates him or herself on a job well

Before, during and after a celebration are all times when th

14

Team work

- The team surrounding the animator prepares.
- They consult with the musicians, cantors, the choir.
- They itemize a list of materials necessary for the celebration.
- Those outside the team, whose help will be needed, are contacted.
- Tasks are assigned to various group members.

- A presider of the assembly is clearly identified.
- Other animators contribute according to their role.
- There are occasions within the ceremony for the congregation to express itself.

- The team does a complete review of the celebration.
- Feedback is obtained by speaking to persons who were present.
- The team makes the necessary adjustments for the next time, based upon its learning experience.

Christian community has a chance to speak its mind.

"*Your Word lives, Lord;
for us, today,
it is light and life.*"

__How do we prepare a celebration together?__

Identify the starting point of our coming together

We celebrate Jesus Christ risen and living in our midst

• as the key event in our own personal history of salvation which we live throughout the liturgical year of the Church; the Bible is for us a "family album" in which we read of the wonders God has worked for his people.

• in those celebrations which particularly touch upon our communal concerns (e.g. the anniversary of the founding of our parish, the harvest, liturgical services with selected themes). Having become conscious of the importance of this event for us all, we bring it to the Father in prayer and, looking at God's Word found in Scripture, we seek to discover a message of hope that will light our path.

• in celebrations which reflect individual joys or sorrows in which the community, too, expresses its concern for the individual — death, birth, marriage, anniversary, etc. Through its participation, the community lends to the occasion a more universal dimension. We look to Scripture to find a teaching which is pertinent to the experience we are presently living:

— What event has gathered us together in the name of Jesus Christ?

— What is the link between this event and the experience of the life of our Christian community?

Liturgies which must be celebrated in the absence of a priest, nevertheless do open up enormous possibilities for those in the community to uncover and better appreciate the connection between their everyday lives and their life of worship, and to express that link through celebrations which have a flexible structure.

Grasp the essentials in the Word of God

The place accorded to the Word of God remains an important criterion by which to judge the value of liturgical celebrations conducted in the absence of a priest. Our concerns about making the celebration understandable, so that those who attend will feel at ease and wish to participate, should not allow us to forget the primary importance of the Word of God in every liturgical celebration.

Before deciding who will read, where the lectern will be situated, how the text is to be enunciated, what hymns will be chosen to follow the Scripture passage — it is essential not only to choose an appropriate passage but also to spend time understanding its message to the community.

In order not to stray too quickly into drawing moral implications or subjective impressions from Scrip-

17

ture, we suggest that the planning team use the grid proposed by the Canadian Bible Society as a study guide to help explain and provide a background to the text. Having chosen texts, after careful consideration, with a view to the theme of the celebration, and having opened oneself to the stirrings of the Spirit, the group can ask the following questions:

1) What does this text tell us about God?
2) What does it reveal about humanity?
3) How does it apply to us here and now?

A further reminder: at least two texts should be chosen — one from the New and one from the Old Testament. And, when studying these, it is better and sometimes easier to begin with the New Testament text.

Determine the character of the celebration

Keeping in mind the time in the liturgical year, the significance of the event to be celebrated, the social experience of the parish, what is the most effective format to be used for the celebration? Will the mood be joyous, or sombre?

These questions are posed so that the group can take into account the needs of each particular assembly, rather than simply rely upon the individual likes and dislikes of the

animators or the parish priest (even if he is not there) in determining the focal point of the celebration and how the theme is to be expressed.

Choose the forms of expression for the celebration

Singing is not to occur haphazardly, here and there throughout the celebration, according to the tastes of those in the group. Visual aids, such as overhead projectors or wallhangings, are not to be used just for their own sake. Animators obviously should not say which they would like, or when they would like them, during the Service.

Agreed! But just what criteria should be used in choosing hymns, etc.?

Without going into great detail, here are a few reminders that can be used as working principles for any liturgical team:

— Choose the means of expression that lend themselves to community prayer;

— Respect the right of the congregation to be part of that expression;

— Vary the forms of expression used;

— Leave room in the celebration for silent prayer, for quiet, for reflection along the lines of the theme suggested;

— Never lose sight of the central theme and the character of the celebration, which will affect the types of expression that are appropriate to encourage the people of God to worship.

1-Choice of hymns and music
— congregational singing, solos, hymns to be done by the choir only
— strike a balance between song and instrumental music

2-Choice and editing, if need be, of prayers (from the written texts)
— the rite of welcome
— the penitential rite (penitential intentions)
— readings from the Word of God; the psalm
— homily
— prayers of the faithful
— communion rite, if necessary

— rite of dismissal

3-Choice and location of forms of expression
— gestures to be used (symbolic, bodily, etc.)
— visual layout, decor, lighting

4-Assignment of tasks
for preparation of celebration; also, for animation during the ceremony

5-Selection of a date to **evaluate** the effect of the celebration upon the life of the community; **input —** positive and negative criticisms to be discussed

Remember: there are other ways of organizing and carrying out a celebration that might be even more effective!

What's important:
- *plan it together,*
- *keep the Word of God uppermost in mind,*
- *be creative,*
  so that the community will be stimulated to pray together.

Let us give thanks to the Lord our God...

It is he who has given us the earth on which to live, the mountains that surround us, the rivers that replenish the soil and bring with them life. For his love endures for ever!

It is he who knows each of us by name, and who says to each of us here tonight (today): I love you, I don`t want you to die. For his love endures for ever!

It is he, the faithful God, the God of our fathers in faith, the God of our forefathers who founded this nation! For his love endures for ever!

It is he — the God who is so close to us through his son Jesus — who is here with us now. For his love endures for ever!

Indeed, let us give thanks to the Lord our God, for his love endures for ever.

The Celebration

Typical format for a celebration

We believe it is important to include the following elements in each celebration conducted in the absence of a priest. In order that they not be seen to be imitations of the Mass, it is critical to give a different form to each celebration rather than the same format for all.

Depending upon the circumstances, a particular element may be more important on one occasion than on another.

This is perfectly acceptable. That way, one is respecting the rhythm of the liturgy, be it festive or more ordinary — and also the mood of the congregation.

The welcome and the gathering

— at the outset, the meaning behind the celebration

— the welcoming of Christians and the calling to mind of the presence of Jesus Christ
— penitential rite
— opening prayer

The hearing of the Word

— the Word is proclaimed
— we respond
— profession of faith

Praise and thanksgiving

— prayer of praise
— Our Father
— communion or other sign of community

Sent forth on mission

— universal dimension of the prayer
— gesture of active commitment
— the sending forth

The welcome

— the physical arrangement of the room
— the atmosphere created by lighting, decor, music
— the visual theme, if needed
— distribution of instruments to assembly (candles, etc.), if needed
— especially, members of the community (male and female) to greet and welcome those attending

— solemn entrance (if need be) of the different personnel: presider, reader with the lectionary; later, bearers of the Offertory gifts, etc.
— entrance music or hymn

Welcoming words by the presider

Familiar greeting in a warm, simple and natural manner

This can indicate: the meaning of the gathering, the central message of the Word of God, an invitation to community prayer, a link — if applicable — to the entrance hymn

Penitential rite

Introduction by the presider

Penitential intentions to be read by another person, each intention to be followed by a sung or spoken response, or perhaps a moment of silence

Concluding prayer by the presider.

A word proclaimed and welcomed.
— brief introductory comment, if necessary, by the presider or commentator
— proclamation by the reader
— response of those assembled: group sharing, or time of silence, or psalm proclaimed with sung or spoken response, or entirely sung by a good cantor.

The acceptance by the assembly may take various forms.

The assembly, in the absence of a priest, could enter into a dialogue about the meaning of the Word of God and its applicability to the everyday lives of those present. Again this must be done with respect and discernment.

A sharing described above would replace a homily. Or, a minister appointed to speak on the text could offer a homily. He should have certain aptitudes, be recognized in and for his ministry and have a mandate from the local Church to perform this function.

Though it is necessary to encourage the emergence of charisms to witness to and proclaim the Good News, it is equally important to treasure a respect for the Gospel, for its teaching, and for the Christian assembly itself.

Interesting experiences are lived in small communities and a sharing on the Gospel can awaken a real questioning of the commitment — both individual and collective — and the quality of that commitment in the Lord's work:

● in what ways does God's Word touch our experience of life today?

● what concrete response does it call us to make today?

● what changes are we, am I, ready to make in order to really respond to this Word?

The commitments made are evaluated the following week.

Assemblies in the absence of the priest: opportunities for growth in the Church, if these assemblies become occasions in which Christians enter into dialogue about Christian experience lived and examined in the light of the Word of God.

The profession of faith

The profession of our common faith is an important element in any gathering convened in the name of Jesus Christ. Here again, it is advantageous to vary the methods for doing so:

- profession of faith, as in the Roman Missal
- profession of faith, composed and proclaimed by an animator or the presider, in the name of all
- profession of faith, recited or sung
- motives of faith expressed spontaneously by the assembly

Praise and thanksgiving

Gathered together in your name, Jesus Christ, it is right and just to praise and honor God our Father whom you have made known to us and whose love you came to reveal. We recall his marvels throughout the history of his people...

A Word proclaimed and welcomed calls for a response made in a spirit of thanksgiving and praise.

A spontaneous response — yes, in the form of intentions coming from the congregation, but also a more structured response which, as mentioned earlier, should not be the eucharistic prayer itself.

This anthem of praise proclaimed by the presider could be composed by the team around the theme of the great feats of God for his people, during the course of the history of salvation: Creation, Covenant with his people, Liberation, Redemption in Christ Jesus — as continued today in his presence to his followers in the Church and through the sacraments.

This prayer should mention and recall the eucharistic celebration to which all aspire. It should be concluded by the Our Father: the prayer, *par excellence*, of any Christian.

In order to avoid any confusion, this prayer of praise should, under no circumstances, take the form of the eucharistic prayer. For this reason, we strongly recommend that the team not borrow from one of the texts of the eucharistic prayers — such as using the conclusion or introduction to one of them (instead, see example given on page 21).

26

Praising God Our Father, in union with Jesus, can also be demonstrated by a sign. The foremost sign that comes to mind is communion. This is most certainly possible in this celebration, and can be a very significant moment for all. On the other hand, to avoid routine or perhaps ambiguity with the Mass, other signs might also be used to educate the faith of the assembly.

The use of symbols which have proven prominent in the tradition of the Church can be extremely interesting. We note several examples:

— Touching the Bible with the hand can be a symbolic gesture of our conversion and adherence to the Word of God;

— The use of holy water can recall our baptism, and be used to signify our new step toward conversion and toward the Father;

— A gesture of faith and confidence in God by writing a prayer or request that we place on the altar or on a cross;

— A symbol of our offering ourselves by presenting the fruit of our labors or some product of our work;

These are just some of the illustrations of the creativity that is open to a team in planning a meaningful celebration that includes symbolic gesture.

Praising God Our Father, in union with Jesus, can also be demonstrated by a sign. The foremost sign that comes to mind is communion.

Sent forth in mission

This last part of the celebration is more than a conclusion — it is also a point of germination. As such, it is indispensable to the celebration. We suggest that the following elements be included:

• Our horizons open us, we open up to the world — recognizing that we live in solidarity with all our Christian brothers and sisters, who suffer, struggle, or rejoice: This concern should be expressed in the prayers of the faithful.

• Called to become committed in our own social setting by the Word of God, we ponder: what am I (are we) going to do to live out my (our) commitment this week?
— individual commitment
— group commitment

• Parish announcements for the week: it is a good idea to underline coming events of interest: (baptisms, funerals, marriages, other activities, etc.).

• Prayer of conclusion; or blessing.

• Recessional hymn or instrumental music.

"May the Lord be with us this coming week that we may truly live what we have celebrated here today."

Particular Questions

Where to celebrate?

At the church, certainly! But why not think of other significant locations as well:

The family home surely could be a place for a celebration, occasionally, to express that within the family circle lies a privileged opportunity to live out the Gospel message.

And it would be suitable, in rural settings especially, to renew the tradition of honoring Mary during certain months, and of making the stations of the cross?

Rooms would be made available in community centres and, in summer, festival tents large enough to accommodate a group for non-eucharistic assemblies. These are oftentimes better than the place of worship within a church, which presents a more formal setting.

We hasten to add, for this reason, that gatherings outside the church contribute greatly to the acceptance and practice of non-eucharistic celebrations — particularly those in which communion will not be distributed.

Celebrating for all?

There must be room in the assembly for expression by those of all ages and social strata.

And there must be openness in the assembly to seek out and find common ground with other gatherings, outside the Church, which are comprised of marginal Christians — those who have distanced themselves from the official Church practice.

There must be two goals for celebrations that occur in the absence of a priest: These celebrations must reflect the Church's sense of mission, and its commitment to accompany all men and women in the journey of faith.

Evaluating?

The work does not end with the goodbye handshake at the conclusion of a well-received, joyous celebration.

Only by systematically evaluating what took place can the team improve the quality of their celebrations.

To assist in the evaluation, here are some ideas:

• Find out how the celebration was received by the community:

questionnaire-survey, telephone pool, ask persons in conversation, etc.;

• Identify, before the celebration, the key goal behind the service and use it, in the evaluation, to determine the success of the gathering;

• Consult the congregation at large, from time to time — especially after an innovation — to obtain feedback;

• Evaluate in order to correct or to improve the celebration, but also to educate and stimulate the animators.

In order that these celebrations may not suffer an awkward introduction, parish priests and their respective teams are encouraged to prepare their parishes as well as their animators. The best way to accomplish this is to involve the parish in the decision-making process, rather than simply present decisions as a *fait accompli*.

Calling the assembly together: *The leader invites the people of the community to come together for Sunday worship. He or she helps them to recognize that as baptized members of the body of Christ they have a responsibility to give public worship to God. A leader who is concerned about this community of God's people will seek to make the celebration as good as possible, working with the other ministers to prepare and celebrate better. Some leaders will invite and encourage members of the community to join in public prayer both on the Lord's day and at other times.*

Leading the assembly: *The work of the leader may be compared in some ways to that of the conductor of an orchestra: the leader encourages other ministers and members of the community to prepare and carry out their own roles in a manner that makes the celebration a good experience of worship. As well, the leader presides over the celebration, leads the major prayers, and leads or gives the reflections on the scriptures.*

Evaluating the celebrations: *A leader has to look back at past celebrations, consider their strong and weak points, and work with the liturgy committee, ministers, and pastor to improve and maintain the quality of the community's worship. Suggested improvements should be discussed and tried out carefully.* from National Bulletin of Liturgy, May-June 1981, pages 104-105

Pitfalls to Avoid

One or more persons who mistake their roles as animators:

— what place within the celebration has been given to the Word of God?

— what room within the service has there been for expression by the community?

— what link, if any, has been created between those present and the priest-pastor who is absent?

An Assembly closed in upon itself:

– has the celebration conveyed any sense of concern for the velfare of the universal Church?

– how have we received others, those who are different :rom us...?

— what collective response and commitment to work in service of the Lord was evoked by our gathering?

— where have we avoided sympathizing and identifying with the needs of others?

A colorless assembly:

— can the specific meaning behind our gathering be clearly identified, by looking at the lived experience of the community and the Word of God used in the celebration?

— is the same, repetitious format being used for each celebration, week after week (songs, music, silence, gestures)?

Resources

General topics

Adam, Adolph. *The Liturgical Year.* 1981, Pueblo, 1860 Broadway, New York, New York 10023.

Deiss, Lucien. *The Christian Celebration.* 1977, World Library Publications, 5040 N. Ravenswood, Chicago, Illinois 60640.

The General Instruction of the Roman Missal, "Introduction". 1974, Canadian Conference of Catholic Bishops, 90 Parent Ave., Ottawa, Canada K1N 7B1. Pages 11-82.

Homiletic Service. Novalis, P.O. Box 9700, Terminal, Ottawa, Canada K1G 4B4.

Homily Service. The Liturgical Conference Inc., 810 Rhode Island Ave. N.E., Washington, D.C. 20018.

Hovda, Robert. *Strong, Loving and Wise: Presiding in Liturgy.* 1976, The Liturgical Conference, 810 Rhode Island Ave., N.E., Washington, D.C. 20018.

Living with Christ. Novalis, P.O. Box 9700, Terminal, Ottawa, Canada K1G 4B4.

National Bulletin on Liturgy. Canadian Conference of Catholic Bishops, 90 Parent Ave., Ottawa, Canada K1N 7B1. Vol. 12, No. 70, September-October, 1979: "Liturgical Year and Spirituality"; Vol. 14, No. 79, May-June, 1981: "Sunday Liturgy: When Lay People Preside."

Sloyan, Virginia, ed. *Touchstones for Liturgical Ministers.* 1978, Liturgical Conference, 810 Rhode Island Ave., N.E., Washington, D.C. 20018.

Western Liturgical Conference of Canada. *God's Word, Thanksgiving, Communion, with Layperson Presiders.* Chancery Office, 3225-13th Ave., Regina, Sask. S4T 1P5.

Specific topics

Bitney, James. *Bright Intervals: Prayers for Paschal People.* Winston Press, 430 Oak Grove, Minneapolis, MN. 55403.

Bitney, James. *Sabbath* (filmstrip on Sunday Assembly), Winston Press.

Duffy, Regis, OFM. *Real Presence.* 1982, Harper and Row, Keystone Industrial Park, Scranton, PA. 18512.

Life is Changed: Prayers at the Time of Death. Novalis, P.O. Box 9700, Terminal, Ottawa, Canada K1G 4B4.

National Bulletin on Liturgy. Canadian Conference of Catholic Bishops, 90 Parent Ave., Ottawa, Canada K1N 7B1. Vol. 12, No. 68, March-April, 1979: "Postures and Gestures in our Prayer."

Searle, Mark. "Gestures at Liturgy," *Assembly* (December, 1979), P.O. Box 81, University of Notre Dame, Notre Dame, IN. 46556.

Worship Without Words. Canadian Conference of Catholic Bishops (address as above).

LAY PRESIDERS AT LITURGY

Adapted from:

Célébrations en l'absence du prêtre
(Novalis), written by Gabriel Gingras,
professor of theology
at the University of Sherbrooke.

Edited by:

Jerome Herauf

Layout:

Jan Gough, Gilles Lépine

Photography:

Cover: Joyce Harpell;
p. 2, 10, 22: Roman Matwijejko;
p. 6, 16: Sheila Sturley, RSCJ;
p. 8: Gilles Lafrance;
p. 13: "Vivants univers";
p. 19: Paul Hamel

Illustrations:

p. 24 and 28: Krista Johnston;
cover 1 and cover 4: Lee Thirlwall

Excerpts from the *National Bulletin on Liturgy, No. 79, copyright*® Concacan In., 1981. Reproduced with permission of Canadian Conference of Catholic Bishops, Ottawa, Canada.

*"In every place
I want the people
to lift up their hands reverently in prayer."*

(1 Timothy 2:8)

Winston Press
430 Oak Grove
Minneapolis, Minnesota 55403

ISBN: 0-86683-738-8

Health Care Ministers

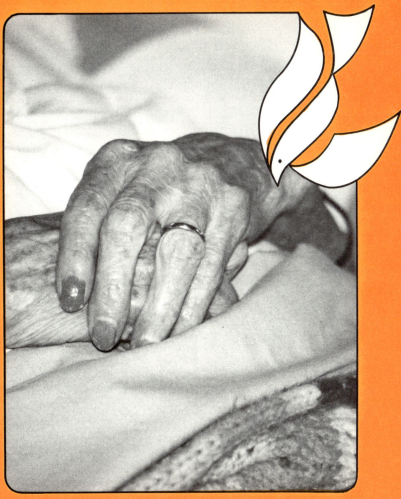

New Parish Ministries

WINSTON PRESS

Contents

New Parish Ministries was originally published by Novalis, Saint Paul University, Ottawa, Canada. This edition is published by Winston Press, Inc., by arrangement with Novalis, Saint Paul University. Copyright © 1982, Novalis. Copyright © 1983, Winston Press. All rights reserved. No part of this book may be reproduced in any form without written permission from the publisher.

ISBN: 0-86683-739-6 (previously ISBN: 2-89088-086-9)

Printed in Canada

5   4   3   2   1

Winston Press, Inc., 430 Oak Grove, Minneapolis, MN 55403

Introduction

To visit the sick, to be with someone in distress, these are not activities to be taken lightly. And yet, as Christians, our responsibility to care for others is central to our faith.

To be a Christian is to be Christ-like. If one were to remove from the gospel accounts of Jesus' life all references to healing, there would be little left that is recorded. Therefore, we must assume that to be Christ-like, each of us has a responsibility in the healing ministry.

"Then the King will say to those on his right hand, 'Come you whom my Father has blessed, take your heritage prepared for you since the foundation of the world... I tell you solemnly insofar as you did this to the least of these brothers of mine, you did it to me'" (Matthew 25:34, 40).

To visit the sick is a personal and a communal responsibility of the parish Christian Community. Some participate by praying for the sick, others in direct ministry, and all by becoming more aware of the power of caring in our interactions with others. A smile, a nod of affirmation, an incline of the head which indicates a listening ear — all are signs of our concern for others.

By reason of our baptism, our daily activity in service to others is ministry, and a furthering of the mission of Jesus. For example: When a husband attends his wife during childbirth, when a mother wipes the tears of frustration from the eyes of a child, when an employee takes time to listen and encourage a co-worker, when a family prays with a dying loved one, when a senior citizen calls on a friend who is lonely — all are participating in the ministry of healing.

It is often through a heightened awareness of gifts and talents discovered in everyday happenings that a call is heard to serve the sick in a more formal way, perhaps on a parish team. This booklet is written to give some insights to those who hear this call, and to initiate ongoing growth in its creative ministry.

The Parish Team of
Health Care Ministers

For the parish health care minister, the importance of a team relationship — even if the team is that minister and just one other person — cannot be overemphasized. The key words for such a team are: community and growth.

Community

The members form a support-community which is commissioned by the Christian community to bring the love, prayers and concern of the Christian community to those who are sick. Through the team, by way of its members, the sick communicate with the Christian community.

Growth

Members are assisted in their growth as ministers to the sick through the group experience of prayer, interpersonal relationships, problem solving, information sharing and education. By reflecting on their experiences in the light of the gospel, members are strengthened by that same gospel.

Objectives of the Team

- To assess needs in the parish.

- To develop a reasonable plan of action.

- To encourage membership on the team.

- To assign tasks, matching abilities of team members with needs.

- To solicit the assistance of the parish priest or another parish ministry team, when appropriate, e.g., the Social Action Team for an elderly person who needs financial assistance.

- To assist one another to grow in faith and an understanding of the meaning of caring for the sick as ministry.

- To be a resource for problem-solving in difficult situations.

- To help members regularly evaluate their ministry.

- To study scripture, reflect and pray as a group.

3

• To provide ongoing opportunities for education and renewal, such as: a small reference library; resource persons on specific topics at selected meetings; funds for seminars which individual members, or the group as a whole, might wish to attend.

How to Carry Out Objectives

To assess needs in the parish

• Parish records will provide the names of family members who have suffered the loss of a loved one.

• New parents often benefit from a visit of the health care minister. Times of great change in lifestyle, such as that experienced when a baby is born in a family, bring about a new kind of self-knowledge and the possibility of growth in our relationship to God.

• A tear-out form in the parish bulletin, which may be filled out when a visit is requested, will remind parish members to think of those in need.

To develop a reasonable plan of action

Teams should receive their mandate out of the Christian community (the parish council) and base their objectives on the needs they have been assigned to fulfill. There is often a tendency to become too organized — so that the organization takes priority over the purposes for which the group came together. It must be kept in mind that the primary concern of team members is to minister to the sick.

The successful team will limit objectives and develop a long range plan of action. Objectives should be reviewed annually in order to assure that they are realistic, and to meet the needs of the group and the Christian community.

To encourage membership on the team

Jean Vanier's book, *Community and Growth: Our Pilgrimage Together*, devotes a full chapter to the topic of "Welcome." He says, "Welcome is one of the signs the community is alive." And "When we pool our strength and share the work and responsibility, we can welcome many people, even those in deep distress, and perhaps help them find self confidence and inner healing."

An innovative way to sensitize the parish to the health care ministry and the need for members on the team is to name a health care ministry week in the parish. The time for such a week might be chosen to coincide with a Sunday on which a homily on the healing mission of the Church would be appropriate.

Following this, a member of the team could be invited to give a short description of the work of the team, the need for new members, and the need for the prayers of the Christian community to support the sick and the work of the team.

A more in-depth workshop could be given, during the week, on health care topics such as:

• the personal and communal responsibility of the parish to serve the sick

• faith and family wellness

• the need for a Catholic presence in health care institutions in the diocese

• moral decision-making issues such as: euthanasia, contraception, genetic engineering

The call for members may bring forth individuals who are able to minister in new ways not previously thought of by the team. For instance, a new member from a particular ethnic group, like the Vietnamese, would be able to help the team understand the special needs of the ethnic group in question and also would be very helpful in ministering to parish members who spoke Vietnamese.

To assign tasks, matching abilities of team members with needs

The parish community has many persons who could bring a broad range of expertise to the health care ministry team. Nurses, doctors, members of religious congregations have professional exper-

tise. Families, as a group, might wish to bring communion to the sick. Students, the retired, and the elderly have unique gifts and, often, time to visit the sick. Those who are house bound and/or handicapped can become members of the team by visiting "over the telephone." They also might be of assistance by serving as a contact person for a group of visitors, or by telephoning members to remind them of meetings.

To assist one another to grow in faith and an understanding of the meaning of caring for the sick as ministry.

Shared experiences on the team will help ministers to understand God's healing power and the many ways that healing takes place: the healing which occurs when the minister comes to know him or herself in relationships with God and others; the healing which follows forgiving oneself, forgiving others. Each of these brings recovery and new life.

To be a resource for problem solving

At times there is a need to consult with others regarding a difficult problem which arises during ministry. An opinion may be needed on whether assistance, outside of that which the minister is able to provide, should be sought. It may be that the minister needs affirmation in an action taken.

*"Welcome is one of the signs
the community is alive ...
When we pool our strength
and share the work and responsibility,
we can welcome many people,
even those in deep distress,
and perhaps help them find self confidence
and inner healing."*

Community and Growth: Our Pilgrimage Together, by Jean Vanier

In all cases, professional secrecy must be maintained by the persons consulted. When consulting with others about a patient, names should be used only when necessary.

To help members regularly evaluate their ministry

The purpose of evaluation is to assist growth in ministry. The most important evaluation is regular personal review. Team members are able to assist one another by affirming actions and bringing out talents in others which might be used in ministry.

A member might wish to ask the group to evaluate an approach to ministry, taken in a particularly difficult situation. Such a discussion would be helpful to all in assessing their ministry and finding new ways to minister. Education sessions will assist ministers to find ways to strengthen weak areas.

It is recommended that each team member meet with a team spiritual director, at least annually, for a more formal evaluation. The outcome of this would be personal recommendations for growth in their service to others.

To study scripture, reflect, and pray as a group

May we refer you here to another booklet in our New Ministries series, "Parish Prayer Groups," for some practical hints concerning how to pray as a group.

To provide ongoing opportunities for education and renewal

Some topics which might be addressed by resource persons at selected meetings are:
- the theology of health care
- the basis for moral decision-making in health care ethics
- listening skills
- suffering
- praying with patients

Membership on the Team

The team will be comprised of individuals who wish to visit

- the lonely and distressed
- the sick in hospitals and long-term care facilities
- the elderly
- the handicapped
- the bereaved

For many sick persons, their greatest need is one of companionship and relatedness to others. This ministry of friendship is a good place for the new health care minister to get a start. In dropping in to say, "hello," chatting for a short period of time, he or she will learn to *be with* someone and to *listen*, to sit quietly without speaking — in other words to *be present*. This presence is a manifestation of the caring of the Christian community, and forms the basis for all other ministry to the sick.

Others on the team will visit the sick to also be present, but in a way that may also relate to their spiritual needs. They will listen as well, but may also counsel, pray, bring the Eucharist, and assist the priest in administering the sacraments.

A spiritual director, knowledgeable about ministry to the sick, is an important member of the team. This may be the parish priest, or another assigned by him, with background and experience in the health care ministry (e.g. a member of a pastoral care team of a local hospital).

Models of Teams and Meetings

In smaller centers one team may serve a number of parishes, or each parish might wish to have a small team of two or three persons and the parish priest. In large urban parishes two or three teams might be needed in each parish. Meetings of the team should be held on a regular basis, at a predetermined time agreed upon by the membership — and not less than once a month.

How to Run a Meeting...

Members might wish to alternate in preparing and chairing of meetings. The agenda should be simple and allow time for: scriptural reflection and prayer (15 min.), business meeting (15 min.), sharing of experiences and problem solving (30 min.), education (45 min.), coffee (15 min.).

The education program might be conducted by one of the members with a particular expertise, the spiritual director, or a resource person. A resource person might be invited to take part in the problem-solving part of the meeting, or to combine this with the education session.

A team which prays together, for each other and for those entrusted to them in ministry, will EXPERIENCE its support in their lives. Communal prayer assists the community to love, to understand, and to grow.

"My prayer is that your love for each other may increase more and more; and never stop improving your knowledge and deepening your perception so that you can always recognize what is best."

Philippians 1:9, 10

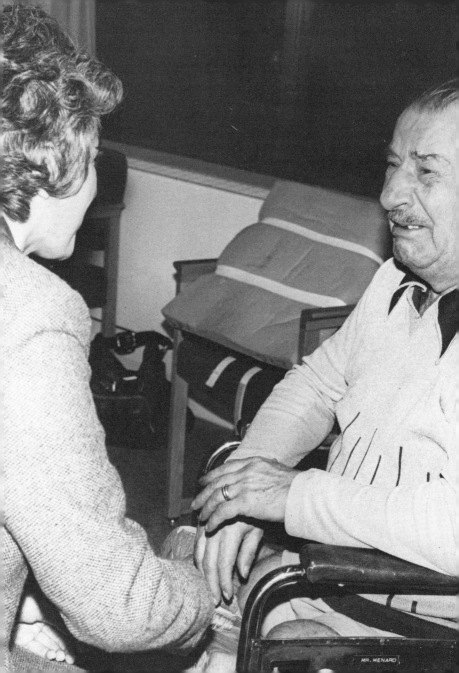

The Lay Health Care Minister

A story is told of a little boy who asked his mother, after she turned off the lights at bedtime, to stay with him because he was afraid of the dark. His mother explained that there was no need to be afraid because God was in the room. The little boy answered that he knew God was in the room, but that it would make him feel much better if there was also someone there "with their skin on." The lay health care minister is present to the sick, the suffering, the grieving, in much the same way as the mother is present to her son.

For the lay person, who understands ministry as a call received by all Christians to attend to the needs of others, these are very exciting times. No longer is the lay person asked to be a passive occupant of a pew. He or she is called to minister!

Each situation to which the lay minister is called is unique, and each baptized Christian brings to that situation his or her own uniqueness. Therefore, the minister must be himself or herself; this is extremely important. Because the patient may already have a sense of a loss of reality, the health care minister will further traumatize the patient if he, himself, is not being authentic.

The Role

The role of the health care minister is to be present to the sick person as a representative of the Christian community; and, further, to listen and to counsel when appropriate, to pray with and for the sick person, to prepare for and to administer the sacraments.

In order to perform this role certain gifts and abilities are needed. The following list is not exhaustive. You may wish to add to it. A discussion of its content could provide the basis for orientation meetings for new members of the parish health care ministry team.

- Willingness to commit oneself
- Maturity
- Awareness of human worth and potential, and the unique dignity of each person
- Warm, sympathetic personality
- **Ability to listen**
- Ability to communicate
- Personal prayer life
- Ability to be with others, no matter what their concept of Church, status in life, or moral outlook
- Responsibility
- Good judgment
- Common sense
- Ability to accept reversals and apparent failures
- Flexibility and a sense of humor
- Discretion and ability to keep a confidence
- Ability to function within limitations
- Ability to pray with others

If important qualities are missing and appear unattainable to an individual aspiring to this ministry, this must be recognized. Perhaps another ministry would be more suitable.

Self-knowledge and Evaluation

The answers to the following questions will help an individual know him/herself as a health care minister:

- What are my gifts?
- What are my weaknesses and limitations?
- What am I doing to grow in my ability to minister?
- What are my reasons for working in this ministry?
- Do I wish to serve the sick?
- Is my ministry primarily self-serving?
- How am I ministered to by those I visit?

- How do I come to know, more deeply, God and Church?

The same questions provide a good basis for periodic, *personal evaluation* of ministry. Assessment by team co-workers, parish priest, or chaplain would also be helpful.

The need for a spiritual life on the part of the minister cannot be overemphasized. By listening to God, in prayer and in our daily activities, we come to know him and thus are better able to communicate his presence to others.

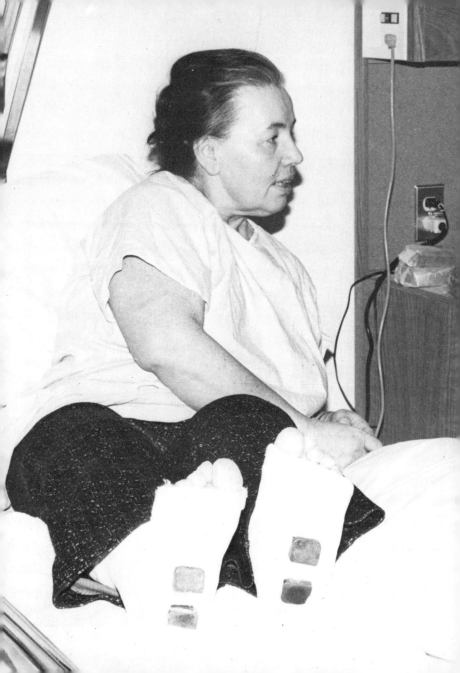

Sickness

Those who are sick contribute to the Church's life through their participation in the passion of Christ; their efforts to deal with their sickness edify the Church. They remind those who are involved in everyday affairs of the fragility of life and the hand of God in the midst of humankind's greatest achievements. In short, the sick remind us that we are on a journey — a pilgrim people with a final destiny.

excerpt from *National Bulletin on Liturgy,* No. 57. © Concacan, Inc., 1977. Reproduced with permission.

Day-to-day relationships with families, friends and co-workers, as well as our daily activities, provide us with a sense of security. However, when we become sick, activity changes and usually is restricted. Relationships are temporarily disrupted. (The hospital visiting hours may be the only time when contact is made with close relatives and friends.) Even the comfortable pew, which for many is the only place where God enters their thoughts, is denied them.

The experience of being sick is one for which few are really prepared. Insecurity and uncertainty often set in — for example, not knowing what is happening at work, or what will be the outcome of a proposed surgery; or having to face death, not as a remote possibility but as an imminent probability.

The Feelings of the Sick

Understanding the feelings of a sick person is one of the first steps to be taken by the health care minister. The feelings of any one sick person might be found in the following list which, although incomplete, takes into account a whole range of feelings which might be experienced throughout an illness: loneliness, fear, depression, loss of control, despair, physical pain, insecurity about the future, denial, anger, acceptance, rejection, frustration, boredom, restlessness, confusion, peace, abandonment, fatigue, fright, thanksgiving, relief, hopelessness, embarrassment.

Awareness of the feelings and the physical condition of the sick person will help the health care minister to relate to needs.

The sick person suffers physically, emotionally and socially. But suffering and living with the lesson that illness teaches about the fragility of life can also result in dramatic spiritual growth. Growth in suffering brings about a serenity which comes from knowing that the "now" of suffering gives way to the good of tomorrow.

In his recent book, *The Gift of Courage*, Dr. James Wilkes, a practising psychiatrist from Toronto, uses the symbols of Easter, Gethsemane, Calvary and the Resurrection to point out how our Judaeo-Christian heritage can give meaning and value to life. Finding ourselves and grasping the meaning of life in dramatic experiences such as these can bring us to the moment of decision. These same dramatic instances can bring the patient to a new knowledge of self and of relationships. The sick person may, for the first time, truly experience God as a loving and forgiving father.

The sick person has the *gift of time*. Illness provides a space in life between what has occurred before illness and what will occur afterwards. The outcome may be a return to what was before, a new life plan, or the end of life on earth. The potential is infinite for growing, for becoming, in this life-space. As never before, there is also at this time a need for love and care. A listening ear is needed from someone who will reflect back with the sick person, counsel when appropriate, and bring the news that the Christian community cares and is praying.

To dare to be with someone during this journey, called sickness, is what the health care ministry is all about.

The Visit

A little girl lost a playmate in death, and one day reported to her family that she had gone to comfort the sorrowing mother. 'What did you say?' her father asked. 'Nothing,' the child replied, ''I just climbed up on her lap and cried with her.'

from an article on "Grief" by Hadden W. Robinson, *Journal on Grief.*

What an unforgettable visit the little girl had with her friend's mother. She was able to be with — to be present to — this woman in an extraordinary way. Yet what happened was a very simple expression of feeling. Words were not necessary or important. The experienced health care minister knows that a simple approach to a visit is the most helpful.

Suggestions for visiting

The following suggestions for visiting a patient in the hospital could also be of help — with some slight accommodations for a visit at home:

● From the information you have received about the patient from the parish team, relatives, hospital chaplain or your previous visit — *anticipate possible feelings and needs of the patient.* Bear in mind that this information may have little relevance to the present visit, if the condition of the patient has changed — due perhaps to intervening surgery, an adverse medical report, etc.

● It is a good idea to *identify yourself to the nursing personnel.* They should be able to inform you of any dramatic change in the patient's condition or outlook. In many cases nurses are even aware of an expressed spiritual need.

"People turn to God in times of crisis; and illness is among those times when people feel the need for spiritual guidance. Nurses, therefore, are in a unique position to bring spiritual aid to their patients and the patients' families."

Marguerite Lucy Manfreda, *Spiritual Care: The Nurse's Role*

19

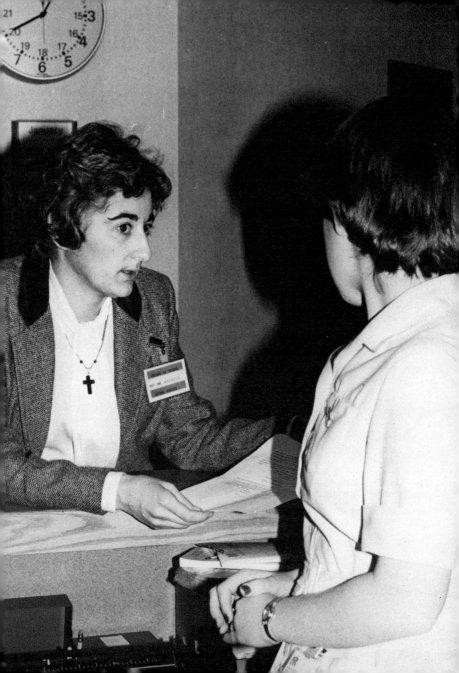

- Before entering the room, *place yourself in the presence of the Lord*, bringing to mind the patient you will be visiting. The following short prayer, or one similar, might be said:

Lord, fill our minds with insights into love
So that every thought may grow in Wisdom,
And all our efforts may be filled with your peace.

The Book of Christian Prayer, 23rd Sunday in Ordinary Time

- *Enter the room. Greet the patient and introduce yourself, if necessary.* If other visitors are present, judge whether it would be better to return another time. If the patient is dying or critically ill, relatives may be comforted by the visit of the minister.

At other times, the presence of a number of business acquaintances might make a visit inappropriate.

- If the patient is alone, appears well enough for a visit, and accepts the visit, *initiate a conversation.*

This should be related to the patient, his or her condition, concerns, etc. However, the patient may just want to be quiet, and this should be respected. An initial visit may have to be less personal. If this appears to be the case, after a short exchange, excuse yourself and suggest returning for a visit at another time.

- Remember the patient is sick, so *do not prolong conversation unless the patient insists.*

- *Try to understand how the patient feels and relate to those feelings* without allowing yourself to be overcome by them. If you are uncertain about what the patient is trying to say, reflect your understanding back to the patient: "Did I understand you correctly, when you said...?"

- *It is not necessary to have answers for the concerns the patient is expressing.* Often the fact that the patient is able to say something about a concern to someone who is not emotionally involved may be all that is needed. Affirmation on the part of the minister is helpful, whenever possible: "Yes, I can see that that would console you."

- *Ask the patient if he or she would like to pray.* Such a prayer might commence with a short scriptural reading, and follow with spontaneous prayer, relating to information received during the visit:

Lord, Mrs. Smith is concerned about the welfare of her three daughters while she is in the hospital. Care for them and give Mrs. Smith peace of mind in the knowledge that they are in your care.

If you are uncomfortable with spontaneous prayer, the Lord's Prayer or another prayer from a book of prayer might be used.

This assumes that the patient wishes to pray during the visit. If this is not so, you might wish to say on leaving, "I'll pray for you." Also, if the suggestion of prayer does not seem appropriate or acceptable, you may consider a few minutes spent in prayer after the visit(s), asking that God receive the patient into his care, and to be intimately present to him or her.

The health care minister may never know how the patient has benefited from the visit — how much one smile, one short prayer, one reading from scripture, a gentle touch or squeeze of the hand may have contributed to the life and emotional and spiritual growth of the patient.

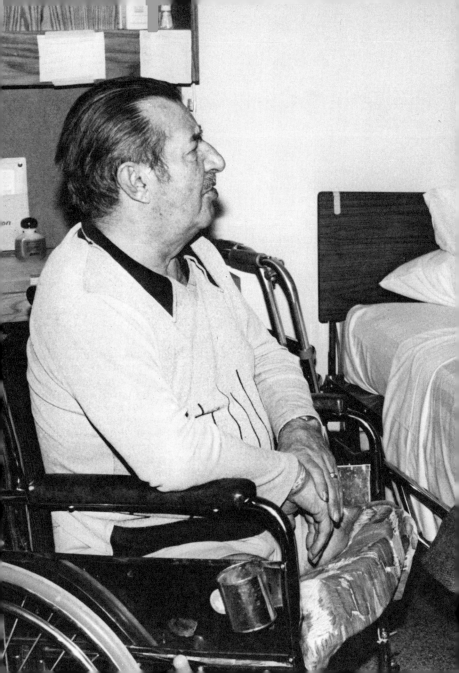

The visit involves a relationship which includes: the minister, the person visited, and God. The patient should be able to depend on the minister, and in some cases may even become dependent. Such a dependency should be allowed to develop temporarily only if the minister is free to say "No" when this dependency interferes with other priorities in his/her life, and if the dependency is not harming the patient. (Here is an instance of where reflection with a team is especially important.)

Laying on of hands to pray for healing is an ancient tradition of the Church. However, if this makes the sick person or the minister uncomfortable, because he or she cannot relate to this type of prayer, it should not be done. It is important that the minister listen for signs which will indicate the patient's experience and image of Church.

The skill of listening is paramount in ministering to the sick. The minister must listen and respond in such a way as to help patients find their own answers. The minister would, therefore, not often say "This is what you should do," but, rather, "What do you

think you should do?" This will affirm the patient as a person of self-worth, capable of making decisions. It is not easy to carry on a listening conversation. It takes practice and understanding to allow another to make decisions, particularly if the minister has a tendency to feel that he or she has "the" answer.

If the patient is unconscious or apparently unable to speak, it is helpful to hold the patient's hand. This touching is, in itself, a healing form of communication. An embrace and a physical contact contains within itself a great deal of meaning. Holding the hand is also a visible extension of the embrace or handshake of the Christian community expressed at the sign of peace, during the Eucharistic celebration.

Initially, the health care minister may feel uncomfortable praying with a patient — particularly in spontaneous prayer. Ease comes with practice. The parish team meetings are a good place to begin. Praying with the family at the dinner table, reflecting the family experiences of the day and asking for God's assistance for family needs will also be helpful. It is important for the minister to know that he or she is more aware of any personal discomfort in this area than those with whom he or she is praying.

The visit may also include bringing communion. By this action, the sick person shares in the bread which was blessed at the Eucharistic celebration of the Christian community. That moment in which the minister of communion (with the words "the Body of Christ") gives the bread to the sick person, is a precious moment in the life of the Christian community as well as in the relationship of those involved.

When the minister brings communion, the following procedure is suggested:

Reading from scripture

● Read a short scriptural text from one of the following: John 6:51-52 and 56; John 6:54-55; John 14:23; 1 Corinthians 11:26.

Prayer

● Recite the Lord's Prayer

● *Minister: Happy are those who are called to the Table of the Lord.*

● *Patient: Lord, I am not worthy to receive You. Only say the word and I shall be healed.*

● Silent thanksgiving

● Concluding prayer
God our Father,
Our help in human weakness,
show (name) the power of your loving care;
We ask this through Christ our Lord.

- Blessing
May God bless you, protect you, and keep you from all harm.

When the minister brings communion, the following procedure is suggested:

Greeting: the minister greets the sick person and all present.
- The minister places the consecrated bread on the table and suggests that all observe a moment of silence and personal prayer.
- The minister invites all present to recall their sins and ask the Lord's forgiveness (by an Act of Contrition, *"I confess..."*, or some other formula).

Scriptural Reading: a short text from one of the following: John 6:51-52 and 56; John 6:54-55; John 14:23; 1 Corinthians 11:26.

The Lord's Prayer: *Our Father, who art in heaven...*

The Communion Rite: The minister introduces the rite as follows: *Happy are those who are called to the table of the Lord... Lord, I am not worthy to receive You. Only say the word and I shall be healed.*

Communion: *The body of Christ.* **Amen.**

Concluding Prayer:

God our Father, almighty and eternal, we confidently call upon you, that the body and blood which (name) has received may bring him (her) to everlasting health in mind and body. **Amen.**

Blessing:

May God bless you, protect you, and keep you from all harm. **Amen.**

The health care minister may be asked to assist when the priest confers the Sacrament of the sick. The Sacraments of the sick and dying are Penance, Anointing and Communion. Communion which is given to a person who seems to be close to the moment of death is called Viaticum. The health care minister should be sensitive to the needs of patients for the Sacraments, and make arrangements for the priest to meet with the patient when necessary.

Blessed oil has traditionally been used by the Church to signify strength and comfort, and sometimes healing. It is used by the priest in the Anointing of the Sick. The health care minister may also use oil as a sign of healing when visiting the sick.

Making the sign of the cross on the forehead and lips, the minister prays:

May God, our Father,
give you comfort and peace.
℟. **Amen.**
May Christ, his Son, help you carry your cross,
and bring you to share his glory.
℟. **Amen.**
May the Holy Spirit
bring you healing and joy.
℟. **Amen.**
May God bless you for ever.

excerpt from *A Book of Blessings*, copyright © Concacan Inc., 1981. Reproduced with permission of the Canadian Conference of Catholic Bishops, 90 Parent Ave., Ottawa, Ont. K1N 1B1

Prayer in Preparation for a Visit

Lord,
With you is Wisdom, who knows your
works,
and was present when you made the
world;
who understands what is pleasing in your
eyes
and what is comfortable to your
commands.
Send her forth from your holy heavens,
and from your glorious throne dispatch
her,
that she may be with me and work with me
that I may know your pleasure.
For she knows and understands all things,
and will guide me discreetly in my affairs
and safeguard me by her glory.

based on Wisdom 9:9-11

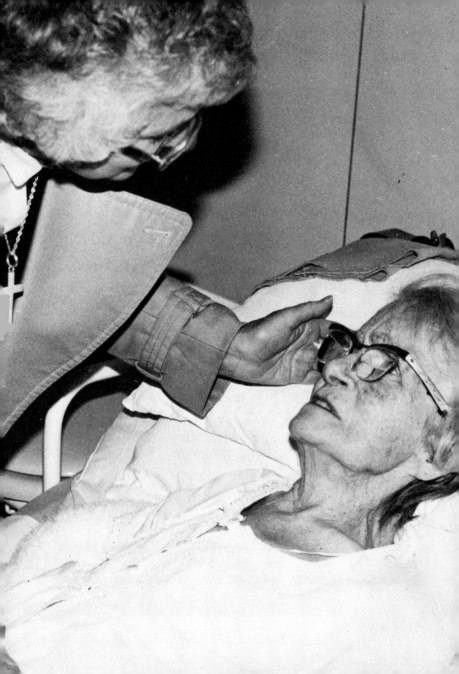

Caring for the Dying

... The story of the good thief best illustrates that Jesus understood the greatest need of a dying person: reassurance, forgiveness and hope. We need only to read the words spoken by Jesus, dying himself, to that criminal: *"Today you will be with me in paradise"* (Lk. 23:43). No greater love could have been shown that man than to assure him that he was all right and that a new life awaited him. The Christian community is called to do likewise.

Ministry of the Christian community: Just as the faith community must be present at the sacraments of initiation to welcome the new Christian into the Body of Christ, so must it come to the support of the dying Christian in his or her passage through death to life.

... Death is a lonely experience, and because of that, the dying person has special need for the support of others, especially from those who are intimately close. Dr. Elisabeth Kubler-Ross strongly advises ministers to the dying to be listeners. Whether the dying person communicates verbally or non-verbally, his or her greatest need is to be supported by ears and hearts that will listen. The aged and the terminally ill are relieved to find someone who will talk and pray with them about death. They need to talk about it and to be listened to.

The studies of Dr. Kubler-Ross are a rich source of information about the psychology of dying. Her findings show that the terminally ill patient is not an object to be treated, pitied or avoided, but a human being in the final stage of growth, and therefore very much in need of loving support and reassurance. A dying person often indicates a desire for community by reaching out with his or her arms.

In their works on the theology of death, theologians such as Karl Rahner and Ladislaus Boros maintain that, at death, people are faced with the final and most important decision of their lives. Death is a moment of personal encounter with God. That moment in peoples' lives, then, is a privileged and a holy one; and the ministers who serve them must keep that in mind.

The initial reactions of persons who find out they are terminally ill are negative and painful. Only later do they arrive at a point where they can accept their condition. They usually go through five stages of the dying process: denial, anger, bargaining, depression and acceptance. It is of paramount importance that those who minister to the dying are aware of this process, are able to recognize what stage these persons are in, and are sensitive to their immediate needs.

... The family and friends of the dying person also go through the **stages** of the dying process just as the patient does, so they too need to feel the reassuring presence of Christ and the community. The Church's rites can be a source of acceptance and consolation for them too.

When the sick person is much closer to death and unable to participate very much, the praying community should be present to assist and commend him or her. This is very important for two reasons:

• the rite for the commendation of the dying, like all rites of the Church, is public and communal;

• the dying person needs community support at this final and decisive moment of life.

Even though the dying person is apparently weak and passive at this time, in reality he or she is breaking through the limitations of this life and is becoming totally free to see clearly his or her relationship with God, humankind, and all of creation. He or she is faced with the choice either of accepting these relationships with grateful love or of rejecting them in utter self-centeredness.

The last senses to fail are touch and hearing, so while the dying person may no longer be able to respond, we need to continue communicating the fact that we are there. Holding his hand, tracing the sign of the cross on his forehead, or washing his face with water can be comforting signs reminding him of his baptism. The short scriptural texts and aspirations from the rite for the commendation of the dying, which contain many beautiful images of salvation and life, should be repeated slowly in a quiet reassuring voice, with everyone present making responses.

The faith community supports a dying brother or sister to the end by presence and prayers. The communal and paschal character of the Christian community is thereby demonstrated. Family and friends find strength and consolation in this, and the whole community experiences the meaning of death and life by facing it in a positive way.

Excerpts from articles written by John O'Brien for the NATIONAL BULLETIN ON LITURGY #57, copyright © Concacan Inc., 1977.

Perspectives on Disabled Persons

In her own words, we learn from Joan Green what it is to be disabled. Too often we let our personal bias and misperceptions get in the way of the true feelings and needs of the handicapped person. We do not seek to visit persons as *they are* but as we feel they should be. By approaching a visit with a handicapped person with openness and *listening*, during the visit, the health care minister will be in a much better position to help the disabled person; but more than that will find that he or she will *learn* a great deal from a unique person whom God has created to give as well as to receive.

I was afflicted with rheumatoid arthritis when I was three years old. Now, I'm 36. This is a very painful disease, and most of the time it feels like there's a furnace inside of me. I give off so much heat that I keep my room like an iceberg most of the time. The heat is worst at my joints, and most of them are now fused together. My elbows don't bend, my knees don't bend, one ankle and one wrist don't bend, and my neck is now partially fused. My jaws are partially locked and my spine is extremely inflexible.

The disease is progressive, which means that the fusing will get worse as I get older. Eventually my neck will completely fuse. When that happens, I will have to find another way to read and write. That bothers me a bit, but I'll come to grips with it when it happens.

I've usually been alone when the pain has been worst, so that I've learned how to deal with it on my own. You just go through the pain and you learn to cope the best way you can. I didn't realize what I was doing during all those years, especially when I was little, but I definitely have developed a skill. I think that is one of the reasons why I have such a high tolerance now.

I keep the reality of my physical condition before me all the time. That way, I can remain at peace with what is going on inside. Nothing is going to take me by surprise to the point where I can't handle it.

I believe in God and I believe that He has created me for some purpose. I am on earth to fulfill that purpose, whatever it may be. I am part of the Kingdom and I have a task to do. If I don't do it, then there will be something missing in the

Kingdom. God is what keeps me going. He's my strength and I know that nothing can overcome me. I know where my heart is and where my priorities lie.

I find that people have some very funny myths about disabled people. For one thing, they think that we are fragile. I find just the opposite, that most disabled people are healthier than the general population. If we neglect our health, then we have nothing to fight back with. We have to have a very strong constitution just to be able to deal with our disability.

The other myth is that disabled people are emotionally fragile, and, therefore, they must be protected from the harsh realities of life. But that doesn't make sense. Disabled people are constantly adjusting on a daily basis to difficulties that many people face only in a crisis. So who are the sheltered people in our society? I'm accustomed to a certain amount of pain and suffering because it's a constant part of my life, but there are times when adjustment and acceptance of that pain seem to be an hourly task. Death is just a normal part of my thinking. None of these things disturb me greatly because I've been adjusting to them every day of my life.

When I cry, people get very upset, and some of them even try to stop me from doing it. What they don't realize is that crying is one of the few ways I have to get rid of physical and emotional tension. Because of my severely limited movement, strenuous exercise is impossible. My only relief is to cry. It serves the same purpose for me as does swimming or running for other people.

The strangest thing about disabled people, no doubt you have found, is that we usually think, feel, and react along the lines of normal people, yet people expect us to react differently. It's funny too because I've never considered myself a disabled person. I hate the word and I am considering haunting the guy who invented the words "handicapped" and "disabled." Normal? What's "normal"? Tell me what's normal. On my scale from 1 to 10, the fact that I have so many disabilities doesn't even fall within the top five slots of what it is to be normal.

A lot of disabled people need to learn their limitations, where and when to expend their energy. We need to discover our capabilities and to identify our priorities. Once you get a firm grip on who you are, then it takes a lot to destroy that image. Your horizons suddenly take on a wider scope, you are open to change, new ideas, and you realize that there is a real joy in being responsible for yourself and in being accountable for your decisions.

by Joan Green, quoted from *Obstacles, Report of the Special Committee on the Disabled and the Handicapped.*

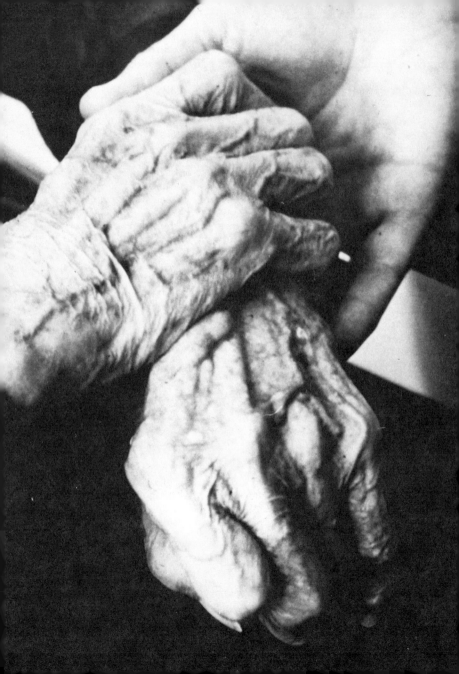

Aging and Eldering

"Eldering" is a new word which has been coined to describe the process of aging, in the senior members of society. The image of elders is a positive one. They are someone to turn to for advice, for their advanced years have provided them with experience and wisdom. The happy task of the health care minister is to help elders to know their wisdom, their self-worth, and to appreciate aging as a time of growth and preparation for the final experience of life, which is death.

Dr. Paul Hiebert, famous as the author of Sara Binks and winner of the Stephen Leacock award for humor, writes in "Reflections at Age 88":

One of the things I am devoutly thankful for is the privilege which has been granted me of being allowed to drift into what we call "old age"...

One of the great advantages of growing old is that one becomes more and more aware of the impermanence of things physical...

What then remains? What then has any abiding value? It is just here that old age makes its assessment. It is just here that one really asks as to the true nature and value which underlies the fleeting existence of the things of this world, and especially the true nature of our own selves which all this time have been clothed within the physical body.

In this search one finds God. God, the context of the true meaning of things.

... There is no doubt that with the clearer vision and understanding of old age we have life more abundantly. For with laying aside of self-interests one also lays aside the self-concern and fears which have beset so much of our lives. Things that worried us in the past, possessions and health for example, are surrendered into God's care.

I admit that this business of growing old is something that I dislike very much, and that, too, must be part of God's therapy. I suffer from aches and pains and impairments from the ankles to the top of the head. Joints, teeth, ears, eyes and various innards all seem to be playing out and perhaps one of the worst aspects of the syndrome is that I cannot remember any words beginning with capital letters.

Names of people and places simply slip beyond recall until later, when they are no longer wanted.

It is all a big nuisance, and yet I cannot but feel that the whole experience is very rewarding. I would never, but never, want to return to the careless but, alas, thoughtless days of my youth. In old age I find treasures that I never knew were there.

taken from *Manitoba Seniors' Journal*, Sept. 1980. 1102 Childs Bldg., Winnipeg, Man. R3B 2A2.

What we find in wisdom.

Whether consciously or unconsciously, willingly or unwillingly, eldering persons struggle to integrate and organize the past events of life into a totality which will justify their existence, the time given to them on earth. Their desire is to finish the script of life with a happy ending.

Reminiscing and narrating, over and over again, the events in life are very often attempts to find meaning and forgiveness, and to allay guilt. The repetition may be mistaken for senility which, in fact, is found in only a small percentage of the population.

Charles Dickens characterizes the process of "life-review" in his story, *A Christmas Carol*. As the three spirits present events in his life to him, Scrooge experiences a dramatic conversion and comes to know his need for forgiveness and reconciliation. There is a little of Scrooge in all of us — the dark side which we would rather not face but which we know is seen by God. Thus, as eldering persons face their encounter with God at the end of life, they may verbalize a need for forgiveness ("I hope my sons' failure wasn't my fault") and reconciliation ("We were young and didn't know better, when we had our differences.") Scrooge's conversion occurred overnight. For most persons there is a more gentle, subtle development through which they grow in wisdom, and come to know the true values and meaning of life.

Ministry to the elderly involves:

- **Listening** and assisting the aging person to know self-worth and the presence of God in the sufferings, trials, failures, and successes of life — in order that death may be faced with a sense of completion.
- Helping the eldering person to find creative ways to relate to God and others, in spite of being house-bound and/or physically handicapped.
- Assuring that physical needs are met.
- Developing an understanding of the social factors which have an impact on his or her well-being, such as, housing, pensions, retirement, institutionalization, care in the home...
- Growth of the health care minister as the result of a relationship with an elder of the Christian community.

"One of the things I am devoutly thankful for is the privilege which has been granted me of being allowed to drift into what we call "old age"...

Reflections at Age 88, by Dr. Paul Hiebert.

Psalms and Prayers

Through prayerful reflection on scripture and related reading, the health care minister will discover those passages and prayers which will best relate to his or her unique ministry. The following were suggested by several chaplains and health care ministers.

Reflection for the Health Care Team

There is a wide variety of gifts but always the same Spirit; there are all sorts of service to be done, but always to the same Lord; working in all sorts of different ways in different people, it is the same God who is working in all of them.

The particular way in which the Spirit is given to each person is for a good purpose. One may have the gift of preaching with wisdom given him by the Spirit; another may have the gift of preaching instruction given him by the same Spirit; and another the gift of faith given by the same Spirit; another again the gift of healing, through this one Spirit; one, the power of miracles; another, prophecy; another the gift of recognizing Spirits; another the gift of tongues and another the gift of interpreting them.

All these are the work of one and the same Spirit, who distributes different gifts to different people just as he chooses.

1 Corinthians 12:4-11

Prayers for Health Care Workers

1 Corinthians 12:4-11

Lord,
Make me an instrument of your health.
Where there is sickness, let me bring cure;
Where there is injury, aid;
Where there is suffering, ease;
Where there is sadness, comfort;
Where there is despair, hope;
Where there is death, acceptance and peace.

Grant that I may not seek so much
to be consoled, as to console;
To be understood, as to understand;
To be honored, as to love...

For it is in giving ourselves that we heal;
It is in listening, that we comfort
And in dying, that we are born to eternal life.

(with some apologies to St. Francis of Assisi... Students of
Masters Chaplaincy Program, St. Paul University, Ottawa)

Prayer in Preparation for a Visit

Lord,
With you is Wisdom, who knows your works,
and was present when you made the world;
who understands what is pleasing in your eyes
and what is conformable to your commands.
Send her forth from your holy heavens,
and from your glorious throne dispatch her,
that she may be with me and work with me,
that I may know your pleasure.
For she knows and understands all things,
and will guide me discreetly in my affairs
and safeguard me by her glory.

based on Wisdom 9:9-11

Prayer Before Surgery

Father, our creator and preserver, you know every fibre of my being. As you created me at birth, so now guide the minds and hands of all those who will operate on me to restore my health, and grant them success. Let my apprehension and that of my relatives dissolve in the precious thought of your ceaseless providence. When I awake from the anaesthetic, may we all have the sense that you are indeed still with us.

The Hospital Prayer Book, J. Massyngberde Ford.

Forgiveness — Sharing in God's Love

It's the truth; it's a fact!
We need only to proclaim it and celebrate it!
We are not to be judged under the law,
    nor are we to be condemned in our law breaking.
When we accept what God
    has done for us through Christ,
    we are delivered completely and forever
    from the guilt of sin.
It is just as if sin never happened.
This is what Christ did for us
    some two thousand years ago.

In the moment that we lay claim
    to God's great gift
    of forgiving love
    it is applicable to us — here and now.
What laws and morals and rules and regulations
    can never do,
    God has done on our behalf...

Every temporal security may crumble.
But God's love and reconciling grace are forever,
    and he will never let us go...

Nothing, absolutely nothing
    can separate us from the love of God...

from *Psalms Now*, Leslie F. Brandt.

The Divine Praises

Blessed be God.
Blessed be his Holy Name.
Blessed be Jesus Christ, true God and true Man.
Blessed be the Name of Jesus
Blessed be his most Sacred Heart.
Blessed be his most Precious Blood.
Blessed be Jesus in the Most Holy Sacrament
    of the Altar.
Blessed be the Holy Spirit, the Paraclete.

Blessed be the great mother of God, Mary most holy.
Blessed be her holy and Immaculate Conception.
Blessed be her glorious Assumption.
Blessed be the name of Mary, Virgin and Mother.
Blessed be St. Joseph, her most chaste spouse.
Blessed be God in his angels and in his Saints.
May the heart of Jesus,
  in the Most Blessed Sacrament,
  be praised, adored,
  and loved with grateful affection,
  at every moment,
  in all the tabernacles of the world,
  even to the end of time.

Prayer of Abandonment

God my Father,
I thank you for all that you are,
And all that you do for me
through your son, Jesus.
In Jesus' name, Father,
I place myself entirely in your care.
I hand over to you myself — my mind,
  memory, will, emotions, body, sexuality.
I hand over to you every person in my life,
  every situation, every relationship, every concern.
I trust you to care for me and others
  in the most loving way.
As I have emptied myself, and handed everything
  over to you, I ask you, Father, to fill me with
  your Holy Spirit and all the gifts and fruits
  of that Spirit.
I ask this through Jesus
Your son and my brother,
In the power of the Holy Spirit. Amen

written by: Brian McNally (Director,
Pastoral Care Dept., Hotel Dieu Hospital,
Kingston, Ont.)
approved: J. L. Wilhelm, D.D. Archbishop of
Kingston, Ontario.

The Power of Prayer

There is no need to worry; but if there is anything you need, pray for it, asking God for it with prayer and thanksgiving; and that peace of God which is so much greater than we can understand will guard your hearts and your thoughts in Christ Jesus.

Philippians 4:6-7

Consolation

Jesus' words to his disciples before his death bring consolation to the dying as well:

Do not let your hearts be troubled.
Trust in God still, and trust in me.
There are many rooms in my Father's house;
if there were not, I should have told you.
I am going now to prepare a place for you,
and after I have gone and prepared you a place,
I shall return to take you with me;
so that where I am
you may be too.

John 14:1-3

Longing for God

God, you are my God, I am seeking you,
my soul is thirsting for you,
my flesh is longing for you,
a land parched, weary and waterless;
I long to gaze on you in the Sanctuary,
and to see your power and glory.

Your love is better than life itself,
my lips will recite your praise;
all my life I will bless you,
in your name lift up my hands;
my soul will feast most richly,
on my lips a song of joy and, in my mouth, praise.

On my bed I think of you,
I meditate on you all night long,
for you have always helped me.

I sing for joy in the shadow of your wings;
my soul clings close to you,
your right hand supports me.

Psalm 63:1-8

Confidence in God

God is our shelter, our strength,
ever ready to help in time of trouble,
so we shall not be afraid
   when the earth gives way,
when mountains tumble
   into the depths of the sea,
and its waters roar and seethe,
the mountains tottering as it heaves.

Come think of Yahweh's marvels,
the astounding things he has done in the world;
all over the world he puts an end to wars,
he breaks the bow, he snaps the spear,
he gives shields to the flames.
"Pause a while and know that I am God..."

Psalm 46:1-3, 8-10

46

Prayer after Recovery

Scriptural Reading:

On his return Jesus was welcomed by the crowd, for they were all there waiting for him. And now there came a man named Jairus, who was an official of the synagogue. He fell at Jesus' feet and pleaded with him to come to his house, because he had an only daughter about twelve years old, who was dying. And the crowds were almost stifling Jesus as he went.

While he was still speaking, someone arrived from the house of the synagogue official to say, "Your daughter has died. Do not trouble the Master any further." But Jesus had heard this, and spoke to the man, "Do not be afraid, only have faith and she will be safe."

When he came to the house he allowed no one to go in with him except Peter and John and James, and the child's father and mother. They were all weeping and mourning for her, but Jesus said, "Stop crying; she is not dead, but asleep." But they laughed at him knowing that she was dead.

But taking her hand, he called to her, "Child, get up." And her spirit returned and she got up at once. Then he told them to give her something to eat. Her parents were astonished, but he ordered them not to tell anyone what had happened.

Luke 8:40-42, 49-56

Prayer

Father, Son and Holy Spirit, I praise and thank you with a heart full of joy because it has pleased you to heal me, even as Jesus healed Jairus' daughter... I am released from spiritual, social and moral isolation. I rejoice in the reunion of our family and friends, and in the prospect of returning to my work and enjoying all the beautiful things your world contains. May I go out of this hospital as a more appreciative and compassionate person. Bless abundantly, either in this world or in the next, all those who have helped me to grow well.

The Hospital Prayer Book, J. Massyngherde Ford.

St. Camillus de Lellis, patron of the sick
and those who care for the sick, pray for us.

47

Resources

This bibliography gives further background for the sections of this booklet. Sections related to the books are indicated by numbers in parentheses. Several of the books contain extensive bibliographies. These are noted by an asterisk.

Henderson, Frank, *Ministries of the Laity*, Canadian Conference of Catholic Bishops, 90 Parent Ave., Ottawa, Canada K1N 7S1 (Section 1).

Peel, Donald, *The Ministry of Listening** — *Team Visiting in Hospital and Home*, 1980, Anglican Book Centre, 600 Jarvis St., Toronto, Ontario M4Y 2J6 (Sections 2, 3, 4, 5, 8).

Vanier, Jean, *Community and Growth*, Griffin House, 461 King St. W., Toronto, Ontario M5V 1K7 (Section 2).

Kennedy, Eugene, *On Becoming a Counselor* — *A Basic Guide for Non-Professional Counselors*, 1977, Seabury Press, 815 2nd Ave., New York, NY 10017 (Sections 3, 5).

Nouwen, Henri J. M., *The Way of the Heart* — *Desert Spirituality and Contemporary Ministry*, 1981, Seabury Press, 815 2nd Ave., New York, NY 10017 (Sections 3, 5).

Fish, Sharon and Shelly, Judith Allen, *Spiritual Care: The Nurses' Role*, 1978, Intervasity Press: Downers Grove, ILL 60515 (Sections 3, 4, 5). Extensive biblical references in notes.

Robinson, Hadden W., *Journal on Grief*, Zondervan Publishing Co., 1415 Lake Drive, S.E., Grand Rapids, MI 49506 (Section 5).

MacNutt, Francis, *Healing*, 1974, Bantam Books/Ave Maria Press, Notre Dame, IN 46556 (Sections 5, 6).

Christian Prayer: The Liturgy of the Hours, 1976, Catholic Book Publishing Company, 257 W. 17th St., New York, NY 10011 (Sections 5, 9).

Kubler-Ross, Elisabeth, *On Death and Dying*, 1969, Macmillan (Section 6).

Canadian Conference of Catholic Bishops, 90 Parent Ave., Ottawa, Canada K1N 7S1, *A Book of Blessings*, 1981 (Section 5).

Canadian Conference of Catholic Bishops, 90 Parent Ave., Ottawa, Canada K1N 7S1, *Pastoral Care of the Sick and Rite of Anointing*, 1974 (Sections 6, 7).

Canadian Conference of Catholic Bishops, 90 Parent Ave., Ottawa, Canada K1N 7S1, *National Bulletin on Liturgy*, "Rites for the Sick and the Dying", No. 57, Jan.-Feb. 1977 (Sections 4, 6).

Ontario Conference of Catholic Bishops, 67 Bond St., Toronto, Ontario M5B 1X5, *One in Jesus Christ* — *A Pastoral Statement about Handicapped Persons among Us*, 1980 (Section 7).

House of Commons, Ottawa, Canada, *Obstacles, Report of the Special Committee on the Disabled and the Handicapped*, 1981 (Section 7).

Nouwen, Henri J. M. and Gaffney, Walter J., *Aging* — *the Fulfillment of Life*, 1976, Image Books, A Division of Doubleday & Co. Inc., 501 Franklin Ave., Garden City, NY 11530 (Section 8).

Green, Edward and Simmons, Henry, C.P., Ph.D., "Toward an Understanding of Religious Needs in Aging Persons", *C.H.A.C. Review*, March-April 1978, Journal of the Catholic Health Association of Canada, 312 Daly Ave., Ottawa, Canada K1N 6G7 (Section 8).

Brandt, Leslie F., with artwork by Kent, Corita, *Epistles Now*, 1974, Concordia Publishing House, 3558 S. Jefferson Ave., St. Louis, MO 63118 (Section 9).

Brandt, Leslie F., with artwork by Kent, Corita, *Psalms Now*, 1973, Concordia Publishing House, 3558 S. Jefferson Ave., St. Louis, MO 63118 (Section 9).

The Jerusalem Bible — *Reader's Edition*, 1968, Doubleday & Inc., 501 Franklin Ave., Garden City, NY 11530 (Section 9).

Ford, J. Massyngberde, *The Hospital Prayer Book*, 1975, The Paulist Press, 545 Island Rd., Ramsey, NJ 07446 (Section 9).

Powell, John, S.J., *He Touched Me, My Pilgrimage of Prayer*, 1974, Argus Communications, One DLM Park, Box 5000, Allen, TX 75002 (Section 9).

Wilkes, James, *The Gift of Courage*, 1979, The Anglican Book Centre, 600 Jarvis St., Toronto, Ontario M4Y 2J6 (Section 9).

HEALTH CARE MINISTERS

Written by:

Nancy McGee,
Catholic Health Association of Canada

Edited by:

Jerome Herauf

Layout:

Jan Gough, Gilles Lépine

Photography:

Cover: *Joyce Harpell;*
p. 2: Mia et Klaus;
p. 8: Jonas Abromaitis;
p. 11, 12, 15, 16, 20, 23, 25, 28, Joyce Harpell;
p. 31: Canadian Government Travel Bureau;
p. 35: Novalis;
p. 38: G. Savoie;
p. 44: Victor Charbonneau;
p. 46: Pierre Coulombe.

Illustrations:

Cover 1, cover 4, and inside illustration:
Lee Thirlwall

"God did not come to suppress suffering,
not even to explain it
but to fill it with his Presence."

Saint Thomas More

Winston Press
430 Oak Grove
Minneapolis, Minnesota 55403

ISBN: 0-86683-739-6

Parish Prayer Groups

New Parish Ministries

WINSTON PRESS

Contents

New Parish Ministries *was originally published by Novalis, Saint Paul University, Ottawa, Canada. This edition is published by Winston Press, Inc., by arrangement with Novalis, Saint Paul University. Copyright © 1982, Novalis. Copyright © 1983, Winston Press. All rights reserved. No part of this book may be reproduced in any form without written permission from the publisher.*

ISBN: 0-86683-740-X (previously ISBN: 2-89088-087-7)

Printed in Canada

5   4   3   2   1

Winston Press, Inc., 430 Oak Grove, Minneapolis, MN 55403

A Simple Reality, but Filled with Mystery

A parish prayer group is a very simple thing. It is just a group of people who regularly come together to pray in the context of a parish. But at the same time it is very important to recognize that this simple reality is filled with mystery. Where two or three, or two or three hundred, or thousands, are gathered in his Name, Jesus is among them (Mt. 18:20). The setting of the group may be very prosaic, but those who take part come together as members of the Body of Christ, and his Spirit dwells in them as in a temple (1 Cor. 3:16; 12:27). And as they pray, they can be sure that the Spirit himself prays with them so that they can proclaim Jesus Christ as Lord, to the glory of God the Father (Rom. 8:26; Phil. 2:11).

Editor's Note:

Although the following pages are written primarily from the author's experience within charismatic prayer groups, we feel certain that many, if not all, of the insights shared here are applicable to any form of Parish Prayer Group.

Part of the mystery of the Church

The mystery found in every prayer group is, then, very closely identified with that of the whole Church, of which Vatican II reminded us. There have always been groups of people coming together in the Church to pray; indeed, this has been one of the basic manifestations of the life of the Church. The early Christians gathered on the Lord's Day, as we do now, to adore God and to celebrate in the Eucharist the mystery of Christ's death and resurrection. Prayer in common has always marked the monastic and religious life. Many other groups too — sodalities, confraternities and so on — have flourished for centuries, with prayer together as their whole purpose or one of their principal features. And now, in recent years, we have seen the growth and spread of many new prayer groups throughout the Church. We have to see this as one of God's great gifts to his Church today — for which we praise and magnify his Name.

Praise and evangelization

At the root of this whole development is a profound spiritual insight: the bringing together –- in practice — of praise and evangelization, the spreading of the Good News. The Gospel, the Good News, is that God has chosen us as his adopted children through Jesus Christ "to make us praise the glory of his grace" (Eph. 1:5). A prayer group, therefore, gathers to praise God; and, in doing this, it becomes a powerful instrument of evangelization.

People may have various reasons for coming to a prayer group. They may come seeking love and communion. They may have some deep pain, some healing they need. They may have a concern for someone they want to pray for. But, as they go on, they discover praise and find that this brings them to know the Lord and his Good News more deeply and personally than ever before. Thus the strength of any group at any stage in its development can be discerned in relation to the level of praise found in its meetings and in the effectiveness of its evangelization.

Times when discernment is needed

In the development of a prayer group there are three moments when such discernment is most needed. The *first* is when the group is just beginning. There are so many questions then, so many doubts and uncertainties. The *second* is when troubles come, when an established group runs into the doldrums or loses its leaders or experiences divisions. In both of these moments it is easy to recognize the need for help, but not always easy to know where to find it. The *third* moment is not so easily recognized: It is the moment of

3

prosperity, the time when the prayer group is flourishing.

The group is growing in numbers and in depth of experience; the love of the Lord is manifest and is being shared in an ever-stronger sense of community.

It is easy, then, not to see the need for discernment; yet it is especially needed then, for the Lord is leading the group along new ways, to heights unknown to them before. At all these times, therefore, a prayer group and its leaders need the best advice they can get.

Guided by the Spirit

At whatever stage it may be, a prayer group looking for discernment has to seek it from the Holy Spirit. The Spirit may speak in a variety of ways: through the voice of the teaching authority in the Church, through the experience of other groups, through a prophetic word of one in the group or a common discernment of many. But always his advice is there when it is needed. It is there in a special way in Scripture.

When I was asked to write this booklet I prayed for a text from God's Word. The one I was given was from the Epistle of Jude (20-21):

But you, beloved, build yourselves up on your most holy faith; pray in the Holy Spirit; keep yourselves in the love of God, wait for the mercy of our Lord Jesus Christ unto eternal life.

This seems to me to contain the best general advice to prayer groups at any stage in their development. Let us, therefore, listen to this advice of the Holy Spirit.

"But you, Beloved"

The Christian life is a life of intimacy with God. Certainly, anyone who joins a prayer group should find himself or herself in a relationship with God and with others, that is filled with love. God has first loved us (I Jn. 4:10). He calls us his "beloved." It is in that love that we must live if we are to know him, for "love is of God, and he who loves is born of God and knows God" (I Jn. 4:7). Whether a group is beginning, struggling or flourishing, always the first thing to be recognized is the love of God. We must praise him for his love, and work to respond to it more perfectly.

In this we can take the example of Mary and join with her in praise. Mary was the "highly favoured" one (Lk. 1:28), made holy by God's grace from the very beginning of her life, but she knew herself only as the lowly handmaid of the Lord, ready to receive his Word (Lk. 1:38). We can see her, in the Gospel, as the first to receive the Holy Spirit when he came upon her in a new way so that she could bring Jesus into the world. At once, then, she went off to see her cousin Elizabeth, and together they held a prayer meeting to share the great things God was doing for them and to give him praise (see Lk. 1:46-55). At Pentecost, too, Mary joined the disciples in prayer for the coming of the Holy Spirit; with them she received him and sang out the wonderful works of God.

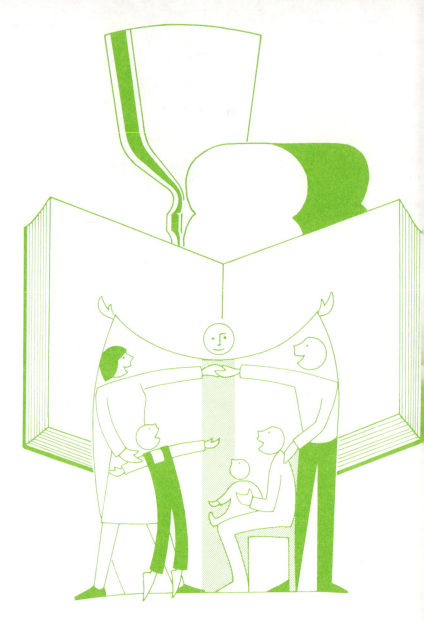

8

"Build Yourselves Up on Your Most Holy Faith"

"Rooted and grounded in love," therefore (Eph. 3:17), we can begin to build ourselves up on our most holy faith. What does this mean? Well, the basic thing it means (in the experience of all of the prayer groups I have known) is to submit completely to Jesus as Lord.

Jesus Christ is Lord. We already believe that. Our common way of speaking of Jesus has been to call him, "Our Lord." That Jesus is Lord is the first teaching of our faith. At Pentecost, when the Holy Spirit had come and the crowd gathered wondering what was going on, Peter summed it up by telling them, "God has made this Jesus, whom you crucified, both Lord and Christ" (Acts 2:36). If, therefore, we really believe that Jesus Christ is Lord we have to submit our whole life to him. He is not just Lord in a general sort of way; he is our Lord — my Lord and your Lord. He must be Lord of our prayer groups.

A good test as to whether this is truly so is whether we accept his whole plan of salvation. Jesus has called us to follow him in his Church, as members of his Body. In the Church we find teaching and pastoral care that we must accept. There we receive the life Jesus gives in the Sacraments. And in the Church we are given the Word of God in Scripture.

How is this to be applied in the moments when our prayer groups need advice? *Whether we are beginning or struggling or flourishing, we need to look to the ways we are being built up on our most holy faith.*

Our Place in the Church

For most of us, the parish is the place where the Lord has called us to live and grow. There we are taught and cared for; there we receive the Sacraments; there we hear God's Word. There our prayer group should find its home. We must not let our group be, or even appear to be, alien to the parish.

This can happen *at the beginning of a group*. Often the first step toward the founding of a group occurs when some people become involved in a prayer group somewhere else than in their own parish. In itself this is a wonderful thing for them. They find the Lord in a new way, are filled with his Spirit, inspired by his Word and learn to pray deeply. But it can, in effect, become their whole life. They can become almost invisible in their own parish. Then they decide, under the guidance of the Spirit, that they should start a parish prayer group, and they are astonished and dismayed when the pastor is not enthusiastic. But why should he be? He knows, or should know, that a prayer group is a serious undertaking: Other people will become involved and he, himself, will have new responsibilities and concerns. Why should he be eager to plunge into such a thing with people he hardly knows? This does not mean that the Holy Spirit is not leading these people toward the founding of a parish prayer group.

But it may well mean that in order to be faithful to him they must first undertake to enter more fully into the life of the parish. This can be done in various ways, and the Lord will show them how to do it. Then, when the idea of the prayer group comes up, it will be seen not as an importation from outside but as a fruit of the Spirit's life within the parish.

Again, *when a prayer group has been going for a time and begins to run into difficulties*, one of the areas to be examined is its relation to the parish. Has the group come to be seen as the private concern of a few? Has it lost its place? One good way to avoid this is to make sure that the group regularly praises God for and intercedes for the parish. The Lord gives many gifts to any parish, and any parish has many needs to be submitted to his mercy. A parish prayer group should be a focus of praise and thanks for the gifts, and a constant centre of intercession for the needs. If a group is not serving this function, it is no wonder that it is having troubles.

And *when a group is prospering*, when new people are coming to it all the time and its experience is deepening, then, too, it is good to look at its relation to the parish. Probably there are a good many people coming in from other parishes. That is a good thing, for which God should be praised. But it may then raise the question of their relation to their own parish. Perhaps the group should en-

courage them to try to form their own parish group; certainly it should try to support them in entering vigorously into their own parish life.

Teaching and Pastoral Care

The Church is not some outside organization imposing rules on us. It is the People of God into whom we are born, the Body of Christ of which we are members.

In this body the Spirit gives different gifts to the different members, and different responsibilities. To some, particularly the Pope and bishops and those with whom they share it, he gives the gift and charge of teaching and pastoring in the Church. *All of us need to accept that teaching and pastoral authority.* In a parish prayer group, especially, this means that we accept the authority of the pastor of the parish under the broader authority of the bishop so that this may be exercised in appropriate ways.

One of the distinctive and precious features of the prayer groups which have developed in recent years has been the role of lay leaders of prayer. The priest, whether he be the pastor of the parish or not, should be careful not to usurp this role. The lay leadership is essential to the experience of the prayer group as a group. This does not mean that the priest should be a passive spectator or should leave the group to its own devices; his role is also essential as teacher and shepherd.

When a prayer group is beginning, the priest is often as new to the experience as anyone there, or even newer. He has to be aware of this and not try to impose restrictions on the action of the Holy Spirit in the group. Many priests have found it an excellent idea to spend some time with an established group elsewhere in order to learn. This may not be possible; the priest may just have to grow with the group. In that case he should have confidence in the leaders (that is one reason why it helps a lot if he knows them well) and work closely with them. And he should not hesitate to teach and encourage. In particular, it is good for him to teach from Scripture, and to do this in a personal way. If the people coming to the group see that the priest meditates on the Word of God in his own life and is willing to share this, they will be encouraged to do the same. The priest will find himself reading and studying and praying more in order to help them.

When an established group has difficulties (and there are always some), the role of the priest can be crucial. *A relationship of mutual trust and love between him and the group leaders is most important.* If this does not exist, the priest will be caught in the position of becoming a focus for discontent. People will come to him with complaints about the leaders and he will not know how to respond. The leaders will feel betrayed. But if the priest and the leaders work at building up their mutual confidence and love — which takes time and prayer and openness — then the priest will be able to defuse complaints or to bring them up as suggestions.

When a group is doing really well, the priest's role will become more that of spiritual director. People will come to him for guidance along the new ways of prayer and contemplation on which the Lord is leading them. He will be able to bring to them his own acquaintance with the spiritual classics and the experience of the saints. He will find himself growing also, able to give sound guidance and to find new inspiration.

Living Sacramentally

For Catholics, one of the joys of the experience of the prayer group should be a growing awareness of the meaning of the Sacraments in their lives.

United in the Body of Christ, we live with his life by the Sacraments. In Baptism we are plunged into his death so as to rise with him to new life — the life of grace — expressed in faith, hope and love, given and sustained by the presence of the Holy Spirit within us. This life is nourished and strengthened by the Eucharist, restored and renewed by the Sacrament of Reconciliation, brought to bear on the central needs and crucial times of our lives in the other Sacraments. The more we recognize Jesus as Lord, the more the Sacraments will mean to us, and the more we shall give him praise and glory for his marvelous gifts.

In the context of the Sacraments, the prayer meeting should be seen as an informal Liturgy of the Word. We come together in the Lord's presence to worship and praise him and to submit ourselves to his Word. We should do so freely and joyfully. The meeting should be ordered in such a way as to facilitate this freedom and joy.

This can be helped by *beginning with a song or two of praise and one to the Holy Spirit. A good music* ministry can help lift a group up and lead it into prayer. That is what is important here; not to demonstrate high musical skill — although that can be a great gift to be offered to God — but to make our song our prayer and to try to have everyone feel free to join in. Our notes may quaver, but God will listen to the song in our hearts.

Sometimes people find it hard to be really free in prayer because they feel that they are not good enough to be heard by God. This, of course, is quite contrary to the life and teaching of Jesus, who came not to call the virtuous but sinners (Mt. 9:13). It can be helpful, therefore, either at the beginning of a meeting or later, perhaps in response to a reading, for us to *admit our sinfulness and to pray together the prayer which Jesus said would be heard: "Lord, be merciful to me, a sinner"* (Lk.18:13).

Then the leader, usually with a passage from Scripture, should call the group to praise and thank God for his merciful love. *Throughout the meeting there should be praise, which again can be helped by song, the reading of passages from the Word of God, the sharing of experiences in which God's love can be seen, intercessory prayer for the needs of individuals, the parish, the Church and the whole world, and sometimes there should be specific teaching.* All of this should be structured by the leader only to the degree needed to help people to feel free. Thus many groups find it advantageous to set aside a time near the end of the meeting for intercessory prayer so that people, knowing this is coming, will be able to set aside their concerns in the earlier part of the meeting and praise God in freedom and joy. Teachings may be planned beforehand or may arise out of something which comes up in the meeting. Anyone who teaches should be careful to work with the leaders to see that what is said fits the needs of the group.

A prayer meeting is not a television program; a period of silence is not necessarily a bad thing. The leader must learn to distinguish two types of silence: the silence of embarrassment, when people need encouragement to enter more into shared prayer, and the silence of communion, which should be cherished. Sometimes the leader should call for a period of silence, a time of love and of listening, asking people to be quiet until a signal is given.

One element of structure which may seem limiting, but which really contributes to freedom is to have a firm closing time for the meeting. Few things take away people's sense of joy and freedom more thoroughly than a gnawing fear of missing the last bus home. The leader must be firm about this.

In some groups this informal Liturgy of the Word is taken as indeed the first part of the Eucharist and is completed by the offering of the gifts and the whole Eucharistic Prayer. In many groups the celebration of eucharistic liturgy immediately before or after the meeting provides one of the principal links with the life of the parish. Special liturgies can also be helpful.

The Sacrament of Reconciliation is another way in which the grace of Christ can be brought to us to make us strong. As people grow in prayer and become more aware of the presence of the Lord in their lives they also become more aware of their own sinfulness. They begin to recognize sin in ways of acting and thinking which they had previously just taken for granted. This is a grace from the Lord which calls for the use of the Sacrament in which the forgiveness Jesus has won for us is given and celebrated.

And the prayer group can benefit from the *Sacrament of the Sick*. There is much healing to be found simply in prayer for one another in the group, but when this can be focused and united expressly with the healing action of Jesus in the Sacrament it can have new power. Many groups hold regular or occasional Healing Masses. These usually include special provision for persons, desiring prayer, to meet with prayer teams after the end of the Mass. The use of the Sacrament in this circumstance can also be very helpful.

Scripture is the Word God has spoken to his people. In the Church we receive and live and develop the revelation given there. Here is a special opportunity for the work of evangelization in a prayer group. Many Catholics lack a true awareness of the place of Scripture in their lives. They have heard it read at Mass, but often have failed to hear it as a personal Word spoken to them. And this is what we need to do.

In our prayer group, we need to let God speak to us in Scripture, taking the Bible in hand and reading it prayerfully, and we need to share it with one another. At whatever stage of development our group may be, God's Word will speak to us and feed our prayer.

When a group is just getting underway, there can be a difficulty arising from the fact that perhaps most of the people involved are not accustomed to a regular reading of Scripture, or are shy about sharing it. One of the best helps, then and always, is for the leader to come ready to begin the meeting with a text that has struck him or her and on which he or she has prayed during the week. The priest and others also have such texts but be alert not to use them if others begin to share. It can also be helpful to encourage everyone to try to follow the readings used in the Eucharist each day. When people do that, they will often find someone else sharing a text that has struck them, and this will encourage them.

When a group is in the doldrums, some of the first questions that should be asked are about the use of Scripture. Look around the group; how many have their Bibles with them? How many have been reading and listening to God's Word on their own during the week? There is a natural tendency for us all to coast now and then. But if most of the group are regularly coming just to listen to others, the few who are sharing will gradually become weary and the sharing will begin to droop. The members need to be challenged and encouraged.

Another problem can come *when some in a group adopt a false or inadequate approach to Scripture.* This can generally be spotted by one or more of three tendencies: People will take texts in isolation from their context and from the rest of Scripture, they will ignore the teaching of the Church, or they will use Scripture to justify themselves and to condemn others. When this begins to appear, the leaders and the priest need to exercise patience and love with firmness. An incident or two may be let go. If a pattern begins to emerge, the person should be talked to privately. Usually he or she will be glad of instruction.

If the problem is more widespread, it may be a good idea to make special efforts to be sure that good teaching about Scripture is made available in reading, tapes or a lecture series. As a last resort some may have to be asked not to share at the meeting, or even not to attend. This can be very difficult and may severely test the union in prayer and love and trust of the priest and the leaders. But it is very important for the group to be able to hold on to the full truth of God's Word spoken to his Church.

When everything seems to be going well, one danger to be looked for is a tendency to draw from Scripture only the comforting words. It can be important then for the leader to meditate on the Sermon on the Mount (Mt. 5-7) and to call the others to hear the Lord's challenges. The whole message of Scripture must include the challenging and even the condemning words as well as the consoling ones. Only by listening to the Lord with open hearts can we submit to him and be built up on our most holy faith.

In our prayer group
we need to let God speak to us in Scripture,
taking the Bible in hand
and reading it prayerfully,
and we need to share it with one another.

"Pray in the Holy Spirit"

All true prayer is prayer in the Holy Spirit. "No one," Paul tells us (I Cor. 12:3), "can say, 'Jesus is Lord', unless he is under the influence of the Holy Spirit." So we cannot bring our adoration, praise, thanksgiving or petitions to the Lord except in the Holy Spirit. To be open to the Spirit should be characteristic of a prayer group.

The Spirit as Gift

The Holy Spirit is the Gift of Love that the Father gives to the Son and the Son to the Father. He is the perfect Gift that the Father and Jesus give to the Church and to each member of Christ's Body. He is sent to dwell in our hearts.

God, of course, is present always and everywhere. He comes to be present in us in a new way, however, when we come to know him and love him. This is the work of the Spirit. He lives in us by grace, and in him we have faith and hope and love. He gives us new capabilities, draws us into new relations and leads us to new achievements.

New Capabilities: The Seven Personal Gifts

The Prophet Isaiah (11:2-3), looking forward to a new king for Judah and through him to the coming of Jesus, prophesied: "The Spirit of the Lord shall rest upon him, the spirit of wisdom and under-standing, the spirit of counsel and might, the spirit of knowledge and the fear of the Lord. And his delight shall be in the fear of the Lord." From this text has come the traditional teaching on the seven gifts of the Spirit.

21

These seven gifts — wisdom, understanding, counsel, fortitude, knowledge, piety and fear of the Lord — are needed by all. They are given to us in Baptism as seven ways the Spirit strengthens us to live the life of grace, or seven sails to catch the wind of the Spirit. It is our common experience, however, that if they are left unused, our sails become tattered and torn.

One of the great experiences in the beginning of our involvement in a prayer group is the way in which the Spirit, already in us by Baptism but to some degree bound by our sinfulness, is released in us. His gifts take on new power. By the fear of the Lord we come to know our own sinfulness in the presence of God's love. By the gift of piety we are enabled to cry out, "Abba, Father." By the gift of under-standing we hear God's Word speaking to us in new ways. Each of the gifts manifests the presence of the Spirit.

God can release his Spirit as he wills. He does it whenever we are open to him. This can happen quite independently of a prayer meeting — as when someone is praying alone or is on a retreat — but one of the values of any prayer group should be that it helps us to be more open to the action of the Holy Spirit. In charismatic groups a special period of shared prayer and shared experience known as the Life in the Spirit Seminar is devoted to this. The heart of the Seminar is in the session in which the participants commit themselves to the Lord and are prayed over individually that the Holy Spirit may come to them in a new way.

New Relations: the Community Gifts

In the life Jesus gives to us in the Holy Spirit we are formed into the new People of God, into his Body. Each member thus takes on new relations to all the others and receives appropriate gifts. These community gifts, therefore, are different from the strengths we all need; these are given, some to one and some to another, so that the whole Body, and each particular section of it such as a parish, a prayer group, a family, may grow in love.

These charisms, as they are called from the Greek word for gift, may take any form that the Spirit chooses and which the Body needs. St. Paul always speaks of them in relation to the Body (Rom. 12:3-8; I Cor. 12:4-11, 27-30; Eph. 4:11-16). Some gifts are special, as for example, prophecy, healing, tongues; others are more ordinary, such as teaching or administration. But all are directed to the common good.

Among these gifts one of the most common in charismatic prayer groups is that of praying in tongues. Speaking in tongues, which requires interpretation, is much less frequently found. This is by no means the most important gift. St. Paul always puts it in last place although he explicitly says that it should not be suppressed, and that he would like everyone to have it (I Cor 14:5, 39). It is a gift which can teach us much. When we pray in tongues it is not that we are speaking some foreign language (although this may sometimes be the case), but that we let the Holy Spirit guide our prayer and especially our praise.

When we begin to praise God and thank him for all his gifts, our hearts are overflowing but our words are inadequate. Then, "when we cannot choose words in order to pray properly, the Spirit himself expresses our plea in a way that could never be put into words and God who knows everything in our hearts knows perfectly well what he means, and that the pleas of the saints expressed by the Spirit are according to the mind of God" (Rom 8:26-27).

When our group is struggling, then, we should look at our openness to the Spirit. Are we letting him guide our prayer? Are we accepting and using all the gifts he gives for the service of the whole? Sometimes we diminish our expectations; when we pray, we do not really expect the Lord to do great things for us (cf. Lk. 1:49). Sometimes we rest in the gifts already given, as if the Spirit could do no more. We always need to open ourselves more to this action.

New Achievements: The Fruit of the Spirit

Jesus tells us, "You will know them by their fruits. Are grapes gathered from thorns, or figs from thistles?" (Mt. 7:16). And Paul describes for us the fruit of the Spirit: "Love, joy, peace, patience, kindness, goodness, trustfulness, gentleness and self-control" (Gal. 5:22). This fruit is experienced when the gifts of the Spirit are lived and shared so that the Body of Christ is built up.

An example of the ways in which the fruit of the Spirit can be seen in a prayer meeting is the way the praise, readings, sharings and petitions will flow together and reinforce one another. A theme will develop, unplanned and unguided by the leader, that leads people to pray together profoundly. This is clearly an action of the Spirit, using the willingness of all to share their gifts. It is one of the ways the Spirit builds up a true community in the prayer group.

True community is always open to the needs of others. A prayer group is not a special-action group and should not try to be; but it must support and encourage the prayer of its members in becoming concrete action beyond the group.

The prayer meeting should not be seen just as a sort of refuge from the pressures of the world where we can find love and joy and peace — although that can be very important sometimes — but rather as a source from which the love and joy and peace the Spirit gives can be taken out and shared generously with others.

"The love of God," St. Paul tells us (Rom. 5:5), "has been poured into our hearts by the Holy Spirit which is given us." And in the Gospel according to John, Jesus tells us that the love he wants to give to one another is the very same as that which the Father has given to the Son from all eternity and which Jesus himself, Son of God become man, has given to us (Jn. 15:9-12; 17:24-26). It is in sharing this love that we can be one as Jesus and his Father are One (Jn. 17:21-23); by it we remain in him and his words remain in us, so that we can ask what we will and the Father will give it to us (Jn. 15:7, 16).

A prayer group, therefore, must be a place in which the love of God is lived and shared. The efficacy of our prayer depends on this, and it is central at every stage.

At the beginning of a group there is a temptation to concentrate on techniques and procedures. This is a mistake. It is much better to concentrate on the love God has given to us and on sharing it with profound respect for one another (Rom. 12:10). The time when the group is small is a precious time for deepening our relationship in the Lord.

And later, if a time comes when our group seems to be floundering about with little sense of direction, we should look at the way we share Christ's love. How do we welcome newcomers? Has our love become a private thing shared only with a small in-group? Are we divided by controversy or ambition? We need to look again at the generous and forgiving love of Jesus and let him speak to us.

This can be very important too *when everything seems to be going well.* It is good then to look at how we tend to regard those outside the group, those who, perhaps, oppose it. Do we really love them as Jesus taught us to do? Or do we tend to judge them as he taught us not to do? When the evil one cannot prevent the growth of communion in Christ's love he will try to distort it, so we have to be especially careful when growth is manifest.

There is a special need for mutual love among the leaders of the group. The structures of groups may vary greatly and the names given to them do not always have the same meaning: "pastoral team," "service team," "core group," "group of elders": terms such as these sometimes have distinct meanings, sometimes are used vaguely and almost identically.

A group of twenty members does not need the same structures as one of two hundred. Each group should find its own pattern. But two things are necessary: responsibility should be shared so that no one person makes decisions for the group, and those who share the leadership must make great efforts to do so in love. There will be differences of opinion and this is fine; one reason for having more than one person is precisely to have a variety of opinions. But what is needed is true discernment in the Lord, and that springs from love and from prayer.

"Wait for the Mercy of Our Lord
Jesus Christ unto Eternal Life"

When Jesus speaks about prayer he tells us to have confidence (Mk. 11:24), to agree together (Mt. 18:19) to remain in him and let his words remain in us (Jn. 15:7), to forgive (Mt. 6:14-15), and as the best sign and evidence of all this he tells us to persevere (Lk. 11:8; 18:5). He invites us to pester him, to ask and seek and knock, and to keep at it.

Perseverance is very much needed at the start of a group. Indeed, it is the essential thing. If two people are willing to commit themselves in God's love to meet together for prayer, then the prayer group exists and God will bless it. It is a common experience that some people will come to a new prayer group with great enthusiasm but then soon drop away (cf. Lk. 8:13). Unless there is a committed nucleus, ready to persevere, the whole thing will fade, but if there are those who will hold fast, then they will bear the fruit of the Spirit in their perseverance (Lk. 8:15).

One of the moments when perseverance is most needed is when the leadership of the group changes. It is healthy to make such a change from time to time, but it is not always easy. In religious communities it has long been found wise to have definite terms for superiors; something like that could be valuable in relation to leadership in prayer groups as well. But more important than any

structure is the submission of leaders to the discernment of the group. In this discernment the pastor or the priest who is spiritual director should take part and his voice should be given great respect.

Jesus made it very clear that anyone who is to be a leader among his disciples must be the least of all and the servant of all (Mk. 10:43-44). No one should feel that he or she has a right to leadership, not even those who founded a group. If those who are committed to the group submit themselves to the Lord and to the guidance of the Spirit, they will be able to discern who should be leaders and make changes if these are needed. Commitment and submission are essential.

And there is a special challenge to perseverance when a group is going along very well. Those who have been with the group for a while have gained experience in prayer and in the ways of the Holy Spirit and the exercise of his gifts. But they can find themselves growing impatient with others in the group, newcomers or wounded members, and be tempted to pull away. It is true that the needs of the experienced members are quite different from those of beginners. Spiritual direction is especially valuable for them. They may have a developing desire for closer community and a deeper

teaching. The development of a special program for this core group may become a necessity at this stage. But it is also important for the experienced members to maintain their place in the whole group in such a way as to fulfill the commandment of Jesus to love one another as he has loved us.

Praise and thanks to God

There are many more things that could be said about parish prayer groups. This little booklet cannot pretend to cover everything. Many practical points will be found dealt with in the books listed in the short list that follows. What remains now is to give praise and thanks to God for all he is doing in our prayer groups.

Truly Father, we praise and thank you. You have called us together in many new groups to magnify your Name, as Mary rejoiced to do when she met with Elizabeth. By the power of your Spirit you have taught us to pray, to lift up our hands, our voices, our minds and hearts in praise. You have spoken your Word to us and through us. You have enabled us to know Jesus Christ, your Son, as our Lord and to proclaim him to your glory. Alleluia, Father, we thank you in the Holy Spirit through Christ our Lord. Amen.

Praise the Lord, all nations,
extol him, all peoples!
For his love is strong,
his faithfulness will last forever.

Psalm 117

Resources

There is a considerable and a growing literature relating to prayer groups and the charismatic renewal. Here I can only suggest a few items.

The Canadian Bishops have made two significant statements in this area. Their Pastoral Message of Pentecost, 1978, entitled *Fullness of Life: Basic Elements of a Christian Spirituality*, offered "Guidelines for the different prayer groups to which many Christians belong." Earlier, their Message of April, 1975, *Charismatic Renewal*, gave a balanced pastoral encouragement to this movement.

For the use of Scripture the best first guide is *Reading Scripture as the Word of God*, by George Martin (Word of Life, Ann Arbor, © 1975). For practical advice in many areas I have found the collection of essays in *Prayer Group Workshop*, edited by Bert Ghezzi and John Blattner (Servant Books, Ann Arbor, © 1979), to be most useful.

For the Life in the Spirit Seminars, especially for those involved in charismatic prayer, there is the *Team Manual*,

Catholic Edition (Servant Books, Ann Arbor, 1979) and the little guidebook, *Finding New Life in the Spirit* (Servant Publications, South Bend). I have written some notes on prayer to accompany this, entitled *Come, Spirit, Come* (Basilian Press, Toronto, 1981). Another approach to this may be found in *You Will Receive Power: A Holy Spirit Seminar* — Eight Sessions of Catholic Teaching, Leader's Guide and Participant's Guide, by Sr. Philip Marie Burle, C.PP.S. and Sr. Sharon Ann Plankenhorn, C.PP.S., (Dove Publications, Pecos, New Mexico, 1977).

Cardinal Suenens and Dom Helder Camara have treated the relation of prayer groups and social action in *Charismatic Renewal and Social Action: A Dialogue* (Servant Books, Ann Arbor, © 1979). This is the third in the series of Malines Documents issued by Cardinal Suenens. The first was *Theological and Pastoral Orientations on the Catholic Charismatic Renewal* (Word of Life, Notre Dame, © 1974) and the second was *Ecumenism and Charismatic Renewal: Theological and Pastoral Orientations* (Servant Books, Ann Arbor, © 1978).

PARISH PRAYER GROUPS
Written by:

James Hanrahan, CSB,
president of St. Thomas More College,
Saskatoon, Saskatchewan

Edited by:

Jerome Herauf

Layout:

Jan Gough, Gilles Lépine

Photography:

Cover: Sheila Sturley, RSCJ;

P. 2: Carmen Roy; p. 6: Ellefsen;

p. 18, 32: Mia and Klaus

p. 26: Ellefsen.

Illustrations:

Cover 1 and cover 4, inside illustrations:
Lee Thirlwall

*"Build yourselves up on
your most holy faith :
Pray in the Holy Spirit."*

(Jude 20 adapted)

Winston Press
430 Oak Grove
Minneapolis, Minnesota 55403

ISBN: 0-86683-740-X

Parish Council

New Parish Ministries

WINSTON PRESS

Contents

New Parish Ministries was originally published by Novalis, Saint Paul University, Ottawa, Canada. This edition is published by Winston Press, Inc., by arrangement with Novalis, Saint Paul University. Copyright © 1982, Novalis. Copyright © 1983, Winston Press. All rights reserved. No part of this book may be reproduced in any form without written permission from the publisher.

ISBN: 0-86683-741-8 (previously ISBN: 2-89088-088-5)

Printed in Canada

5 4 3 2 1

Winston Press, Inc., 430 Oak Grove, Minneapolis, MN 55403

Introduction

So you've heard murmurings about something called a "parish council" which is going to appear in your parish? Or perhaps you're already faced with one, and you're puzzled? You've probably heard a story that sounds like one of the following... or maybe you've already lived through the experience yourself, and want to explore it a bit further:

"The Parish Council at St. Miriam's has really helped the parish. The pastor encourages people to think about some of the problems the parish is having, and present ideas to help solve them. Things seem to be a lot friendlier in the last couple of years."

"Well, did you hear about the situation at St. Mary's? My friend Trish is on the Parish Council there, and the pastor presents all the ideas, and if anyone disagrees, or has another idea, they don't have a chance of a hearing. What Father says goes. It's just like it always was."

"At Holy Family, we've got another problem. Seems that a lot of parishioners feel that the only people running the Parish Council are these "modern" Catholics who like everything new. The rest of us don't have a chance."

"Our parish doesn't have a Parish Council. What's it about? How does it happen?"

Sound familiar? Can you put different names, faces, or places into the situations? Has the appearance of a Parish Council in your parish puzzled you? Where did it come from? Why? How did these people — or yourself — get picked? or nominated? or appointed? What sort of responsibility goes with the job? What does being part of a Parish Council mean?

It seems that our present situation is critical for whatever will happen in the future. We have collected a certain number of experiences of "Parish Council" since the vision of Vatican II first encouraged this mode of lay participation in the life of the community. Some of these experiences were highly successful; others were total flops.

1

It would be impossible in a booklet like this to analyze each situation in order to find out what went wrong — or what worked. But one of the suspicions we have had, when things have gone wrong, is that maybe we have gone about "it" in the wrong way in the beginning. We became very preoccupied with committees, reports, elections and all sorts of administrative details, and we allowed the key dimension of building the Christian community to fade from our range of vision. Then some important questions began to emerge: Why did we seem to be repeating the same reports, meeting after meeting? What was wrong, that we couldn't quite put our finger on?

Parish Council As Ministry

The task of building up the Christian community must remain our constant measure and challenge in the years ahead. That is why we are just beginning to talk about the Parish Council in terms of *ministry*.

Ministry has the fundamental task of giving life to nourishing and building up the Christian community, the body of Christ. And so it involves the people of the parish community, with all their various talents and gifts, building up the body of Christ.

If someone asked you *"Which of the following most closely resembles your idea of Parish Council?"* what would you respond?

• a group that meets to discuss finances?

• a group that tells the rest of the parish what to do?

• a group that advises the pastor of the needs and preoccupations of parishioners?

• a group that reflects ''in miniature'' the gifts, joy and pain of parishioners and tries to enable the whole parish to respond more creatively to one another?

Depending on our experience and prejudices, any number of descriptions could come to mind. *The task for Parish Councils is to search out creative ways of becoming a ministry-type Parish Council,* or of deepening this kind of Council, if we already have one.

Although very little has been written to encourage Parish Councils to think of themselves in ministry-type terms, we can certainly begin to look at some of the words that seem to "happen" together with ministry.

We have already seen the word *Church*. Ministry is that action which "brings to birth" and nourishes the life of the Church as a community gathered by word, sacrament, and service in the name of Jesus the Christ.

A second word is *gift*. "There is a variety of gifts, but the same Spirit" (1 Cor. 12:4ff). Each individual has talents — actual or potential — which flourish according to that individual's personality, education, environment, job. These talents may change over the course of an individual's life journey, although certain basic ones will remain constant. They develop in different ways as they interact with the gifts of others. A uniqueness develops which enables each person to respond to a variety of other people's or group's needs.

This is closely linked with a third word, *service:* "The doing what is necessary to provide for people's needs." Bernard Cooke points out the wide range of tasks that this has included in the Church's history: preserving the unity and vitality of the people, healing, reconciling, caring for those in temporal need, basic administration and hospitality.[1] A tall order for today, but one which merits more than a passing glance!

So, given all this, what can we propose as a description, for our purposes here, of a Parish Council?

A Parish Council is a group of people, called from and by the community, to foster with the pastor the building of the Body of Christ, and the actualization of the "kingdom" in that parish.

It is a ministry *on behalf* of the parish community. Impossible to effectively call together 1000 people! But 20 people "of the people" can hopefully bring the community, with their gifts, desires, needs, questions and challenges, not only to the pastor, but also to one another. In this sense, Parish Council is a ministry *to the parish community,* for it becomes a facilitator enabling members of the community to become aware of their gifts, creativity and needs, and encouraging them to put these into circulation to build up the community.

What we will describe in the following pages is one possible manner of setting this ministry in motion within a given community.

Notes

[1] Cooke, *Ministry to Word and Sacraments*, pp. 343-402.

4

Getting Started

Elections or appointments, or a combination of the two, have been the usual means of establishing a Parish Council. Each approach brings with it unique problems.

Electing people who are relatively unknown has little value. *Parishioners electing a Parish Council should be able to meet the candidates, and to hear from each of them what sort of community vision they offer* (for example, have a candidate "meet the people" at coffee time after liturgy, two or three weekends before elections). In this way, the electing body is given the possibility of a choice which is at least minimally informed.

How and when can this election take place? Many parishes have opted for elections during or after Sunday liturgy, a time outside liturgy, at an open parish meeting — where voting can take place. To encourage participation, those on the parish census list might be sent a ballot, to be returned at the time of the meeting. An accompanying invitation could contain basic information about the "how and why" of the Parish Council. Reminders could be posted on the church announcement board, and in the parish bulletin... even in the local newspaper, on local cable TV, and in radio public service announcements. Such a meeting could give candidates a chance to express their views, respond to questions, and meet parishioners. Obviously what is essential is that anyone who wishes to stand for election, or who has been asked to stand for election, has reflected on what he or she believes his or her contribution to the growth of community life can be.

Another option — in parishes where large numbers of people are already active in different ministries — is to call these people together for a period of reflection, after which an election takes place. From these people, already ministering, a Parish Council would be chosen which would foster, with the pastor, the growth of the Kingdom in their parish.

"*The parish offers an outstanding example of the community apostolate, for it gathers into a unity all the human diversities that are found there and inserts them into the universality of the Church. The laity should develop the habit of working in the parish in close union with their priests, of bringing before the ecclesial community their own problems, world problems and questions regarding man's salvation, to examine them together and solve them by general discussion. According to their abilities, the laity ought to cooperate in all the apostolic and missionary enterprises of their ecclesial family.*"

Decree on the Apostolate of Lay People, No. 10.

After the election

At the first Council meeting, there may be fifteen people or so gathered around the table. In the one or two years for which they have been elected,[2] they have goals to achieve. So, what happens next?

They will elect a chairperson who, in consultation with the pastor, will prepare an agenda. Members will be elected, or will perhaps volunteer, to take responsibility for various committees. Times for meetings will be set up and, at each meeting, reports will be made from the various committees. But be careful! If their activity continues only in this manner, it is quite possible that the members of this group will go their own ways as strangers to one another and to their deeper calling, until their term of office expires.

Although the mechanics of the meetings are necessary, they must not dominate the Council's purpose (for more on the mechanics, see pages 25-33). *Members need to discover the other people on the Council, their vision of Church, their perception of the parish situation,* *and the gifts they bring to the Council.*

Some people are doers — they want to get straight to the heart of the action. Others ask questions, tend to deal with ideas, and have a bit more trouble turning them into concrete action. Someone is always ready with a joke to break tension; another brings a meandering discussion back into focus.

This sort of interaction needs to be consciously observed, for if a Council is composed, for instance, only of "doers," it will have to try harder not to suppress the reflective elements from its meetings. Each of these styles of operating has real elements of leadership in it. A key element is to be aware that there are weaknesses corresponding to the strengths.

Besides recognizing the difficulties inherent in any group that tries to work and talk together, the Parish Council has a responsibility to get acquainted with some of the dynamics involved in nurturing the body of Christ.

---

[2] Usually some members of the parish Council are elected for a two-year office, and others for a one-year term.

Establishing Priorities: Tools for Understanding and Action

As baptized people, members of the Body of Christ, we are called to participate in bringing the Kingdom of God to its fullness. This Kingdom is not a place, but a bringing of God's power to act on behalf of his creatures. Jesus talks about this kingdom in stories, the parables, which are startling tales parachuting us into a strange world. Here, what is thought to be undesirable, useless and broken, actually becomes the foundation for the working of God. A Parish Council needs to learn to take very seriously this paradox of strength in weakness. It is hard not to notice that the people Jesus associated with are tax collectors, prostitutes... a really "unique collection." Poor people keep turning up at dinner, and cheaters are rewarded with his favor. Administratively, Jesus' world is chaotic! And... what is most astounding is that in Jesus' Kingdom these people are not simply served by that Kingdom, they are its foundation. They are the gifted ones! Luke, in his version of the Beatitudes (Lk. 6:20-23), makes this very clear.

This leaves us with the question: How is the Kingdom happening here and now among us? Is our effort at organization and administration, our encouragement of people's gifts helping that Kingdom to "happen?"

Therefore, perhaps the first item on the agenda of any meeting would be one of these parables of the Kingdom (a list is presented on page 39). A good starting point might be the story of the banquet in Luke, Chapter 14, verses 16-24. Here are some questions which might guide the group's reflection:

What is the banquet?
What does the banquet look like in our parish?
Who is there?
Who isn't there?
Who [has been] is invited? How?
What is served?
Who is host?
Why should anyone come?

Be realistic. The only judgment made on the responses given will come from the group itself. The point is not to lament the past, or to celebrate it. The point is that the Kingdom of God is happening here and now, through us, and sometimes in spite of us. (At the same time however, a Council needs to be aware that the choices

9

it makes now, in response to this action of God, will have consequences one year or five years down the line. Present members of a Council may not have to deal with those consequences, but others will... and a parish will have to live with them, too.)

Take, for example, the elderly in a parish. How do we involve them in the community in such a way that their gifts, their experience, their wisdom may benefit the group? Certainly they have special needs (e.g., transportation, housing, health care), but we should be wary lest by only fulfilling their needs and not asking for the gifts they are able to give, we end up marginalizing them. The same can apply to other groups, such as: young; handicapped; single parents; divorced; homosexual; sick; ethnic or racial minorities. Each has something to *offer* to the parish community, as well as something to receive from it. We must constantly remember that we do not get our standards for participation and membership from ourselves, or from our society (often preoccupied with productivity, youth, beauty or wealth). Nor do we have to search far to find these standards. They are already given: in the gospel.

It certainly is not always easy to get down to cases and talk about who we are and what we might do, from this perspective. It seems far simpler to just "get on with the agenda." Yet, this fuller kind of communication is possible. *The following pages illustrate some ways for Parish Council members to help one another discuss individual and common visions, and to translate them into action.*

When a group of people get together, they inevitably bring with them different visions of Church and of what a parish should be doing or being. These visions often produce in other individuals that grating feeling of "I don't like this, even though I can't quite say why"... which may lead to some of the conflicts around the Council table, and a disheartening inability to act.

An effective tool for helping Parish Councils and other groups to begin to understand how they envision their parish is Leon McKenzie's game, "That's a Nice Parish.[3]"

Participants in this exercise are asked to distribute 15 scoring points among a list of 15 characteristics of a "nice parish." The lowest number indicates the person's highest priority. After completing the exercise individually, small groups are formed, where a group ranking is arrived at through a compilation of the individual scores. Individuals are asked to explain their priorities; at the same time they are forced to deal with the fact that *their* priority could be "lost" in a group priority different from their own.

[3] McKenzie, *Creative Learning for Adults*, pp. 41-43; p. 139.

11

The context is non-threatening and should provide a forum for differences to emerge without their being labelled as "wrong." Tensions may emerge but because no concrete issues are being dealt with at the moment, and by this group, such tensions can be handled more easily now than around the sometimes emotionally laden Council meeting table.

Participants in such an exercise should be encouraged to listen to one another and to try to understand the viewpoints of others by asking questions. Respect and gentleness are very important here: Sometimes people forget that a lot of living has been invested in what we treasure as our understanding of Church. Even if we disagree with a viewpoint, we must do our best to handle it with care.

Parish Features	My Ranking	Group Ranking
A. Air-conditioned church		
B. Superior parish school		
C. Superior parish catechetical program		
D. Warm and friendly clergy		
E. Involvement of laity in parish activities		
F. Vital Sunday liturgies		
G. Warm and friendly people		
H. Effective adult education program		
I. Ecumenical involvement with neighborhood churches		
J. Spacious parking facilities		
K. Interesting Sunday homilies		
L. A working parish council		
M. Concerned with social justice		
N. Large Sunday collections		
O. Accessible parish clergy		

Models of the Church

Our priorities, with regard to parish life, spring out of an individual and group image or understanding of Church. To take our last exercise one step further, we can look at our highest priorities. (Often there will be a pattern emerging in individuals or groups of individuals.) These groupings of priorities can be said to form certain images or models of Church. With their different viewpoints and resources, these groupings are indeed a richness to be tapped; however, they can become a barrier to communication and functioning, if they are not understood and examined.

The American theologian, Avery Dulles, has worked extensively with these groupings of characteristics of Church. He calls them "models" and offers this explanation:

"The peculiarity of models, as contrasted with aspects, is that we cannot integrate them into a single synthetic vision.... In order to do justice to the various aspects of the Church as a complex reality, we must work simultaneously with different models."[4]

This is precisely the sort of "juggling act" that Parish Councils will so frequently find themselves engaged in, either i) as individuals or ii) as a Council

[4] Dulles, *Models of the Church*, p. 14.

i) As individuals

Because of his or her experience of family, life and Church, each member of the Council brings to the working of the group an internalized model of Church — with fairly well-delineated structures of responsibility, of "what a nice parish is," of what a parish does, who does it, and how. Each of these visions has its own validity. HOWEVER, when people get together, with their different models, the group risks a certain number of seemingly unresolvable conflicts on all levels of group interaction, if these differing perspectives and experiences are not discovered and clarified.

ii) As a Council

The different perspectives and experiences of Church found in the individual members of the Council reflect a tension which the Council must eventually deal with. Not only in a parish will we find countless viewpoints on the image of Church, but we will also find groups of people coming together who share common experiences of Church and life. The special interests which these groups perceive and make known to a Council (Third World problems, divorced persons, art in the liturgy, etc....) and the spontaneous identification of different Council members with these interests, can either become a source of growth and discovery in a parish, or they can almost completely divide a community.

Rather than to alienate these groups, one of the functions of the Council is to learn to create the situations where these groups can creatively contribute to parish growth.

Models and Their Meaning for the Parish Council

a) The Hierarchical Model

This model, most familiar to us as the one we grew up in, emphasizes the Church as the perfect society. It tends to be characterized by: institutional structures, the clergy as source of power and initiative, obedience to rules, adherence to approved doctrine, and the reception of the sacraments.

In this sort of situation, it would be very difficult to find a Parish Council that could be anything more than a "rubber stamp" for the pastor. Parishes in which either the Council members or the pastor believes that the priest must be the source of all initiative, tend to experience some frustration, ill will, and hurt feelings. To the chagrin of the community looking to participate more fully in its own life, it has had to deal with a Council perceived to be composed of fifteen clerics — rather than just the one they were accustomed to dealing with!

There is a positive side to the hierarchical coin, however. *It also includes a great many of the traditional administrative structures of the Church.* This means that a Council does not have to "reinvent the wheel" for every contingency with regard to structures, particularly in dealing with the diocesan Church. It can borrow whatever will better enhance its functioning for building the community.

b) The Mystical Communion Model

Dulles calls his second model of the Church the "mystical communion" model. Here, meeting one another face to face in some sort of stable group — with some experience of intimacy — is a dominant characteristic.[5] It is a lot like a big family, or an old-fashioned neighborhood, where everybody knows one another, a bit of the family history, and maybe a few of the "skeletons in the closet." People rally together to help one another through difficult situations, and come together to celebrate weddings, births and other happy events.

In the context of Church, *this model highlights our meeting with Christ in one another.* As the body of Christ, it can grow, change, be renewed. Because this model sees a profound spirit of charity as the basis for being Church, it can open up to other denominations, other groups. But Dulles warns against the disillusionment that can result from people expecting too much in terms of "warm fuzzies" from the community. He also points out the danger that can develop when the drive to create a warm community obscures the much-needed sense of mission and identity.

[5] Ibid., pp. 52-53.

For the Parish Council, however, this model is certainly much more hospitable. Community members wanting to find out who their members are would be encouraged to facilitate friendship and understanding. This would probably involve much more than updating the census: It would embrace the concerns of the community — their needs, their vision of community, and the gifts they feel able and prepared to offer. Caution must be exercised to maintain the openness of the community so that exclusivity or elitism does not creep in, producing a real country club situation.

c) The Sacrament Model

Using one of the most famous statements of the *Dogmatic Constitution on the Church* (from Vatican II), Dulles describes a third model in which the Church is a "kind of sacrament of intimate union with God and of the unity of all mankind; that is, she is a sign and instrument of such union and unity." (LG, n. 1)[6]

In this model of the Church, there is a real and vital tension between the inside and outside. *Here is the awareness that the total reality of human beings and the world they live in, taken both individually and as a group, reveals the working and the presence of Jesus Christ.*

Most frequently, this tension has been reduced to a focus on the community's liturgical life, or its celebration of the sacraments. But sacrament is more than liturgy; it is the realization that all human reality is capable of revealing the creative, saving presence of God. Needed here, then, is a concerted effort to take seriously the humanity and the human experience of the community (any parish could provide hundreds of different angles to that experience!). The key question becomes: How might we celebrate this, make it visible, give it to the whole body in tangible form, so that it may contribute to the growth of all of us in Christ? This is a very different question from "What songs should we choose to sing this Sunday?"...

d) The Herald Model

Here, the proclamation of the Word in various forms is primary. The Word, the real presence of God communicated and encountered, gathers and creates the community, which in turn is challenged to pass this Word on to others.

The Liturgy of the Word, well-celebrated, and education are of great importance in this model. So also will be the other situations where the Word is encountered: Energy is devoted to adult education in all its dimensions; the catechumenate is a concern; the community seeks to create a situation which assures that each of its members, young and old, will have access to a systematic and organized encounter with the sav-

[6] *Vatican Council II: the Conciliar and Post-Conciliar Documents*, edited by Austin Flannery, O.P.

ing mystery of Jesus Christ, the Word made flesh.

This outreach goes beyond the immediate community to include the whole dimension of mission. As a community, the group wants to share this Word with those who have not yet heard it, wherever they may be.

e) The Servant Model

Here, the model is that of the "community for others." As a community, it reaches out to all people to feed the hungry, welcome the homeless, clothe the naked, work at bringing justice to the oppressed.

The danger for this model lies in divorcing this outreach from the gospel which inspires it and gives it energy and strength.

The tremendous positive value of this model is the opportunity it provides to make the community more aware of other people in situations often profoundly different — culturally, economically, politically, religiously — from that of the community. Social Action, Development and Peace projects, refugee committees, concern for political prisoners: All of these fall among the characteristic actions of the Church as "servant."

The spirit of the Lord has been given to me,
For he has anointed me.
He has sent me to bring the good news to the poor,
To proclaim liberty to captives
And to the blind new sight,
To set the downtrodden free,
To proclaim the Lord's year of favor.

Isaiah 61:1-2; Luke 4:18-19

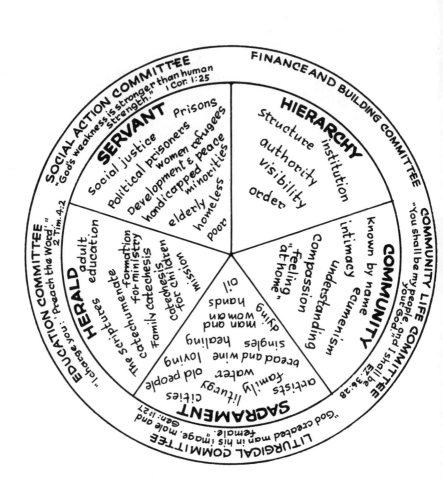

SOCIAL ACTION COMMITTEE
"God's weakness is stronger than human strength." I Cor. 1:25

FINANCE AND BUILDING COMMITTEE

SERVANT
Prisons
Social justice
Political prisoners
women refugees
Development & peace
handicapped
minorities
elderly
homeless
poor

HIERARCHY
institution
structure
authority
visibility
order

COMMUNITY LIFE COMMITTEE
"You shall be my people and your God." Ez. 36:28

COMMUNITY
known by name
intimacy
ecumenism
understanding
compassion
"feeling at home"

EDUCATION COMMITTEE
"I charge you: Preach the Word." 2 Tim. 4:2

HERALD
adult education
the scriptures
catechumenate
formation for ministry
family catechesis
catechesis for children
mission

SACRAMENT
oil
dying
hands
man and woman
healing
singles
bread and wine
loving
old people
water
family
liturgy
artists
cities
female

LITURGICAL COMMITTEE
"God created man in his image, male and female." Gen. 1:27

Several features emerge as we examine the model "pie" (see page 18).
• we need all the models to create the whole
• all the models meet and touch one another in the center
• no model is dominant, because none contains the whole. Hierarchy, like "servant" is an integral and integrated part of the whole.

Each slice represents one dimension of the reality of God's kingdom growing in our midst. And each slice should cause us to ask ourselves a few questions:
• have we neglected this dimension? If so, why?
• have we overemphasized this dimension? If so, why?
• have we isolated this dimension, e.g., as the concern of a particular group?
• have we failed to integrate this dimension into the life of the community?
• what can we do to improve?

It is perfectly natural, in the evolving life of the community, that different dimensions of this reality called "Church" will at different moments in its life be more prominent than at others. The task of integrating all of this is a life-long one which, however, cannot be left to chance. Particular caution should be exercised to ensure that the hierarchical dimension is neither isolated from the whole nor allowed to dominate it.

If we return now to the priorities we uncovered using "That's a Nice Parish," we can examine them to discover how these models of Church emerge from our choices. Each individual should study his or her priorities. What model(s) do they seem to indicate? What types of action do they therefore emphasize?

What are the priorities of the Council as a whole? (Using the total derived from adding together the individual rankings for each characteristic, you can approximate the group's emphases.) Do you think this is healthy for the parish as a whole? Whatever model emerges from certain priorities needs to be considered thoughtfully. How balanced is our vision of the community? Where do we need to do the most work?

Parish Features	Related to model
Air-conditioned church	Hierarchy (institutional feature)
Superior parish school	Hierarchy (Institution); Herald (education)
Superior parish catechetical program	Herald (education)
Warm and friendly clergy	Hierarchy; Mystical Communion*
Involvement of laity in parish activities	Mystical Communion
Vital Sunday liturgies	Sacrament; Mystical Communion
Warm and friendly people	Mystical Communion
Effective adult education program	Herald; Sacrament; Servant
Ecumenical involvement with neighborhood churches	Mystical Communion
Spacious parking facilities	Hierarchy
Interesting Sunday homilies	Herald; Sacrament
A working parish council	Mystical Communion; Sacrament; Servant; Herald
Concerned with social justice	Servant
Large Sunday collections	Hierarchy (but see section on finances!)
Accessible parish clergy	Mystical Communion; Hierarchy

* A lad of about eleven who was present at a meeting where this was being discussed remarked: "The priests can be as nice as can be, but if the people don't get involved, nothing has changed." Out of the mouths of babes...! Warm, friendly clergy are a bonus; however, the personality of the priest should not become the only foundation of growth in the parish, nor the only criterion for his successful ministry. Accessibility is more necessary. We must keep in mind that oftentimes the priest is appointed elsewhere, but the community remains.

The question of balance

How do we manage to keep from putting all our eggs into one basket? Often, this is the basket which is most familiar, or the one for which we seem to have people ready and willing to work...? (It may be particularly tempting to claim that people are not ready for an experience of Church as "servants"; for instance: Social justice issues may seem too far removed from ordinary, everyday, parish life.)

This is where Councils must recognize the wholistic nature of their task. A project in social action might well be an impractical first venture. But the resources of the whole community can be drawn on, so that through educational programs, speakers, preaching, parish bulletin announcements, bulletin board displays, etc., the first steps towards raising people's awareness can be taken.

With this sort of foundation laid, projects with a more concrete action-line can be undertaken, involving just about everyone's particular expertise. Members of a community life committee can always be wondering: "What does this mean for us as a community? How has it changed us? How can we be sure it doesn't die?" A liturgy committee can ask: "How can we celebrate this experience? How can our liturgical celebrations help us to experience more deeply the reality we're struggling with? What does this have to say about our manifestation of ourselves as a people?"

To illustrate how this process of the interaction of models works, let us take a rather significant test case... that of finances.

"Your money where your mouth is!"

Almost inevitably, groups using "That's a Nice Parish" find that one of the lowest items on their list of priorities is "large Sunday collections." Why?... Is it our reaction to the legendary pastor who "never talks about anything except money?" Is it a feeling that because the love of money is "at the root of all evil" we Christian people really should not have anything to do with it? Is it a reaction to high interest rates, a devalued dollar and escalating inflation? Who knows for sure!

What is certain is the need to confront the issue of finances openly. There will always be certain maintenance needs which must be met: building costs, heating and repairs, clergy and pastoral team salaries. But beyond that, the parish must examine its fiscal investments carefully. It is one thing to declare that adult education will be a priority; it is quite another to provide the resources to take care of it. The resources will include personnel, materials, space. All of these cost money.

Perhaps the classic example of all this emerges in the context of hiring a musician. A Parish Council, under the eager influence of a liturgy committee desiring quality music at a liturgy, begins the search for a musician... It is aware of what sort of salary demands can be made. It is also aware of what sort of salary, given the other concerns of the parish, it might be prepared to offer.

The situation can be resolved in one of several ways:

a) A retired organist with excellent training and experience has just moved into the parish, and offers his or her services for an honorarium which is half of the salary under consideration. [This rarely, if ever, happens!]

b) A good musician, with experience in several other places and some ability to train choirs and leaders of song, applies. References show that this person has formerly served other communities ably. The person would agree to the proposed salary.

c) "A dream come true!" The "ideal" musician — with a Master's degree in music, who is a published composer, an organist playing several other instruments, and a director who has done choir work on radio and TV — applies. This musician insists on a salary which is half again what is being proposed.

There are many gifts
but always of the same Spirit;
there are many services to be done,
but always to the same Lord;
working in all sorts of different ways in different
*   people,*
it is the same Lord who works in them all.

1 Corinthians 12:4-7

The Council deliberates. Several factors emerge:

1) A number of people on the Council feel that hiring (c) would be a "feather in the cap" of the parish. When confronted with the problem of finding an additional sum of money to respond to the musician's salary-demands, this group proposes budget slashes in other areas — namely, education and the installation of access ramps for the handicapped, envisaged in the year's budget.

2) Another group prefers to hire (b), pointing out that staying within the proposed salary suggestions will allow the needs of other groups to be more satisfactorily met. They indicate that while postponing the access ramp is possible, the opening of the new senior citizens' residence in the parish — in the next few months — will soon make the ramp an even more necessary addition to the Church. Furthermore, it would be highly possible that the scripture program set to begin — using resource persons from the local university and religious education office — would not get underway because of lack of funds. (And this is the first time a lot of people have expressed an interest in committing themselves to this sort of study as a group.)

3) On further investigation, (a) indicates that his services might not be available at certain key moments in the liturgical year: His spring holiday in Florida often coincides with Easter.

Each of these options offers a certain viability and certain limitations, just as does each model of the Church. This is not the place to make a final judgment on the situation. However, the Council's final decision, backed by its financial investment, will indicate its priorities with regard to the life and direction of this community, both present and future. If the Council chooses (c) it must remember that its investment, while providing excellent returns in the short term, may eliminate not only some present options, but others in the future.

An option to develop just one model of the Church, be it "sacrament" or "servant," "mystical communion" or "herald" can be dangerous. There is not only a static relationship among the pieces of the pie; there is also a dynamic movement which strengthens each model by drawing on the resources of the other, in varying degrees. (See diagram on p. 24.)

The "model pie" as it functions in the community and within the parish council: Different elements converge, overlap, pile on top of one another, mix, to give the complex of parish life.

24

Structures of Responsibility

One of the elements of community life which has emerged in the last ten years is responsibility to one another. In the parish, the pastor is ultimately responsible to the bishop for the life of the community. He can, however, choose to share that responsibility with other ministers, among whom can be members of the Parish Council.

If the pastor's desire is really to empower the people, then both continuing formation and patient support must be offered them.

Mistakes are inevitable when one is learning anything — and this includes ministry! — and Parish Councils should not be expected to learn their ministry overnight. With patience and formation, lay people can develop their gifts in such a way that their involvement with the pastor will be not only mutually enriching but also enriching for the life of the community. This enrichment of the community is the ultimate goal of all structures of responsibility in the Church.

Structures of responsibility:

In the Church, as the universal people of God, ministry is a dynamic structure, or flow of responsibility. Bishops, responsible for the local Church, delegate their responsibility to pastors, who minister to the local community, with the collaboration of members of that community.

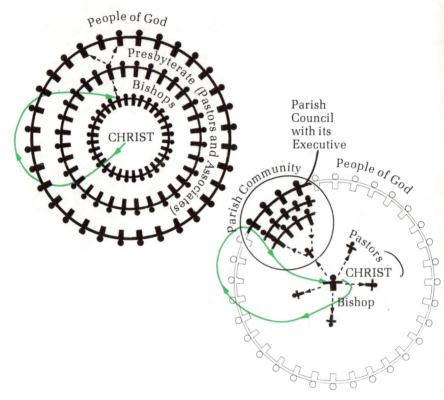

Structures of Responsibility:

In the diocese, there is a similar flow of responsibility. The pastor ministers to the community entrusted to him in collaboration with the pastoral team and members of that community. Where a Parish Council exists, it can become one of the arenas where this collaboration is concretized both as ministry *to* the community, and as ministry *on behalf of* the community.

Meanwhile, all the work of the Council does not fall on the Council members alone. Usually a number of committees are formed, composed of people who are not part of the Council, but with a Council member as chairperson.

Normally there will be a number of *permanent committees:* finance and building, community life, liturgy, social action, education, mission (see pie, page 24). These committees will deal with the basic, ongoing dimensions of life in the community.

The formation and abolition of *other committees* is very organic: As needs or issues arise, specific committees can be formed on an *ad hoc* basis, to gather information, plan and involve the community in action. They may last, and become part of the formal Council committee system, or they may dissolve when their usefulness has been fulfilled. Setting out the goals of a committee at the time of its origin will help all concerned decide when its purpose has been fulfilled. Such an *ad hoc* committee should then be publicly thanked for its work, and dissolved until it is needed again. Until then, of course, its members will likely have much of value to contribute in other areas of community life.

The lists on the following pages are not meant to be exhaustive. They are given to indicate some of the people who should not be overlooked, when the moment comes to set up committees. Your own parish situation will surely suggest other people who should be involved.

The linking between committees by representatives from other committees is by no means mandatory, but is encouraged. It can be done formally, by having a representative appointed to these committees; or it can be done by informal invitation issued, for example, at a Parish Council meeting. Chairpersons could inform each other of the date, time and location of their committee meetings. The linking between committees encourages mutual support, understanding, and cross-fertilization of ideas.

(See pies: pages 18 and 24)

Community Life

Representatives of various organizations: Council of Catholic Men, CYO, Youth Group, etc.

Groups such as: elderly, handicapped, singles, couples, liturgy hospitality group.

Representatives of other committees.

Liturgy

Organist, lead guitarist, leader of song, cantor, representatives of different choirs, and their directors.

Representatives of other liturgical ministries: Liturgical Readers, Ministers of Hospitality, Lay Ministers of Eucharist, non-ordained Presiders, Planning Committee.

Artists — not just for the execution of their art, but for the quality of their perception of life!

Representatives of other committees.

Education

Representatives of: catechists, parish school staff.

Several interested parents from different parts of the parish.

Persons responsible for catechumenate, preparation for baptism and marriage, pre-school programs, adult education.

Representatives of other committees.

Social Action

People involved in community services: nurse, social worker, doctor, politician.

Representatives of different trades; of senior citizens homes, of nursing homes in the area (staff and/or resident, not necessarily parishioners); single parents, divorced Catholics groups; ethnic or racial minorities.

Representatives of other committees.

Finance and Building

Pastor; parish administrator; an accountant or banker, if there is one in the parish.

Representatives of other committees.

The Committee Chairperson

Much of the Council's essential work is done at the Committee level, where groups of people meet on a regular basis to discuss, brainstorm, develop ideas and formulate plans for action to be proposed to the Parish Council. The Committee chairperson has a special responsibility for the smooth functioning of this aspect of Council life. The following is provided as an incomplete checklist for committee chairpersons; each one will have to add to it according to the area he or she is dealing with:

a) for Committee Meeting:

☐ Send a reminder to your committee members as to date, time and location of committee meeting. (It is a good idea to try to keep meetings on the same night of the week.)

☐ Follow this up with a reminder phone call the day or evening prior to the meeting.

☐ Draw up an agenda of issues, questions, situations to be dealt with, remembering to allow time for new business.

☐ Be constantly alert for other people who would be assets to your committee, either as members of the committee, or as people who could be involved in committee projects.

b) for Parish Council Meeting:

☐ Prepare your report of the committee's activities, including suggestions for possible action, for presentation to the Council meeting. It is helpful to have a copy of your report to give to the Council secretary.

☐ Prior to the meeting, submit to the Council chairperson or secretary any extraordinary items (i.e., anything outstanding in your regular report) which your committee thinks would need a special place on the agenda.

☐ Make sure that any information which the whole Council might need — such as dates, prices, program outlines — is reproduced for circulation at the Parish Council Meeting.

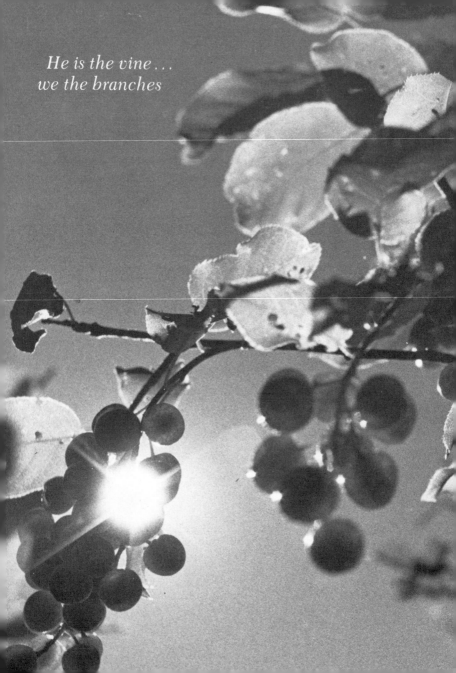

He is the vine . . .
we the branches

The Executive and the Council: Some Responsibilities

The Parish Council chairperson and secretary are important to the smooth functioning of the Council's practical dimensions, particularly to the success of Council meetings. A checklist is provided for each of these people.

The Secretary

☐ Prepare a list of Council members' names, addresses, phone numbers, and the areas for which they are responsible.

☐ Receive, record and answer correspondence, in consultation with the chairperson of the Council.

☐ Send a written reminder to Council members at least a week before the meeting, indicating date, time, and location of the meeting. The agenda could be included.

☐ A reminder phone call to Council members the evening prior to the meeting might be helpful.

☐ Bring materials for taking notes, plus files of minutes of previous meetings, and committee reports to the meeting.

☐ Note those present; announce regrets, if any; note the major lines of discussions only; note who suggested what.

☐ Be sure to note the exact wording of any motions or resolutions passed, the names of those moving and seconding the motions, and the results of any votes taken.

☐ Type, duplicate and circulate Council meeting minutes as soon as possible after the meeting. Keep a copy of minutes for Council and Parish files.

☐ Be sure someone (not necessarily you!) is designated to prepare coffee for the meeting.

The Chairperson

☐ See that you are acquainted with your responsibilities, as outlined in the Parish Council constitution, and that each Council member knows the Constitution and its terms. The format for these varies from parish to parish and from diocese to diocese. Sometimes there is a diocesan formula established.

☐ Prior to the meeting, using the material submitted to you by committee chairpersons, assemble the agenda, in consultation with your pastor. Prepare any questions you feel are pertinent to the various reports.

☐ Prior to the meeting, send this agenda material to the Council secretary to type and distribute. Make sure you allot sufficient time for this.

☐ Prior to the meeting, make sure that you or another Council member is prepared to preside at the group's prayer at the meeting.

☐ During the meeting, set up a context of prayer. Free some time for the group to calm themselves, take a deep breath, relax and have an opportunity for prayer. Consider using a hymn on a tape or record, a scripture reading, a period of silence with a brief prayer. Encourage different people to take responsibility for this time.

☐ "Call the meeting to order" — welcome everyone, particularly non-members who might be attending. Ask for any changes anyone might want to make to the agenda, keeping in mind that even though meetings may be normally held only once a month, some people cannot always avoid double commitments for the same evening. Therefore, someone may have to leave early, and want to make his or her report.

☐ Change the order of reporting during the meeting to avoid giving the impression that any one committee or issue is always first in the order of importance.

☐ Do not let reports become monologues followed by "Thank you." Encourage questions and discussion; be prepared to ask at least one pertinent question yourself.

☐ Schedule your coffee break for the middle of the meeting. People experienced in the dynamics of a meeting recognize that often solutions and ideas are born over the informality of coffee chit-chat.

☐ If any issue generates hostility, if a situation is becoming too heated, or particularly if it is becoming personal, intervene firmly to suggest a cooling off period, and try to devise a more restrained way of re-approaching the issue.

☐ Keep discussions to a humane length. Too many questions which are unanswered may be an indication that the issue should be sent back to its committee for more work. Don't let the meeting get bogged down trying to respond to questions for which you or other Council members do not have the resources to answer at that time.

☐ Try to begin meetings on time, and set a time limit for the length of meetings — to be violated only under extraordinary circumstances, and with Council's approval. This facilitates getting things done!

☐ Acquaint yourself with parliamentary procedure (see Robert's *Rules of Order*). It will help keep the meeting moving, and help you deal with situations which arise.

The Council and the Parish

Different possibilities can be considered in order to maintain open communication with the rest of the parish community: Open meetings of the Council can be held every several months. The Council can develop a newsletter which could be published once a month with the parish bulletin. Parishioners can be encouraged to phone Council members, or to write in with their suggestions. The Council should issue an annual report to the parish. Through its committees, it should be constantly encouraging the participation of others in the building up of different aspects of parish life.

Burnout, Ongoing Development and the Parish Council

What do we do to prevent the moment when tempers flare, and people say, "I have nothing more to give; I hate this; I want to throw the whole thing in the lake, or the river, or over the side of a mountain"?

The suggestions listed below all have one common element: They do not deal with specific items on an immediate agenda. Each in its own way provides a distancing, a change of atmosphere — a breather — as well as ongoing education and development.

Parish Council Retreats

Remember how it all started? The Council may literally need time to get back to its roots. The time the members spend together (hopefully at an available retreat center, or another facility begged or borrowed for the occasion) should provide them with time to relax together, share meals, break bread, play and reflect together.

Spouses might also be invited to attend, so that they might develop another insight into their partner's ministry. The parish could look into providing babysitting for those who need it and, if necessary, could assume the cost. Part of the time should be devoted to regaining the larger perspective of their ministry — which can so easily be overshadowed by preoccupations with administrative concerns and immediate questions. This helps put many situations into perspective. An agenda can be worked out with the staff of the retreat center, who might be invited to give some input into the weekend.

Creativity takes vision, insight, planning, and understanding. Because of this, each Council member needs to do some reading and reflection in the area he or she is most responsible for. This reading keeps one in touch with the ideas, experience, problems and achievements of others with whom we normally might not have contact.

Members should also be on the mailing list of the relevant diocesan offices. If for some reason this does not seem feasible, the pastor should see to it that the information relevant to each sector — which comes into his office — is passed on to the appropriate persons. This should also include information about lectures, workshops, and other educational opportunities for which at least partial financing might be made available.

Periodicals and books should also be made available to individuals or groups wanting to explore them, for example, statements from the various sectors of the National Conference of Catholic Bishops.

Group Study

At times, all members of the group will need to study a specific issue. Pertinent documentation should be circulated, and time for members' responses to and questions about an issue should be included on the agenda of the meeting. If possible, someone with more experience in an issue should be invited to join the meeting, as a resource on a particular subject.

The Council as a whole should be encouraged to attend at least one workshop together per year. (In more remote areas, where this is not easily available, dioceses should try to offer at least one workshop per year for Parish Councils.) The topic might correspond to a major thrust the Council wishes to explore in a given year, or to an area it has never touched. When the group undertakes this sort of activity, a reflection on the experience should always be part of the next meeting's agenda. Some questions to pursue might be:

● What were the main points under discussion, as I understood it?

● What relevance might they have to our situation? Why? Why not?

● What sort of planning or action might we undertake as a result of this experience?

● Whom else might we involve in this?

Most Parish Councils traditionally open their meetings with prayer. But how is that prayer treated? Perhaps one of the most important aspects of prayer is that it is freed time — time that is not bound to the achievement of a particular goal or task. Councils need this time — and not only at the beginning of a meeting. Moments of decision, particularly when the direction is not immediately evident, are times when we should stop, relax, reflect, and listen to the One who speaks inside us. Prayer can clear our sensitivities and bring fresh insight and vigor — and humor — to our decisions. Hopefully it will not become the signal for the beginning and the end of proceedings!

The different members of Council responsible for preparing a time of prayer for each meeting could consult the scripture readings which have already been mentioned, and which are indicated below on this page of the booklet. Any one of them could serve as the basis for a short prayer service. For further information on this, see the booklets on Parish Prayer Groups and Lay Presiders at Liturgy, also in this series.

"Each of us brings a different kind of vulnerability into the world. For this reason, ministry is compassion or shared pain. It is also joyful because the compassion creates gratitude, celebration and mutuality. The incarnation manifests all this, as God comes into the world vulnerable and as Jesus speaks of compassion, and forgiveness, even love, as the essence of our ministry to one another."[7]

Only with this compassion as its source and goal can any parish council hope to minister effectively to the community of which it is a vital part.

The parables of the Kingdom in Luke's gospel:

6:47-49; 7:31-35; 7:41-42; 8:4-8; 8:11-13; 10:11-15; 11:5-8; 12:16-21; 12:35-38; 12:39-40; 12:42-48; 13:6-9; 13:18-19; 13:20-21; 13:22-30; 14:7-11; 14:16-24; 14:28-33; 15:4-7; 15:8-10; 15:11-32; 16:1-7; 18:19-31; 17:7-10; 18:1-8; 18:9-14; 19:12-27; 20:9-18; 21:29-31.

Anthony Padovano, *"Our vulnerability needs ministry,"* National Catholic Reporter, October 23, 1981, p. 9.

Resources

Cooke, Bernard, *Ministry to Word and Sacraments.* Philadelphia: Fortress Press, 1976. (2900 Queen Lane, Philadelphia, Penn. 19129, U.S.A.).

Downs, Thomas, *The Parish as Learning Community: Modeling for Parish and Adult Growth.* New York: Paulist, 1979. (545 Island Road, Ramsey, N.J. 07446).

Dulles, Avery, *Models of the Church.* New York: Doubleday, 1978. (501 Franklin Ave., Garden City, New York 11530).

Flannery, Austin, O.P. (ed.) *Vatican Council II: The Conciliar and Post-Conciliar Documents.* New York: Costello, 1975. (P.O. Box 9, Northport, N.Y. 11768).

McKenzie, Leon, *Creative Learning for Adults: the Why, How and Now of Games and Exercises.* West Mystic: Twenty-Third Publications, 1977. (P.O. Box 180, West Mystic, Conn. 06388).

Padovano, Anthony, "Our vulnerability needs ministry," the *National Catholic Reporter,* p. 10ff, October 23, 1981. (*NCR,* Box 281, Kansas City, Mo. 64141).

Power, David N., *Gifts that Differ: Lay Ministries Established and Unestablished.* New York: Pueblo Publishing Co., 1980. (1860 Broadway, New York, N.Y. 10023).

Schillebeeckx, E., *Ministry: Leadership in the Community of Jesus Christ.* New York: Crossroad Publishing Co., 1981. (18 E. 41st St., New York, N.Y. 10017).

Rademacher, Wm., "The Real Mission of the Parish Council," *Today's Parish,* Nov./Dec. 1979, pp. 21-25. (Twenty-Third Publications, see above).

Sweetser, Thomas P., *Successful Parishes: How They Meet the Challenge of Change.* Winston Press, 1982. (430 Oak Grove, Minneapolis, MN. 55403).

PARISH COUNCIL

Written by:

Bernadette Gasslein, catechist,
liturgist and adult educator
at Mt Carmel Spiritual Center, Niagara Falls,
and St. Dominic's Parish, Mississauga, Ontario.

Edited by:

Jerome Herauf

Layout:

Jan Gough, Gilles Lépine

Photography:

Cover: Ken Harris;
p. 2, 8: Jonas Abromaitis;
p. 6: Novalis; p. 11: Roman Matwijejko;
p. 14, 25, : Ken Harris; p. 30: Joseph McMurray;
p. 34: Henri Rémillard; p. 38: Kathy Clarkin
p. 37: "Vivant univers";

Illustrations:

Cover 1 and cover 4: Lee Thirlwall;
inside illustrations: John E. Lewis, Lee
Thirlwall

St. Patrick's Seminary Library

10000000024729

*"The whole group of believers
was united, heart and soul."*

(Acts 4:32)

Winston Press
430 Oak Grove
Minneapolis, Minnesota 55403

ISBN: 0-86683-741-8